2

Made in Sheffield

Made in Sheffield

my story

NEIL WARNOCK

with Oliver Holt

HODDER &
STOUGHTON

Firs ~~[ ]~~ toughton

The right of Neil Warnock to be identified as the Author
of the Work has been asserted by him in accordance
with the Copyright, Designs and Patents Act 1988

A Hodder & Stoughton Book

2

A CIP catalogue record for this title is available from the British Library

ISBN 978 0 340 93720 4

Typeset in Minion by Hewer Text UK Ltd, Edinburgh
Printed and bound by Clays Ltd, St Ives plc

Hodder Headline's policy is to use papers that are natural, renewable
and recyclable products and made from wood grown in sustainable
forests. The logging and manufacturing processes are expected to
conform to the environmental regulations of the country of origin.

Hodder and Stoughton Ltd
A division of Hodder Headline
338 Euston Road
London NW1 3BH

Dedication

I would like to dedicate this book to Sharon and my kids,
Amy, William, James and Natalie,
whose support has never dwindled over the years.

Being a football manager is a great but sometimes lonely job
and it's not possible without a good woman.

I love Sharon more now than when we first met.
Family comes before everything. It makes you realise
what is important. It keeps your feet on the floor.

It is to my big brother John, too, who I know I can always turn to.
To my sister Carole who I now know made so many sacrifices
for me when I was young.

To my mum and dad who I know will be looking down
on their little black sheep and will be feeling so proud.

To my best mate, Paul Evans, and his wife, Julie. Without Evo around,
this story would have been impossible. Our friendship started when I
scored a hat-trick for Chesterfield juniors against Sheffield Wednesday
and Paul was in goal (I had to mention that somewhere) but the
bond between us has got stronger down the years.

They say if you have one true friend in life, you are lucky.
I have got a handful and, although I have not mentioned everyone,
they all know how much I value their friendship.

And finally, to all the clubs I have managed and to their fans,
to the ones to whom I have given joy and the ones I have upset:
it's nice to know I've given you something to talk about.

CONTENTS

ACKNOWLEDGMENTS

This is a book that I have thought about writing for a number of years. The pre-season training has started and for the first time in nearly forty years as a player and manager I have not been involved in club football; this has enabled me to crack on and finish my story.

I would like to thank Roddy Bloomfield at Hodder & Stoughton for his tremendous belief and encouragement along the way. Roddy is someone I knew was right from the first time I met him. I also would like to thank some other members of the team – Maggie Body, the copy editor, statistician John Ley, and the fact checker Phil Shaw for their excellent work, Gabrielle Allen the picture researcher for coming up with a few crackers from the archives, and Hannah Knowles, the assistant editor, for her patience with me through all the proof readings – many thanks.

Throughout my career I have encountered some wonderful local journalists and we have enjoyed good working relationships. To name just a few, my thanks must go to Rex Page during my Burton Albion years, Terry Bowles at Notts County, Dave Thomas at Torquay, Mel Booth at Huddersfield, Rick Cowdrey at Plymouth and James Shield at Sheffield United. Thanks also to Andy Pack the Press Officer at Sheffield United who was tremendous in my time there. Every manager needs support and these gave me that in abundance.

Thanks as well to David Luxton my literary agent, and last but not least Oliver Holt, my partner in crime. I have always loved reading Oliver's articles and I was delighted when he agreed to help me with my autobiography as his quality is unquestioned. I put him through many days of hard work and it was well worthwhile. It's difficult to get someone who writes a story exactly the way you want it to sound, but Ollie has done just that. The times we spent together were always enjoyable and I will be forever in debt to him for his wonderful writing.

Finally, of course, my special thanks to all my friends and family to whom I have dedicated this book. Everyone needs a good family, and I have been lucky enough to have had wonderful support in the ups and downs of my life.

Photographic Acknowledgments

The author and publisher would like to thank the following for permission to reproduce photographs:

AFP/Getty Images, Paul Barker/PA Photos, Barratts/PA Photos, Roy Beardsworth/Offside, *Burton Mail*, Andrew Cowie/Color-sport, Mike Finn-Kelcey/Back Page Images, Stu Forster/Getty Images, Laurence Griffiths/Getty Images, Fiona Hanson/PA Photos, *Hartlepool Mail*, Ross Kinnaird/Getty Images, Mark Leech/Offside, Claire MacKintosh/PA Photos, *News and Star/ Carlisle*, *Nottingham Evening Post*, Bradley Ormesher/Mirrorpix, Ross Parry Syndication, Photoshoot/Offside, Popperfoto.com, Matt Roberts/Offside, Mark Rodgers/Sheffield United Football Club, *Scarborough Evening News*, *Western Morning News*, John Whitehead/*Herald Express*, Julia and Mervyn Biggin/Callington Studios, Alwyn Morris.

All other photographs are from private collections.

INTRODUCTION

I T WAS POURING with rain when we left Bramall Lane and started the short drive home. It was funeral weather and I felt like a mourner. My elder kids, James and Natalie, were with me. I could see that Natalie had been crying. My wife, Sharon, and my younger kids, Amy and William, had been weeping, too. No one knew what to say. I still felt in a daze. I couldn't believe that my Sheffield United team had lost to Wigan Athletic at home on the final day of the season and that West Ham United had beaten Manchester United at Old Trafford. I couldn't believe we had been relegated.

It was a bleak day on every level. The Manchester United manager, Sir Alex Ferguson, a man I had always looked up to, had put out a weakened team against West Ham. I was numb about that. And then Carlos Tevez, football's equivalent of a murderer out on bail, had scored the goal for West Ham that had kept them up and put us down. So much for the integrity of the Premier League then. So much for fairness and justice in English football.

I looked out of the window at our fans trailing home through the downpour. I wondered how the Premier League chief executive,

Richard Scudamore, would feel if he could see them. It was a Premier League commission, after all, that had said one of the reasons they had not docked West Ham points for playing Tevez when he was ineligible was that it would not have been fair on their supporters. Well, what about our supporters?

We got home. I went to bed. Against my better judgment, I watched *Match of the Day*. That was hard. It was hard seeing Scudamore sitting in the same Old Trafford directors' box as Eggert Magnusson, the West Ham chairman. It was hard seeing Magnusson celebrating with Kia Joorabchian, the agent – some said the owner – of Tevez.

It was difficult seeing our game, too. Seeing the shot from Danny Webber that rebounded off the inside of the Wigan post. Seeing Phil Jagielka fouled in the box and no penalty given. And seeing the mistakes we made that helped Wigan on their way. I felt bitter about the unfairness of West Ham's treatment but I knew we had contributed plenty to our own downfall over the course of the season.

When the programme finished, I took two sleeping tablets but I still couldn't sleep. I started to think about my job. I began to realise what the defeat to Wigan meant for me.

I'm going to have to go, I thought as I lay there with the television flickering in the dark.

Over and over again, the same thought. 'I'm going to have to go.'

And then more thoughts.

'I don't want to be told to go.'

'I want to be able to bring William back to Bramall Lane to watch games.'

'If we lost a couple of games early doors next season, there'd be fans outside the ground, throwing bricks through the windows.'

'There would be car park demonstrations.'

'The squad's more than good enough to win the league, even with somebody else in charge.'

'If a new manager comes in, the type of fans who are waiting under the floorboards for me will have to give him a bit of a chance.'

'But they wouldn't give me that chance. Look at the bad spell Steve Bruce had at Birmingham the season they were back in the Championship. They went for five games without a win some time in September and October. If that happens at Bramall Lane, they'll be setting cars afire.'

I got an hour's half-sleep between 5 a.m. and 6 a.m. Sharon woke up about quarter to seven. I was wide awake again by then.

Kevin McCabe, the chairman of the club's PLC board, was supposed to be going to America on Tuesday. I wanted to go to Brussels, where he's based, to talk to him before he went.

'Listen, darling,' I said, 'I know it's going to mess up the kids' schools but I've got to leave the club. I can't stay at Sheffield United. It's the right time to go. I've got so much of my appetite back for the game and I don't want to finish on a relegation. I want to go to another club, a completely new club I don't know anything about. I want to do well with that club and give it my best shot.'

I didn't know if Kevin would be able to see me on Monday but I phoned him early. Just like I'd phoned him early when I rang to apply for the job seven and a half years earlier. I told him I had to come and see him. I told him I had been up all night. He told me to get over to Brussels.

Before I left, my secretary rang to say Sir Alex's secretary had called and asked me to call Sir Alex back. I thought about it for an hour. I didn't know whether I wanted to ring him. But I did.

He said he was sorry about what had happened at Old Trafford.

'We fucking battered them, Neil,' he said. 'We had twenty-five shots. And the stats would back me up on that. The team was good enough to win.'

'I know, Alex,' I said. 'It's just the psychological boost the other team gets when they see all those names not on your team sheet.'

'I can't tell you how sorry I am,' he said.

Curbishley must hope he gets Manchester United the last game of the season every season. On the last day of 2005–06, Sir Alex presented him with two tickets to New Zealand, the next season it's six players missing from his first team. It's going to have to be something pretty special the third time around to improve on those two.

Even as I was talking to Sir Alex, I was thinking, what about the team you picked to play against us, what about all the stars who played in that?

'Anyway,' I said, 'thanks for ringing. We'll speak another day.'

He was quoted the next day as saying everything was all right between us again now. But it's still difficult for me to digest what happened.

I got a flight from East Midlands Airport at lunchtime. When I landed in Brussels, a car picked me up and drove me to the part of the airport where the private planes land. There are some offices there. Kevin was sitting in one of them. I sat down and we began to talk. I don't know whether he wanted me to stay or not. I thought he did at the time but a few days later he said some hurtful and unnecessary things that made me think differently about him.

I had wondered if there was part of him that wanted me to go anyway. I was the lowest paid manager in the Premiership in 2006-07 and it had crossed my mind several times that he was abusing the fact that I loved the club so much and didn't want to leave. Maybe he had wanted to get rid of me earlier. I don't know.

We talked and talked. We reminisced about all the things that had happened since I joined the club in December 1999. Sheffield United was at a desperately low ebb then and together we had transformed it. I had taken the club to the semi-finals of the FA Cup. We might have got to the final if the referee, Graham Poll, hadn't interpreted the Arsenal game the way he did. We had been through the agony of an unsuccessful play-off final and fought back a few years later to win automatic promotion to the Premier League. We could have beaten the mighty Liverpool on the opening day if it hadn't been for what I thought was an absurd decision by Rob Styles. I felt emotional about it all. This was it. This was the end of my time as the manager of my club.

When I left that building on the perimeter of Brussels airport, I was no longer the manager of Sheffield United. I had resigned and Kevin McCabe had accepted my resignation. I was the ex-manager of the club I loved. But I didn't feel distraught. I actually felt as though a weight had been lifted off me now that I had made my decision and got it over with. I felt like it was a release.

A car took me back to the main terminal. I caught a plane back to East Midlands and then dashed off to the League Managers' Association do in Nottingham. I had thought about not going but I was supposed to be collecting an award to mark my one thousandth game as a league manager, a milestone I had reached against Arsenal at the Emirates Stadium the previous September. I thought it would be churlish not to turn up.

The LMA do was at the Crowne Plaza Hotel in Nottingham. Sky were waiting for me, asking questions which I evaded. I was shown to my table. The Portsmouth boss, Harry Redknapp, came up and said how much everybody felt for me over what had happened. Harry had reached a thousand games about the same time as me but he had already been up for his award. Before I knew where I was, the Sky presenter, Clare Tomlinson, was asking me to come up to the stage to collect mine.

There were a lot of things I wanted to say but I tapered it down. I talked about how low I had felt on Sunday, as low, for a few moments, as when my mother died when I was a lad. I talked about Sir Alex's team selection and Rafael Benitez's a week earlier when Fulham beat Liverpool. I talked about the chairman of the Premier League commission and said I wished he had been with our fans on Sunday night.

'The only good thing about the entire bloody weekend,' I said, 'was seeing Graham Poll retire. I just wish Rob Styles had done the same thing twelve months ago.'

It brought the house down. I got a great reception when I was going back to my seat. The applause drowned everything else out, even though I knew there would be a few of my old enemies out there at other tables. Gary Megson, probably, Stan Ternent, Wally Downes, people who were happy because they thought I had got my come-uppance.

So what. Love me or loathe me, I've always been the type of bloke people have had an opinion about. I've given journalists plenty to write about. Good things and bad things about me have filled their columns over the years but I've never hidden. And I've made a habit of picking myself up when I've been knocked down. I haven't had it easy in football. I've spent a lot of time in the lower divisions, grafting and scraping. I've worked and worked and worked to get to the top.

That night at the LMA do, it felt better being out than shutting myself away. As I made my way back to my table, the applause rang out and I started to get the old feeling back. I started to think I'd show people. I'd show them all I could come back from this. I could get the fans behind me at another club. I could get them chanting my name.

Bloody hell, I thought, I'm going to do it again.

_____1_____
CHILDHOOD

MY CHILDHOOD was not easy. There is no point disguising that. It was not without its moments of happiness and its moments of love but my mum had multiple sclerosis and everything stemmed from that. When she was heavily pregnant with me in the winter of 1948, she was walking home through the snow and slipped on a grate in the street. She wasn't injured but it was a bad fall and she was shaken up. She was diagnosed with MS when I was a baby and people told me that it was probably the fall which triggered it. I was brought up thinking there was a good chance I helped my mum contract the disease that killed her. I was always my mum's little boy, I was always her baby and I loved her like mad. As she withered under the onslaught of the disease, I used to think I was to blame.

I don't remember mum without MS. I remember her being able to walk with the aid of tripods but never without any help. The disease would go into remission now and again. She would get better for a little while and then a lot worse. She would move forward a little bit but then fall even further back. So for a while she was on tripods. She would get a bit better but when that period of relief ended, she had to go back in her wheelchair. She would rally a bit, then the next time it got worse she became bed-bound. Then she'd be back into her wheelchair and when she got worse, she was hospitalised. It was a progressive degeneration but there were these cruel windows of hope when I thought each time that my mum might be getting better and that our nightmare might be coming to some miraculous end. It was a horrible disease. I hated it. There were isolated tales of people supposedly recovering from it and there was always talk in our house of an injection remedy from the Russians that was on the way. Half a century later, it still hasn't happened.

Because my mum was so sick, my elder brother, John, my sister, Carole, and I didn't see much of my dad during our childhoods. My dad was a crane driver for the English Steel Corporation in Sheffield, lifting the steel with his crane and then lowering it on to the machinery that blended it and shaped it. At first, he worked at the Stevenson Road plant but then they moved him out to a massive new site they used to call the Ponderosa at Tinsley. They called it that after the 1,000-acre ranch in the television pro-gramme, *Bonanza*, I think. You can see it from the M1 now. Anyway, he worked all hours to provide for us, sixteen-hour shifts every weekday, Saturday mornings, too, and he'd do extras on top of that to get more money.

John did the shopping, Carole did all the cleaning, I just played football. Carole was cleaning the kitchen floor every day by the time she was eight years old. She had her second knee replacement operation a couple of years ago and I'm sure it's because of that. Even with all the extra hours my dad put in, we didn't have a lot of money. I got my brother's shoes when he had finished with them but nobody realised that, even though I was younger than him, I had bigger feet. I didn't want to say anything but it was a terrible squeeze for me to get into them. I got a couple of hammer toes because of that but I presumed it was normal. I had them operated on in later life to get them put right.

We lived on a nice quiet leafy little road called Youlgreave Drive in Frecheville on the southern outskirts of Sheffield but we didn't have many amenities. We didn't have any central heating for a start. There was a coal fire downstairs and the chimney ran up alongside one of the walls in our bedroom so we got what warmth we could from that. In the morning when I woke up, I used to pretend I was smoking because you could breathe your hot breath out in clouds into the cold air. The windows were either steamed up or frozen on the inside. You never seemed to get colds in those days for some reason. We only had an outside toilet, too, and newspaper for toilet paper. My dad was a working man so he was a *Daily Mirror* reader. That meant I wiped my backside on the *Daily Mirror* every single day.

I didn't appreciate all the graft that my dad put in for us until I was a lot older. At the time, I just saw him as a very strict father. If we made a noise at night time, he would warn us once or twice and after that he would come upstairs. Nine times out of ten, he would slap me. If I was really bad, he'd belt me a few times. If Carole and I had been nattering, Carole always used to blame it on me when my dad came up. She'd say, 'It's him', and point at me when my dad came into the room. So I always used to get it and then Carole would cry when dad had gone because she was sorry I'd been hit.

We lived in a two-bedroom semi-detached house in which mum and dad had the front bedroom, John had one single bed and my sister, Carole, and I slept top and tail in the other. My dad worked so hard that he didn't have a lot of time to be with the kids. By the time he got home, we were usually in bed and he just sat downstairs and ate his tea. I didn't realise that he was working Saturdays and Sundays to make sure that we got clothes to wear. As far as I can recollect, my dad never once told me that he loved me but that was what it was like in that era. There weren't a lot of new men in working-class Sheffield communities. A couple of times he gave me cuddles and things like that. Mum was always telling me how much she loved me and now and again I would be farmed out to relatives for the summer holidays and it was nice to be loved in some of those places. At home, though, it was difficult for dad to look after us all and give mum the care she needed.

Our lack of money wasn't helped by the fact that dad smoked about fifty John Players a day. Later in life, he used to light up in bed before he got up in the morning. But he wouldn't have a day off. He went to work even when he was ill. English Steel used to give workers a towel for a present if they took less than a certain number of days off during a twelve-month period. Dad got one of those towels every year. When he retired, they gave him a watch for forty-five years' service. And another towel. I didn't realise until much later in life just what he must have had to do to keep that family together.

We did have happy times. It was just that they were outnum-bered by the difficulties we faced and maybe they felt bitter-sweet because of that. But we used to go to Wallace's Holiday Camp at

Cayton Bay, near Scarborough, when I was really little and for one hour a day, which was all we could afford, I was allowed to rent a child's car. That was one of the highlights of my childhood. My brother and sister would help me climb into that little car and that hour would be sixty minutes of pure happiness for me.

We went camping a lot, too, often to Sutton-on-Trent by the side of the Trent because dad had some relatives there. One day, we put our washing out on the line in the morning and went over to the Trent which was two fields away. When we got back at dusk, ten cows had appeared in the field and they were gathered around the remains of our tent and our clothes. They had eaten big holes in everything, all the trousers and shirts. There was one cow with its head inside the tent. Dad spent all night trying to repair it and we noticed that one of the cows had a really bad cough the next day. God knows what was stuck down its throat.

Fishing was the main thing dad and I did together. A bit of cricket sometimes and Sheffield United, too, but mainly fishing. English Steel had their own group of ponds at Aston and even though I only had a small fishing rod, I always thought I was going to be able to find that space where nobody had fished before and that's where all the fish would be. Once I was about thirty yards away from dad when the float went down lovely and slowly. I started bringing it in with the old wind reel and then all of a sudden, it just shot off. I shouted, 'Quick, dad, quick, dad.' He ran down the bank and he just managed to get hold of the rod before I lost it. It took him about thirty minutes to reel it in. What had happened was that I'd caught a roach and as the roach had gone away, this pike had got it. When it came out, it was the most monstrous fish I had ever seen. Dad got that pike on to the bank and killed it because they ate all the other fish and that was the rule in those days.

My dad was a funny mix. He was stern and he was a disciplinarian but there was a part of him that lived for the day. When he was confronted with the possibility of buying our rented house from the Community Association for £1,000 or blowing the money on a Standard 9 car, he bought the car. Every other Sunday, when he didn't work, we put mum in the car and drove out with her to this Atco at Eckington. It was a gardening machinery place. They had a big field at the side of it and we would get mum out and put her in her wheelchair and get her into the field. Then we'd play cricket while she watched us or read a book and then we'd have a picnic. They were the happiest times because mum was there. Once John and I pushed her down to the Rex cinema on the other side of Frecheville to watch *Seven Brides for Seven Brothers*. We put her wheelchair at the end of the row of seats and she was so happy to be out doing something with us that allowed her to feel normal. Within a year, dad had smashed up that Standard 9 in an accident in the tramlines outside the Rex. So much for not buying the house.

We didn't have any pocket money. We didn't have anything material. The only time I got money was once a year when the Boy Scouts did bob-a-job week. I wasn't in the Boy Scouts but I gave a mate of mine a shilling to borrow his cap for a week. I went doing bob-a-job, got my own piece of paper and pocketed the money. It all went fine until one year this old lady got me digging up her front garden for her bob-a-job. It took me about four days, I had blisters and my back was killing me by the time I'd finished. She gave me a shilling. That finished bob-a-job week for me. I thought that either word had got round about me or bob-a-job week wasn't quite what I thought it was. I got a paper round at *Frecheville News* instead.

Apart from the odd camping trip, we never really had holidays. Mainly because it was so difficult for mum to move around. I used to go to my Auntie Alice's and Uncle Lol's at Hunter's Bar, ten minutes outside Sheffield, and stay with them for a holiday. They were a lovely couple. The first time I went there, I'd got a bit of muck on my knees and my forehead because I'd been playing football. So Uncle Lol said he was going to put me in the bath. We didn't have a proper bath at home, just a tin thing, so I was scared of having a bath and when I heard the taps roaring away I was frightened to death so I ran under this big table he had in the kitchen for posh dos.

'If you don't come out of there, you're going to be in big trouble, boy,' Uncle Lol said.

But I wouldn't budge. I just stayed all quiet in the corner and he had to crawl under the table to come and get me. So they gave me a bath and got me all prim and proper and then Auntie Alice did me bubble and squeak from the weekend's veg. I loved that. I used to do the Pools with Uncle Lol and pick the numbers out for him. One week he won £400 which was a fortune in those days and I thought I was going to get a handsome cut. But he had a driving school called Slack's and he said to me that when I was seventeen, he'd teach me to drive for free. I was sick as a pig. Seventeen seemed too far away for that promise to be worth anything but he kept his word.

Sometimes I'd be sent to Uncle Ernest and Auntie Flo as well. They had a fish and chip shop at Meersbrook. We used to watch telly with my cousin Alec, and his sister, Pat. Then about quarter to ten, when it was quieter, Ernest and Flo would come in with as much fish, chips and mushy peas as we could eat. Boy, did I enjoy that meal. If I couldn't go and stay with either of my aunties, sometimes mum and dad would send me to a children's home at Ashby-de-la-Zouch and I didn't like that at all. I used to tell my mum that I was frightened to go there. It used to scare me, sleeping with all those other kids in great big dormitories, but when I was off school, dad was working, mum was poorly and they needed to know I was being looked after somehow or other.

Sometimes unscrupulous people sensed we were a vulnerable family. As the youngest, they picked me out as the most vulnerable of all. One summer, when I was nine or ten and my aunties couldn't take me in, a mate of dad's said he would take me to Ingoldmells near Cleethorpes. To me that meant a week at the seaside and I was really chuffed. We set off in this estate car with a wooden veneer and I was so excited about the trip. But about an hour into the journey this bloke reached over and put his hand on my knee. I wondered what the hell he was doing. I had to fend the guy off for the whole week. We stayed in a caravan and I knew once we got back to it in the evening that he was going to be trying to touch me. I told him that if he didn't stop, I'd tell my dad and that my dad would sort him out. It put him off a little bit but the whole thing was still incredibly unnerving. I was sixty miles away from home, I didn't have any money, I only spoke to my dad once that whole week on the phone and I'm there with a bloke who's supposed to be his mate.

I had another incident a year later with a local bread man who befriended me. He said he'd take me to the pictures one night and my mum said, 'Go on, get yourself off.' We sat in the pictures and his hand came on my leg. On the way home, he stopped near this park and I told him that if he didn't take me straight home I'd get my brother and his mates to batter him. I never had any problems again. It just shows you, even in those days, there were people lurking. The bread man used to give me free buns to give to my mum and I thought he was just being nice. I suppose that's how it's done. Grooming, or whatever they call it.

I was quite lucky really. That guy in Ingoldmells frightened me to death. He was an opportunist. He must have realised I didn't have proper holidays and that my parents would probably be grateful for the chance for me to have a holiday by the seaside. When it happened to me again a year later, I began to think, bloody hell, is it me or what? I know I haven't got any bloody hairs on my legs but this is summat else. It did frighten me but I didn't tell anybody. I worried that people would say it was my fault. I did tell my mum about the Cleethorpes bloke in the end and she went ballistic. But I didn't say anything about the bread van man. I never have until now, even though I know his name and he's probably still in Sheffield.

After that, it was hardly surprising that I preferred staying at home. I liked just hanging out with my mates in our street. We had a tight-knit working-class community in Frecheville. It was like they always say about the old days where you never locked the doors or the windows or worried about security. We used to go over the hills and play in the parks. We had good times on our road. We used to play hand tennis with Steven Herbert who lived opposite. It was good for hand tennis on our road because there were lines across it in the concrete which we pretended were the net. We used to play football with a stone. We didn't have a ball. Mum used to complain about the scuffing of my shoes then.

We made our sporting arenas out of our imaginations. The passageway down the side of David Fox's house at 32 Hopefield Avenue was our Lord's. We had England v Australia Test Matches there. Loads of them. There were two steps at the top of the path and we used to incorporate those steps to complete the bowler's run-up and then ping the ball down. If a shot hit the side wall, it was a single. If it went back past the bowler, it was a four. If it went back past the bowler and over the steps to the privet hedge, it was a six.

Everyone's garden was a centre for a melodrama of some sort. I used to crawl under our hedge in our back garden to nick a windfall apple that had dropped off Mrs Ebbatson's tree in next door's garden. They always tasted better than the ones in our garden. Sometimes she heard something and came out shouting about there being someone in her garden and I'd be lying there on my belly, hiding, my heart nearly beating out of my chest. We had a different kind of sport with the old couple next door on the other side. Mr Barratt was a hen-pecked old soul but we were on the other side of the fence one day when he finally snapped. 'I've taken this rubbish from you for sixty years,' he was yelling at his wife, 'and I'm not going to take it any longer.' We cheered inwardly. He died soon after that, the poor old sod. He must have been happier for getting that off his chest.

We had an air-raid shelter in the back garden, too, a relic from the Second World War. It was at the far end of the garden, beyond our little lawn, the small orchard, the greenhouse and the sandpit where we had battles with soldiers. Sheffield had been heavily bombed during the war because it was a centre of the steel industry and we often ran down the steps into it, imagining that we could hear the fighter planes overhead and the exploding bombs all around us. It was a good place to go if you were in disgrace, too. You could hide away in there with your thoughts and your grievances.

There was only one television on the road, round at the Ansons' house, four doors down from us. They were a wealthy family. When Yorkshire were playing cricket and Freddie Trueman was about to come in to bat at number ten, word would get around. All the kids would stop whatever they were doing and a dozen of us used to crowd into the front room of the house with the telly. You knew that Freddie Trueman was going to be in for twenty minutes at the most. He would either get a few sixes and several fours or he'd be out first ball. But just seeing him walk down the steps of the pavilion at Headingley was real excitement to us.

I got into my share of scrapes and adventures like every lad. When I was a small kid and Guy Fawkes' Night was coming around four of us said we would get sixpence each and go and buy some fireworks. Each of us pinched sixpence from our houses and went and got fireworks and started to set them off on this patch of waste ground a few streets away. Then PC Donaldson, the local bobby, came out of nowhere. Whenever you saw him in our area, you just scarpered. This time, he was standing over us before we knew it, looking at our collection of bangers and rockets.

'Where did you get them from, lads?' he said. He was fixing his attention on me because he knew my family circumstances.

'A shop in Normanton Springs,' I told him. Truthfully.

'And how did you pay for them?' he said.

'We all got some money from home and bought them with that,' I said.

'Who gave it you?' he said.

'My mum,' I told him.

'How much did she give you, son?' he said. I was starting to panic now. It was the bloody Spanish Inquisition.

'Sixpence,' I said.

'I don't believe that your mother would give you sixpence to waste on fireworks, my lad,' he said.

I started to protest but he grabbed me by the ear and dragged me the half mile up the road to our house. I knew I was going to be in big trouble.

When we got inside, he started speaking to mum.

'I'm sorry to trouble you, Mrs Warnock,' he said, 'but your lad says you gave him sixpence to buy fireworks. Is that true?'

Mum shook her head. 'Where did you get the money from, Neil?' she asked.

'I'm sorry, mum,' I said, 'I got it out of your purse.' Then I started crying my eyes out.

Donaldson just gave me a clip round the back of my head and

said that if I ever did it again, I'd be in prison. That was the most frightening thing that ever happened to me as a kid. From that day forward, I never got in trouble. But you know what, that guy would have been charged today, wouldn't he. PC Donaldson, he'd have been sent to court for giving me a clip round the earhole. But it stood me in good stead. I know what people say about hitting but there are times when you have got to discipline your kids. I have never hit my kids but I don't think it did me any harm.

I got hit at school anyway. I was bullied for a couple of years at Westfield senior school. There were a couple of older lads who smoked on the bus and they picked on me. They told me I had to get them a cigarette a day each or else I'd get thumped. So I took a couple of fags from my dad's packet every morning for a while. I hated getting that bloody bus. Not great times, those. For a while, I thought that if I started smoking, too, I might stop getting bullied. I went through a spell where I'd pick tab ends up off the floor, get the tobacco out of them and roll my own cigarettes. I once had a smoke in the outside toilet at home and as I opened the window to blow the smoke away, my dad came out and caught me.

He took me in the house. He said, 'Oh, you can smoke can you?'

He smoked these John Players which were just about the strongest things around and he handed me one.

'Here you are, my son,' he said. 'Smoke that.'

I put it to my lips and took a puff but I didn't inhale it.

'Not like that,' dad said. 'Tek it all in.'

He made me smoke the whole cigarette and I went green. I was sick as a pig.

'Let that be a lesson to you,' he said. Didn't stop him smoking his fifty a day, though.

At Frecheville Infants, I got plenty of discipline, too. I even got caned for playing marbles in the wrong place on the grass. As I got caned, the teacher said, 'Why can't you be a good boy like your brother?' with every thwack. It was like a mantra. I began to associate pain with our John for a number of years. I was the mischievous one and John was good at everything. He was clever academically and good at sport. He was a good footballer. And he never misbehaved. So I always used to get it rammed down my throat about that. I suppose they were right about the two of us. I certainly took advantage of him when I could.

When I was seven or eight, John started going out with Norma, who he later married and they have got four lovely kids now. Sometimes, mum would be taken to a disability centre for the day to do some weaving and give her a change of scene. John would be courting with Norma and he would want to be in the house on his own with her. I was in the way and I knew only too well I was in the way. So he'd tell me to go and get some sweets and, to make sure I was out of the house for as long as possible, he'd give me threepence each way bus fare and sixpence for sweets to go to Manor Top. That meant a good five-minute walk down to the bus station and then a ten-minute bus ride each way. So it was a good hour round trip by the time I'd waited for buses and pondered over my sweets. But I soon realised I could get the same sweets from a shop that was walking distance away and save the money from the bus fare for myself. I saved quite a lot of money that way and spent the extra time just sitting with my mates.

I didn't get quite as much leeway at school. There was a teacher called Mr Murton who was very, very hard with the cane. You got to know that if you were in trouble, you ought to put two or three exercise books down your pants and risk being punished further because if you didn't, you had marks for days and days. We got clued up to that. When we were in the juniors, Mr Murton asked me what I wanted to be when I grew up. I said a footballer. And he said no, son what *real* job. I kept saying footballer until in the end I could see another caning coming so I said engine driver or summat just to appease him and get him to move on. He wouldn't have it that I wanted to be a footballer.

But I did want to be a footballer. I loved playing and I loved watching. Even though my dad worked all hours, he did have Saturday afternoons off. I liked United rather than Wednesday right from the start. I identified with United because they were the underdogs in Sheffield at that time. Wednesday had the biggest crowds and the biggest ground. Hillsborough had FA Cup semi-finals and they were generally reckoned to be the club with all the tradition. My sister was a Wednesdayite because she had a crush on their left winger, Colin Dobson, and the first game I went to see was a night game at Hillsborough. But Wednesday didn't do anything for me. I felt like I was the black sheep of our family. I felt I lived in the shadow of my elder brother, that he was good at everything and that I was always causing problems. And so United and me were a fit.

Dad worked from 6 a.m. until 2 p.m. on a Saturday. He'd get home about twenty past two and get changed and then we would run back down to the Intake bus station. We would get to the bottom of Granville Road about ten minutes before kick-off. I had a wooden rattle and if I'd been a good boy, dad would buy me a rosette and we would go up into the Kop. As I went through the turnstile, I'd look up at the bank of people and it was enormous for a little boy. I'd scamper up to the top and smell the hot dogs at the back where they were selling them. You'd get up and just see the backs of the heads of the fans and catch glimpses of the players already out on the pitch. My dad would tap a bloke on the shoulder and say, 'Boy coming', and they lifted me up on to their shoulders and passed me all the way down to the front. I stood in front of the railings with four or five other boys whose parents had done the same thing. My dad stayed up at the back and then we met up a couple of minutes after the final whistle.

He even took me to London once to watch the Blades. Dad used to contribute five bob a week to an English Steel social club and once a year they had an outing. They used to go down to London to watch a game. The game this particular year was Arsenal v Sheffield United at Highbury. Dad couldn't afford to pay for me, too, so he smuggled me on to the bus for the journey south. We stayed at the Imperial Hotel on Russell Square and to a little boy it looked like the biggest place in the world. I slept in his bed and we went to Highbury the next day. I crept under the turnstiles to get in and when I saw the stadium it seemed like one of the wonders of the world. The clock at the Clock End looked like Big Ben to me and the noise at Highbury was unbelievable. They beat us 1-0 but Joe Shaw, the little centre half who played for us, was absolutely magnificent. I wished and wished that I could play like that.

United and Bramall Lane were in my blood. My grandma lived in Denby Street at the back of the ground. On the opposite side of the cobbled street there was a big engineering company and the gates to its premises. I used to play football with a tennis ball against those gates. I pretended it was Sheffield United against Sheffield Wednesday. I put a little goal up and played a ball into this goal and wherever it went when it bounced back off the gates, I had to get it back in with my first touch. I went through all the goals and the celebrations of the United players. There was a pub called the Sheldon near grandma's and she used to give me threepence to walk up to that pub on the corner to go and get a gill of beer for her. When you walked up the road in the sixties, every door was ajar and you could hear the theme tune to *Coronation Street* coming out of every house.

I lived for playing football. When John went off to have a game with his mates after he'd done his homework, he always used to take me with him. And even though I was six years younger than him, he'd say, 'If I can get you in, I'll get you a game.' And he always got me a game. He was brilliant. I wasn't out of place either. The lads would always treat me normally. I played in the school team and dad came to watch me a few times . He saw me play my first game for Frecheville for the Under-9s against Charnock. I'd been a bad lad and the headmaster had said he wouldn't let me play. I was distraught and then on the day of the game, the head relented. My dad had bought me a new pair of boots from Timpsons and I had put dubbin on them. I felt so delighted with those boots. Just wearing them made me feel a bit special. I scored three goals and I was ever so proud because dad was there.

When I was a little bit older, they built a football pitch on the open fields at the back of our house. Frecheville's a suburb of Sheffield but there was open countryside at the back of our house, wild land with big hills and fields. We used to climb there every night and have hide-and-seeks. Then one night there was this big sound and we looked out of the windows and saw this massive land-leveller machine, one of those Wimpy things, and it was working its way into position at the back of the house. It started levelling and when we asked them what was happening, they said they were building a football pitch and that our house would be next to the half way line. They carved a pitch out of the hillside and then flattened the earth down. It felt like it was too good to be true.

They got more and more of the land-levelling machines in there and the drivers got to know me and John and would stop and pick us up and drive us round. It was so exciting being in these giant machines. So they levelled it and turned it into Frecheville Community Football Club. They put fencing up around the pitch and made a bank to stop people getting in. But they had to have a couple of little gates in the fencing because if the football went over the top, they had to have a way of getting it back. So me and my brother used to go on to the pitch every afternoon after school. It was our Wembley.

We played at the far end of the pitch, as far away as possible from the pavilion. But when the Warmans, who were the father and son who ran the centre spotted us, they would yell at us to get off and, when we ignored them, they'd come after us. We always used to leave it until they were about 100 yards away from us before we sprinted off. They never caught us because we knew where to hide. But I never played a proper game of football there and that ambition stayed with me all through my youth and my middle age. Then, when I took over at Bramall Lane, I took a United team up there to play against a Sunday team that was managed by a mate of mine, Mick Howard, for a charity match. I was going to play but I'd got whacked the week before and I thought better of it. It was the right move because the Sunday team kicked us to death and they would have given me the hatchet.

I went back the following year with the full United team. The game was staged in aid of motor neurone disease because the guy who ran the club, Billy Naylor, a local football celebrity, had been struck down by it. People queued for 300 yards to get into the game, all the way up to the main road where the shops were. There must have been 4,000 people inside that little village ground that night. It was a great night. It was solid. The supporters were packed in on the banks. I went round afterwards and showed the United lads where I was born. There is a young couple living there now who have done it up and he's a Unitedite. When I knocked on the door, he was a little bit taken aback but he let me have a look at the bedroom where I was born. The couple have just had twins and it was nice to know that kids would be around the old place again.

It was a good little community when I was growing up. Mum always used to make me go to church, best shirt and tie on with

Brylcreem in my hair. I went to the Methodist church at Frecheville to go to Sunday school, but before we got there, us mongrel kids would dart into another church up the road at Hopefield Hall. I've got no idea what religion it was but they gave you a voucher if you went to their ceremony, which was all singing and tapping your feet, and then after the service, you could claim your voucher back for sweets.

I got round a few of the churches, actually. They used to have a talent competition in the church hall at St Swithin's along from the Methodist church. Steven Herbert, another mate of mine, played the piano and I went along and sang 'Tammy' by Debbie Reynolds. We came second. I had another mate, Geoff Rastall, and we used to go on stage strumming tennis rackets for guitars and singing Everly Brothers numbers. I sang a couple of Cliff Richard songs at an old ladies' do at the church hall, 'Living Doll' and 'Travelling Light'. There was a lot of singing at that time. You had to make your own entertainment.

After church, I went to a community centre at the top of the village. There was a big pond there and tennis courts. Everybody used it as the big meeting place for the weekend. The pond was fantastic. There were fish in it and the odd boat. There were swings and a bowling green, too. Occasionally, we used to go up and pay and have a game of tennis. The courts have all been vandalised now. The grass court, that we used to pretend was Wimbledon, is all overgrown with weeds. Only the netposts remain. One of the other courts was smooth red clay. It's a pockmarked basketball court now with bits of net dangling from the rim. The kids play football on them but there's no tennis. The bowling green's still being used but it's got a fence all around it to try and stop intruders getting in.

The pond looked a bit decimated the last time I went up there, too. I used to love fishing and we used to get a day ticket. Everybody knew there was a great big pike in that pond. Nobody could ever catch it but you always thought you had a chance. Everybody talked about it. It was like the bloody Loch Ness Monster. There were one or two old guys still fishing when I went back and they were saying they used to have a name for this old pike. They called it Randolph or summat. One of the fellas said there was still a big fish in the pond but there were a couple of tyres in it, too, and some tin cans bobbing on the surface. Around the sides it's clogged with all sorts of flotsam and jetsam, McDonald's cups, plastic wrappers, a half-submerged For Sale sign from an estate agent. Just seems to be the way society is going. When people say we have moved on and everything's better, I don't think everything's better. The respect we had as kids for other people was far greater. If we went on a bus and I didn't stand up immediately for a woman, I would get a clip around the ear from my dad and if I didn't open a door for a woman, I would get another one. Nowadays, you could get on a bus and a young kid could be sat next to his mum and never make one inch of movement if there's an old lady standing up. I think that's sad.

As I grew towards my teens, mum's life ebbed away. She hated her illness because she'd been such an active person before she got it. She always used to be round at her mum's in Denby Street near Bramall Lane, helping her out. She loved me to bits, my mum. I was her little boy and the best parts of my childhood were spent sitting on the floor in front of her wheelchair at teatime with the fire crackling and my mum running her hands through my hair. She had been in pain for many years but she very rarely complained or moaned. Very occasionally, when she couldn't do something routine that everyone else could do without thinking, that made her feel she was less of a mother to us than she should have been and she would say, 'I wish I was dead.' Most of the time, she suffered in silence. All I remember from her is love and affection. When I sat there at her feet, she used to murmur to me. 'You will be somebody special one day,' she said, 'make no mistake.'

When my mum got bad, I used to prune the privet hedge at the front of the house and people used to come up to me.

'How's your mum?' they'd say.

'Well,' I'd say, 'she's inside, she's all right. She's only just inside the door there. She'd love to speak to you if you've got a couple of minutes.'

But they were always in a rush. You'd think my mum had got leprosy or summat. She was only ten yards away, just the other side of a pane of glass, propped up in her bed, but they wouldn't go in and see her. She wanted people to talk to. It made me think how horrible people were.

She got worse and worse until she became bedridden and then they admitted her to Nether Edge Hospital and there was a ward with five or six people who had multiple sclerosis. There was talk of a miracle there because one of the ladies was supposed to have left and mum said she had recovered. The doctor said you had to have faith if you wanted to recover but mum said it was so hard to have faith when you were getting worse and worse and worse. I went to visit her every day. I got a bus from Frecheville down to Pond Street where the station was and then a bus to Meersbrook. I'd get off it near Bramall Lane and walk up the cobbled streets to my grandma's house for my tea. She always had pastries and parkin and then I'd walk half a mile and catch another bus up to the hospital. I sat with my mum from seven until eight and then caught a bus back to Pond Street and went straight home. I did that for a couple of years.

When she was getting really bad, my dad used to be the manager of a football club called Swallownest Miners' Welfare. My brother and I played for them sometimes. They were a great bunch of lads. It was a bit like a family. Anyway, he was taking training one night and he joined in and fractured his femur. In those days, you were wired up for months with a broken leg and you didn't move. When we went to see him, he was in traction. Mum was getting worse every day and he was in hospital on the other side of Sheffield for quite a few months. I wasn't aware that mum was on her last legs but she could hardly talk by then. Dad was desperate to get out of hospital but they refused to discharge him. And then mum died. It destroyed dad that he wasn't there. He hadn't seen her for months. He had been asking the hospital non-stop if they would let him out just so he could go and see her but they wouldn't let him. It seems inhuman now. On the day she died, he discharged himself and came home just in time to see them bringing in her coffin.

It was 1962 and mum was forty-six. Even though she had been ill all my life, it still felt like my world had ended when she died. John came home and sat us down.

'Look, I've got some news,' he said. 'You've got to be brave. Mum's passed away. She won't be in pain any more.'

I didn't cry straight away. Mum always used to say to me that I had to be strong and that she wouldn't be there forever, that I had to be a big boy and look after everybody else when she was gone. I couldn't cry for a few hours. I just wanted to be strong, like she'd said. Then a few hours later, it hit me and I couldn't stop crying then.

When she was in the hospital, John had promised mum that she would come home so when she died we brought her coffin into the front room the night before the funeral and laid it on the table which was commonplace in working-class families in those days. Dad was thin and drawn and there were buckets of sweat pouring off him. He sounded like he could hardly breathe. He was obviously in agony. My mum looked peaceful at last. I looked into her coffin and said goodbye. Candles were flickering all around the room and I felt scared and lost.

I went to mum's funeral and when we got back home, Mrs Ebbatson had done all the sandwiches. The house was full of people. A lot of them were the ones who had passed by and didn't want to see mum when she was ten yards away. There were a lot of relatives there who could have come to see her but hadn't. Auntie Edith had a chat with me and said mum was happy now and that God would look after her. But I told her I didn't understand how a God could ever let anybody go through the pain that mum had been through.

I looked at all those people in there and couldn't understand why they hadn't come to see my mum when she wanted someone to speak to. I hated them all and I ran up the garden and went into the air-raid shelter. I told Auntie Edith that I didn't think there was a God and I was full of the unfairness of it all. Me, a thirteen-year-old boy, being deprived of my mum. I went off religion for twenty years. In that house, I just couldn't stand to talk to the people who were pretending they'd had affection for mum but hadn't been to see her. I didn't want to be hypocritical. I confronted some of the people that were having the sandwiches and told them they could have come to see mum when she was alive. It all got a bit awkward. They shuffled me out.

Dad became more of a sympathetic character when he grew older but I never grew closer to him. When mum was in hospital, I was allowed to sleep in his bed for a treat and cuddle up to him. I used to count his breathing. I wished I could breathe like him because he breathed so slow and steady. I took two or three breaths to every one of his and I'd stay awake at night trying to match my breathing to his. Dad started going ballroom dancing after mum had died, up at the Embassy Ballroom near the Rex. I got resentful because he began bringing women home. It was only platonic stuff but I told him he couldn't have any other women in our house because it was mum's house.

I spoiled a bit of his life because there was one time, when I was about sixteen or seventeen, when he met a woman who he wanted to settle down with. She was a nice woman, loving and friendly, and she spent a lot of money modernising our house and putting an inside toilet in it with the idea that she was going to move in with us. I kicked up a song and dance about it and, in the end, it didn't happen. I felt guilty then. It was probably his only opportunity to make a new life with a new partner but I felt it would have tarnished mum's memory.

Dad died in April 1977 when he was sixty-six. It said pneumonia on his death certificate but I don't think the smoking helped. I had felt very proud when he'd come to watch me playing for Chesterfield and Rotherham early in my career but I had also felt the need to escape his dominance as I grew up. Dad was Labour through and through. Like I said, the *Daily Mirror* was the only paper he'd ever have. He used to talk about Labour all the time. 'This party's for the workers, son,' he said, 'just remember that, because no one else will help us but them.'

So the first time I was eligible to vote, he took me down to the polling station. He took me inside and talked me through the ballot paper. He pointed to the name of the Labour candidate.

'That's where you put your cross and that's who you vote for,' he said.

'Okay, dad,' I said.

Then he went outside and I scrawled my cross opposite the Conservative.

'Did you put your cross in the right space?' he said when I came out.

'Yes, dad, I did,' I said.

It was my first act of rebellion against him. That'll teach you, I thought.

2

FIRST OF MANY

I KNEW EARLY in my playing career that I wasn't going to be a superstar. I wasn't a bad footballer. I was a winger, quick but brainless. I thought I got stuck in, too, but other people have told me they never saw me make a decent tackle. Well, wingers are never going to be the bravest. I was direct. I used to get past full backs and cut in from the left to hit it with my right. I could beat a player and I could put crosses in but I just couldn't do it consistently enough to play at the top level. So I played out my twenties and my early thirties in the lower divisions, going from club to club, trying to keep one step ahead of the hangman. Every season, when I got past Christmas, I started to get a heavy feeling in my heart because I knew the time was coming when a manager was going to take me to one side and tell me that he was going to have to release me.

One of my teammates, Kevin Randall, once told me I was the only footballer he knew who had made a success out of being a failure. I was a journeyman but somehow I managed to eke out a career as a professional for thirteen years and 326 appearances. It worked like this: I had a couple of good games every season and towards the end of each campaign, the team I'd played well against came in for me and signed me.

Pretty soon, ambition, for me, meant getting another contract at the end of the season. When first Chesterfield and then Rotherham United let you go at the start of your career, it tends to bring it home to you that you're not going to be the next Tom Finney. But I loved my time as a player. I made the most of what I'd got. There was nothing I left undone and no amount of effort or extra work would have turned me into a top-flight player.

Mainly I was just happy not to be working in the steel industry like my dad. When I left school at sixteen, dad got me a job helping with the accounts in the offices at English Steel. I loved the accounts part of it. I wanted to be an accountant, really. Seriously. But soon I realised that working at a steel plant called for its own kind of sacrifices and they were the kind of sacrifices I didn't want to make.

It was summer and I was hot after the walk from the bus stop, so before I took the short cut through the barmill, where they rolled the steel, to the offices where I worked, I whipped my jacket off and tucked it under my arm. I had a white shirt on underneath and when I came back out into the sunlight, one of the office girls stopped me and asked what I'd got on my shirt. I looked at it and it was covered in millions of minute specks of steel that were obviously floating around in the air.

I was horrified. I thought that if all that stuff was on my shirt, what was it going to be like on my chest? How much harm was it going to do me if I worked there all my life? I thought of my dad coughing like mad in the morning when he was waking up. Some of it might have been down to the fifty John Players a day he smoked but working at the Ponderosa at Tinsley Park couldn't have helped him either. I said to him that night that I didn't think I could work there any more. He smiled at me. 'I've got to do it,' he said. 'I've always had to bloody do it.'

But I didn't do it. I fancied myself as a bit of a ten-pin bowler and I got a job at a twenty-four-hour bowling alley close to our house in Frecheville. I worked there for a year and I was that good at it that I used to do a bit of teaching as well as everything else. I oiled the lanes, repaired the mechanisms, worked in the café and made the frothy coffees. I worked all the hours God sent and one morning I gave a lesson to a lady whose husband turned out to be Cliff Mason, who played for Sheffield United.

When Cliff came to pick her up, I bent his ear. I told him about what a good player I was and how I was playing for Sheffield Club and North East Derbyshire schools. I talked a good game even then because when we'd finished chatting, he offered to put in a word for me at Chesterfield and try and get me a trial. Sure enough, they invited me over and I got a place in their Northern Intermediate League Under-19s squad.

I stopped working at the bowling alley after that. It was glamorous but the hours were killing me. So I moved across Sheffield to enemy territory near Hillsborough and got another job in accounts, this time at a firm called Burdall's who made gravy salt. They were the Bisto of their day. I was seventeen then, so at the end of every day I caught a bus from Burdall's back into Sheffield and then ran down to catch an East Midland bus up to Pitt Street in Eckington where Chesterfield trained.

It was a great set-up. The trainer was a bloke called Reg Wright who had been there donkey's years and put the fear of God into everyone. He stopped me smoking, Reg Wright. I was that scared of him smelling a fag on my breath that I gave it up in my first year at Chesterfield. He was tough with everyone. He expected total commitment and if he didn't get it, he made it fairly plain he wasn't happy.

That's how I got my break. The first choice right winger for the Under-19s was a lad called Micky Viney who was one of the most talented young players at the club. But in the second pre-season I was there, Micky told Reg that he wouldn't be able to play in the first two games because he was going to Butlin's on his holidays. Well, Reg couldn't believe that anyone would choose to go to Butlin's once the football season had started so he put me in the Under-19s in Micky's place and told me that if I did well, I'd stay in.

He was true to his word. I did okay and when Micky Viney got back from Butlin's, he couldn't get his place back. I really thought I'd made it when I cracked the Under-19s. That was the life. When we went up to Middlesbrough or Sunderland for an away game, we'd always stop at Scotch Corner on the way for a pre-match meal and have a fillet steak and toast at midday. Big Time Charlies, we were.

I scored a lot of goals for the Under-19s, so I got pushed up into the reserves. The captain was a guy called Dave Blakey and he was the last of the old brigade who wore boots with steel toe-caps. He said he wanted hard boots for playing at centre half. He said it with a glint in his eye that unnerved me a little bit but at least I didn't have to play against him. In my second season in the Under-19s and reserves, I got about forty goals and towards the end of that season, I made my first team debut, my league debut, on 6 April 1968, at home against Rochdale. I was nineteen years old and still an amateur.

I was playing against a left back who was thirty-eight, old enough to be my dad, and all the lads said I'd run him ragged. But he was a wily old sod, we lost 2-1 and I didn't think I did that well. Still, when I picked up the newspaper the next day, they'd put a star next to my name to show they thought I'd been the best Chesterfield player. And before the start of the next season, the boss, a Scot called Jimmy McGuigan, told me he was going to offer me a contract.

Before I went into see him about my deal, I'd spoken to all the lads and they had told me that I ought to be getting £35 a week and £15 appearance money and then more for every goal I scored. McGuigan told me to come at a certain time and wait outside his office. I could smell his aftershave from down the corridor. I was trembling when I went in there.

He started talking in his thick Scottish brogue and he was very complimentary in a gruff kind of way. He said I hadn't done badly, I'd scored a lot of goals and I had a long way to go but that he was going to give me my first contract.

'There are a lot of players playing Sunday league football with more skill than you but you'll make a living son and do you know why?' he said.

'No boss,' I said.

'Well I'll tell ye,' he said, pointing at his heart. 'Because you've got that under your shirt and it'll get you by. Anyway, this is what I'm offering you.

'You'll be on £12 a week, £5 appearance and £1 a goal,' he said. 'Sign here.'

I just signed it. I would have signed anything. It was a one-year deal. The first of many.

I went back into the dressing room and the lads said, 'Well?'

'Top notch,' I said. '£30 a week.'

I went to see my boss at Burdall's and told him I was quitting to be a full-time footballer. His name was Mr Hyland and he tried to talk me out of it. He told me that one day I could have his job and be earning £25 a week. He knew I was on £6 a week at the time and that I'd just saved up to buy my first suit, which had cost six shillings. He said that I could be finished in football if I got an injury. 'Look at these bricks and this mortar,' he said, pointing around at the factory walls. 'They'll never fall down.' I knew he might be right but I had to go for it at Chesterfield. I went back to Burdall's five years later and the factory had closed down. So much for the talk about bricks and mortar.

I was desperate to do well at Chesterfield. We did our pre-season at a beauty spot called Froggatt Edge in the Peak District. We did some right runs over the rocks. It was about twenty minutes down and twenty minutes back up. I always won the second leg and the rest of the lads said I wasn't trying hard enough on the way down. I loved it there. I associate it with the start of my football career. I've still got an affinity for that place.

McGuigan taught me a lot. Mainly about set pieces and how to attack them and defend them. He went into it in a lot of detail, which was relatively new in those days. I used to love watching our forwards, Ivan Hollett and Kevin Randall, too. They were one of Chesterfield's most prolific attacking partnerships and Hollett had this bicycle trick that he used to do which was an ancestor of the stepover. It wasn't quite Cristiano Ronaldo but it worked every time. Randall was good, too. He had a big backside so it was bloody difficult to knock him off the ball. I respected him as a player – he would have been worth a fortune today and in the early part of my career, he was the player I went to for advice. I must have seen something in him because I even made him my chief scout at Bramall Lane.

But most of what I learned at Chesterfield was about the footballer's way of life. I was still a kid, wide-eyed and raw, and the other lads got a lot of amusement out of playing the odd joke on me. I got my first insight into professional footballers on the road when I went on an away trip with Chesterfield to Swansea in November 1968. The Vetch Field was a lovely atmospheric old ground in those days and Ivor Allchurch, one of the greats of Welsh football, was still playing in his long shorts with his silver hair. We drew 0-0 and after the game, when we were standing outside the ground waiting for the bus, the inmates at Swansea Prison, which was just across the road, were at their windows, rattling their spoons against the bars, while we shouted our greetings up to them.

We stayed down in Swansea that night and the lads told me I was rooming with an Australian goalkeeper called John Roberts who was a good looking bloke and always pulled a bird. We went out for the night and when we got back, I went up to the room and the door was locked. So I knocked on it and this Aussie came to the door and he said, 'Sorry, mate, you can't come in here tonight. See you in the morning.'

I was like a lost lamb. In the corridor of this hotel, on my first away trip, thinking where am I going to sleep. The rest of the lads were pissing themselves. One of them, Tony Moore, who became one of my best friends, came out of his room and said, 'What's up, Warny?' and I told him and he fell about laughing again. Tony took pity on me in the end and I went to sleep on his floor. In the morning, we took the Aussie breakfast in his room so we could have a good look at his companion.

I had some happy times there. I played against Halifax at The Shay at Easter and my family came to watch. I scored a couple of goals for the first team and I loved the social life. All the players used to go down to a casino called the Carlton Club in Chesterfield on a Sunday night when there was a Tamla Motown evening. The music was great in those days and it was also a casino.

But the football didn't go well for me. My proudest moment at Chesterfield also marked the beginning of the end for me at Saltergate. We drew Derby County in the League Cup, the Derby of Brian Clough and Peter Taylor, the team that was getting closer and closer to the league title they would win in 1972.

They won the Second Division title the year I played against them at the Baseball Ground and it was a thrill to be up against men like Kevin Hector and Alan Hinton with his white boots. We played well that night but Cloughie had just signed Dave Mackay and he ran the game. Most of the time, he stayed in the centre circle. He never moved more than thirty yards but he still dominated everything. Everything flowed around him. It was tremendous being on the same pitch as him.

We played ever so well, even though we lost 3-0, but about ten minutes before half time, I stretched for a ball and felt a muscle go under my backside. I stayed on but I wasn't the same for the rest of the game and afterwards, when we got back to the changing rooms, I was struggling. There were these lovely big baths at the Baseball Ground but I couldn't lift my leg high enough to get into one of them.

Treatment in those days was hardly hi-tech. Especially not at Chesterfield. Ollie Thompson was the physio. He used to lean over me with a fag hanging out of his mouth and a tube of Deep Heat in his hand, rubbing the ointment into my thigh. I could tell when he thought things were really serious because he'd get out his anglepoise lamp and shine it on my leg for about half an hour. Generally, the advice consisted of three words: run it off.

But I couldn't run it off. The pain started right under my bollocks and ran right down my side. I was out of the game for four or five months. I kept coming back and then breaking down almost straight away. It got to the stage where McGuigan and the rest of them were getting exasperated about the injury. None of them really knew what it was so in the end they started to wonder if it was genuine. I think they thought I might have been trying it on.

After such a long time out, I was getting despairing myself, so I booked a private appointment with Bobby Little, the Sheffield Wednesday physio who had his own practice. He said I had a deep-seated groin injury, that I shouldn't be playing and that I needed to rest for a month. When I told McGuigan, he went ballistic. He said I shouldn't have gone to another physio. I didn't get fit again until three or four weeks before the end of the season.

I did my best to rebuild my reputation in those weeks but it's quite intimidating being a winger at Saltergate. The crowd is right on top of you, so close you can almost feel their breath on your back. You can certainly hear everything they are saying. I think that's why I'm a bit hunchbacked in the way that I walk even now. I picked up the habit of walking with my shoulders hunched there because it felt as if the crowd were right on your back. At full time I used to walk off and never look up in case I got a mouthful of abuse from the supporters.

I hoped I'd done enough to win another year's contract but towards the end of the season, the phone went at 8.30 one Friday morning in the house in Frecheville I still shared with my dad. I walked downstairs and picked it up. It was a mate of mine called Terry Rose, one of my pals at Chesterfield, and he began com-miserating with me.

He'd seen a copy of the *Derbyshire Times* which came out every Friday and there, among the list of players who were being given a free transfer, was my name. He assumed I knew. He said he was sorry about my release and started asking whether I'd got any offers from any other clubs. My name was right there in the paper alongside Keith Kettleborough's and a few others who had been released.

I felt it was terribly unjust that I had had this groin injury and that no one had believed me and then I was released just like that. I was bitter that McGuigan hadn't had the guts to tell me to my face. Since I've become a manager, I've always thought about that experience that morning and made sure I tell people in person, even if it's sometimes hard and you feel desperately sorry for them.

I sat there at the bottom of the stairs. I was distraught. The tears started to well up in my eyes but I was too embarrassed to let Terry know that I hadn't been told. 'Oh, don't worry, it was expected,' I said. We chatted on for a while but I wasn't listening to what he was saying. I haven't got a clue what he talked about from the instant he told me I'd been released. I didn't know what he was saying and I didn't know what I was saying. Eventually, the call ended. I put the phone down and cried my eyes out.

3

FINDING DIGS FOR A DOG

WHEN ROTHERHAM UNITED came in for me a few weeks later, I thought I'd won the Pools. They were in Division Three for a start and they were a better, bolder club than Chesterfield. Tommy Docherty had just blown through there like a whirlwind while he was still on the rebound from resigning at Chelsea but he'd left good training facilities and a progressive attitude behind him. Oh yeah, and Rotherham paid me more money than Chesterfield, too. But I would have signed for nothing just to stick it up McGuigan and prove him wrong.

The boss was a bloke called Jim McAnearney. His brother, Tommy, signed me later in my career for Aldershot. Jim was straight with me. He said I'd had two good games against them the season before and he thought I was a genuine player but he wanted me as cover for his first choice wingers, Jimmy Mullen and Lee Brogden. I ended up playing more games than either of them in the two seasons I was at Millmoor.

We had some great players in that Rotherham team. The best was Dave Watson, who was to go on and become an England centre half. When he was in his prime a few years later, playing for

Sunderland and Man City, an argument raged about who was the better player, him or Roy McFarland and I would always have said it was Dave. He was one of the best footballers I ever played with. The guy was a man mountain and if you were on his team in the five-a-side at Rotherham, you knew you weren't going to concede too many.

Not long after I got to Millmoor, Dave was beginning to get serious attention from bigger clubs and when he heard Sunderland wanted to sign him, he was keen to go. The board were holding out for more money than Sunderland were offering and things came to a head one day when we were sitting on the team coach outside the ground waiting to leave for an FA Cup tie away at Grantham.

The chairman was a larger-than-life old boy called Eric Purshouse who always wore a fedora, the kind Malcolm Allison liked to strut around in. As we were sitting there, Mr Purshouse got on the bus and walked past where Dave Watson was sitting near the front. He kept going past those of us who were sitting at the card table and plonked himself down next to our left back, Dennis Leigh. It soon became obvious to us that he thought Dennis was Dave and that he was expecting a difficult conversation.

'Listen, son,' he said, 'at the moment we can't let you go. We think you're worth more to us than what Sunderland have offered but I don't want you to think ill of us.'

Dennis Leigh's eyes had been getting wider and wider.

'I don't want to go anywhere, chairman,' Dennis said. 'I'm very happy. It's a family club and I don't want to go.'

Mr Purshouse looked a bit taken aback.

'Well, that's great,' the chairman said, 'because I didn't want you to be disappointed when we turned down the offer from Sunderland.'

'No, chairman,' Dennis said, getting quite animated, 'I won't be disappointed, chairman. I love it here.'

The chairman got up and walked down the bus with a big smile on his face. Dennis sat there with a bloody soppy grin and the rest of us cracked up laughing. Dave Watson sat down the front, oblivious to it all. He would have done his nut if he'd heard that conversation but he got his move eventually.

We had two very good goalkeepers at Rotherham, too. Roy Tunks and Seamus McDonagh both had the ability to be top-flight keepers and went on to have excellent careers. More than ten years later, when Seamus was coming towards the end of his playing days, I took him on loan at Scarborough when I was the manager there and we needed him for a match at Swansea. A lot of us were going to the PFA dinner in London afterwards so we'd taken our dickie bows down with us on the coach.

We lost the game 3-0 and we had a bit of an inquest. Usually, after the game I sit the boys down and have a few words with them individually. I started with Seamus.

'I think you'll be a little bit disappointed with a couple of the goals, Seamus,' I said.

Well, he stood up and went ballistic for about fifteen minutes. I've never had a bollocking like it before or since in all my time in management.

'What do you part-time bastards know about goalkeeping,' he

yelled. 'You're all off to your fancy PFA do with your fucking tuxedos. You're more bothered about getting pissed up in London than you are about stopping goals going in your fucking net. This lot haven't got a fucking clue how to defend.'

He ranted and he raved. His eyes had gone. At the end of it, he sat down like he was exhausted. The room was totally silent.

I thought I had best pretend it had never happened. My captain, Cec Podd, was sitting next to him.

'And as for you, Cec . . .' I said.

Years later, Seamus and I laughed about the incident. McAnearney never had to put up with anything like that from Seamus at Rotherham. The gaffer was a nice bloke, probably a bit too nice, and it was difficult for him trying to fill the gap that Docherty and his charisma had left. But we played some nice football and I nearly got to play against Leeds United in the FA Cup in January 1971. I was in the side to take on Don Revie's team, up against Norman Hunter, Billy Bremner, Peter Lorimer, the lot of them. I was looking forward to trying to get some change out of their left back, Terry Cooper. Then the fog came down over Millmoor and the game was postponed. When it was played a week later, I was left out. It was one of the biggest disappointments of my playing career. We drew 0-0 and took them to a replay at Elland Road. I was left out of that, too.

Towards the end of my second season at Rotherham, Jim McAnearney came up to me before a reserve game and told me he might be letting me go in the summer. He said a few people had come to watch me that night so I could do myself a few favours. It didn't occur to me then that playing myself into a move to

Hartlepool United might be classed as doing myself a favour but at the end of the game, McAnearney told me that the Hartlepool boss, Len Ashurst, was waiting to speak to me. I told him he must be joking. I didn't want to go all the way to bloody Hartlepool to play my football. But McAnearney pleaded with me. He said Ashurst had come a long way to talk to me and that I should at least do him the courtesy of hearing what he had to say. He said it would make him feel better, too.

Well, Len Ashurst spent one and a half hours talking to me, telling me what I would do for them, where I fitted in with his vision of the side and where Hartlepool were going. He told me all about the grand plans he had. You would have thought he was the manager of Real Madrid, the way he was talking. He was that enthusiastic about Hartlepool. He was enthusiastic about me, too. He made me feel so important. As the time ticked on and we stayed shut in that little room at Millmoor, I started to think I'd love to play for him. He won me over and once I'd decided to sign for him, I never regretted it. I got more out of playing for him than anyone else in terms of what it taught me about management because he had this fantastic ability to make everyone feel confident. That's a real gift when you're a boss at a football club. Any football club.

So I drove up to Hartlepool in the summer and settled myself down. I got some digs with a couple called Mr and Mrs Green. They were great and they kept me well fed. But there was one catch. They didn't allow dogs in the house and I had just acquired a yellow Labrador puppy called Dusty. So I had to get separate digs for the dog. I sorted her out with this old fella who treated her like a princess. I walked her on the beach after training and kept her in the car while I was out and about and then I took her round to her digs in the evening. He let her sleep in front of his coal fire and gave her the biggest bowls of dog food you've ever seen. I had to run her and run her on that beach to keep the weight off her.

Pre-season was . . . well, it was different. They got an ex-Commando called Tony Toms in to do the fitness work and instead of the long runs over the sand dunes we'd been used to, it was all about sharpness. We did quick sprints up and over hurdles. We did ball work in squares. We never did more than 400 metres at a time and I felt really sharp when the season began. I've insisted on the same regime since I've been a manager because the old-fashioned distance work just made me one-paced. But the short, sharp sprint work wasn't the different part. The different part was an idea Tony had for a bit of team bonding.

One night he took us all out on to the North Yorkshire Moors, somewhere near Whitby. All we were allowed to take with us was a bar of chocolate, our clothing and some polythene sheeting for shelter. He told us we were going to stay out all night and when we had been dropped off, he took us out over the moors, through the heather and across the marshes, into the middle of bloody no-where. After a while, he stopped. One by one, he pointed each of us in a different direction and told us to take fifty paces and then stay down and keep still. I took my fifty strides and stayed down. I stayed there for what seemed like hours and I began to think they'd forgotten me. The night was black as pitch and it got nerve-wracking. Then, suddenly, out of nowhere, I felt this hand on my back. I've never shit myself so much in all my life. I never heard a twig snap, he was that quiet.

It turned out he'd been going round the whole group, getting them all the same way and then taking them all to a meeting point by the side of a river. But the fun still wasn't over. We had to have a competition to win a ration of extra food. The winner got the food. The loser got chucked in the river. There was lots of nervous laughter. We thought he was joking but he wasn't. So we played this game where you go round the group counting up from 1 to 50 and whenever you got to a number that was divisible by three or five, you had to say 'beep' instead of the number. If you fluffed it, you lost a life. The first one to lose three lives was heading for the river.

That was almost as scary as waiting in the dark for Tony the Commando. I was a couple of lives down when Mally Dawes lost his third one and that was it. We had to lift him up and lob him in the water. He came spluttering to the surface, clambered back up the bank and then started to dry himself up. Tony had started a fire by then and Mally sat very, very close to it. We stayed out there under our polythene sheets until dawn came. Then we were supposed to find our way back to Hartlepool by our own methods. I went to the nearest phone box, reversed the charges and got somebody to come and pick me up without anybody knowing.

We did a lot of bonding exercises at Hartlepool. I learned a lot about how you can tell the players that will let you down from things like that. A man's attitude is the same in life as it is on a football pitch. The lads that will go a little bit further and do that little bit more to help out the rest of the lads and not shirk their responsibilities on a cold night on the Yorkshire Moors will be the same lads who will put the extra effort in for you on the pitch when you're losing by a goal to nil and the chips are down.

We needed all the bonding we could get that first season I spent at Hartlepool. We lost to Jim Smith's Boston United in the FA Cup and we all thought Len Ashurst would resign the next day. We were near the bottom of the league, deep in the re-election zone, which was Hartlepool's usual station in life. But when Ashurst came in the day after, he didn't resign. Instead, he locked us all in a room together and tore into us one by one. He had written all our names up on a blackboard and he read down the list with growing anger.

He called one a coward and another one a bullshitter. He called one a fraud and another one an embarrassment. Bill Green was a centre half and he called him a 'big softie'. He got to me and I feared the worst. He said, 'You should win us more games, you only do it in fits and starts and you have got to be stronger.' I thought I'd got away quite lightly, given some of the stuff the other lads were getting, but he told us that if we went down, none of us would be offered another league club because we were all wasters so we'd better do what we could at Hartlepool.

Ashurst said Hartlepool was going to be a different place from now on and that he was going to sort us all out. He said we were going to move up the table and there was no way he was going to finish in the bottom four. We were second from bottom at that stage but what he did had its effect. We went on a run of eleven or twelve games undefeated. In the penultimate game, we played our local rivals, Darlington, away, knowing that if we won, we were safe with a game to spare. There was a full house at Feethams, an 8,800 gate, and we took a big following.

I was up against a right back called John Peverell. He was known as a bloody big bruiser who kicked hell out of everybody. If he could get anywhere near his winger, he would kick lumps out of him. Sure enough, he caught me a right one early doors on the ankle. That was just his idea of an aperitif. Next, I went up for a challenge with him and he planted his knee hard in my back. So I was feeling a bit sorry for myself at half time. We were 1-0 down and I was going to tell Ashurst that I was going to have to come off but, before I could speak, he absolutely laced into me. He said I had to do more. He said I was a nonentity and a coward and he went on and on about how I hadn't got the guts to deal with Peverell.

After that, there was no way I could tell him how I was feeling. So I kept my mouth shut and went back out. In the second half, Bill Green got an equaliser in the seventy-first minute and then I made a great run four minutes from the end and put in a cross and Willie Waddell scored. Everybody went ballistic and we won 2-1. In the dressing room afterwards, Len was euphoric. 'I knew you could do it, son,' he said to me. But I have never felt so bad in my life. I put my hand on my side and I had got a lump the size of a football on the side of my back. I asked the physio, Tommy Johnson, to have a look at it. He was horror struck. 'I've never seen owt like that,' he said. He looked like he was in shock, which didn't make me feel any better. The swelling was so bad because I'd ruptured my spleen.

My wife, Sharon, and my youngest kids, Amy and William, on the cliffs at Trevigue, one of the most beautiful places in Cornwall, where we renewed our wedding vows in 2007.

Uncle Ernest, dad, mum, auntie Edith and grandad Hopkinson at my parents' wedding.

Auntie Edith, mum and dad taking tea as the photographer turns a few heads.

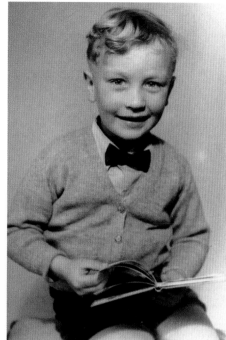

My sister, Carole, my brother, John, and me in the early days in Frecheville.

Me as a little boy. I'm not sure what I was reading but it might have been a Sheffield United programme.

The whole family, sitting in our back garden in Frecheville with me on mum's lap.

Mum doing a bit of fishing on the Trent.

One of the greatest thrills of my young life was seeing Joe Shaw, Sheffield United's centre half, playing for the Blades at Highbury. He was one of my earliest heroes.

I loved playing for my school team at Eckington Westfield. I'm sitting on the front row, second from the right.

Dad was the trainer of the Swallownest Miners Welfare team I played for in the mid-1960s. I'm on the far left of the front row, dad's on the far right, with the bucket.

I broke into league football with Chesterfield in 1968 and was devastated when the manager, Jimmy McGuigan, released me at the end of my first full season. That's me on the front row, third from the left.

Me as a Rotherham United player as my career in the lower leagues of English football began to take shape.

I never thought I'd find myself playing football in Hartlepool but, even though we struggled, we had a great team spirit at the Victoria Ground.

On the moors with Tony Toms, second from left, an ex-marine, who had joined Len Ashurst at Hartlepool. It was a nerve-wracking experience.

I tried some amateur dramatics in my spare time when I was at Hartlepool, including a role in the Gilbert and Sullivan opera, *The Pirates of Penzance*.

Dusty and I were inseparable pals, especially when we shared a caravan together at Henley-on-Thames.

I won the only Player of the Year trophy of my career when I was at Hartlepool after I played a leading part in our stirring escape from relegation.

Left: By the time I got to Scunthorpe United in 1973, I had my seventies look down to a tee.

Below: Like a lot of great wingers, I didn't score many headers but when I did, they were spectacular.

They called for an ambulance and they took me to Darlington Memorial Hospital. There were no beds in accident and emergency – shortages even back then – so they put me on a geriatric ward and I have never heard moaning and screaming like it. I begged them for painkillers because my ankle was killing me as well. They gave me a few but they didn't work and the following morning, I felt sick with pain. I told them I couldn't take any more. Eventually, they took me for an x-ray and found out I had a hairline fracture of the ankle.

I was in hospital for few days but I got quite a welcome when I got out. The *Hartlepool Mail* called me a hero for playing on through that second half with a ruptured spleen and a cracked ankle. I suppose it was about as close to critical acclaim and public glory as I ever got in my career in the lower leagues. I got Hartlepool's Player of the Year award that 1971-72 season, too. The lads said it was a sympathy vote. But it was the only time I ever won a Player of the Year award anywhere. When they presented it to me, they said I'd get a replica when I gave it back. I made sure I got that replica, too, even if I did have to nag them for quite a few years. I got it in 1997 in the end.

Things were never quite as good for me at Hartlepool after that Darlington game. That was a blip of hero-worship. How did I follow that? Not that there weren't a few more highlights. There was one particularly memorable coach journey back from Gillingham where the poker game got totally out of hand. It might not quite have reached West Ham standards, where Matthew Etherington was rumoured to have lost £38,000 in a single poker session in 2006, but the stakes got so big that it scared me off poker for life.

We were about an hour outside Hartlepool when we got involved in a mega-hand. There were about three or four people who thought they could win it. Fortunately, I wasn't one of them so I handed my cards in early doors and sat back and watched. After a couple of rounds, there were still four of them in big time. Another couple of rounds and there was just Mally Dawes and Robbie Smith. By then, the pot in the middle was about £150 which was a lot of money for Fourth Division players in 1972. It got to the point where Robbie Smith had to pay Mally £150 just to see him. He thought about it for a while and, because he had no money left, he put his car keys on the table. He had a Ford Anglia which was worth a lot more than £150. 'Are you sure?' Mally said. Robbie Smith nodded. They turned their cards over and they both had a full house but Mally had a better full house. I asked him a few months later if he ever went round to collect the car. 'Fucking right I did,' he said.

I steered clear after that. I went home at weekends anyway because I had started going out with a Sheffield girl called Sue, who I married around that time. Up in Hartlepool, I managed to keep myself occupied. Apart from walking the dog, I got into amateur dramatics. I joined a musical production of a Gilbert and Sullivan show and sang in the chorus. I got dressed up and everything. I was a philatelist, too. I used to think that was a dirty old man until I realised it was stamp collecting. I collected first day covers. Still do, actually. I love stamps.

I liked it up there but towards the end of the 1972-73 season, I knew the tap on the shoulder, the quiet word and the sympathetic look weren't far away. It came on deadline day in March. Len Ashurst said they'd accepted an offer from Scunthorpe for me. It was £3,250. That was big money in those days for me.

4

FUNNY DOWN SOUTH

S CUNTHORPE WERE fourth from bottom of Division Three when I arrived. The manager, Ron Ashman, said he'd seen me play twice. He said he thought I'd make a difference. Anyway, he said, the only way for Scunthorpe from where they were was up. He was wrong about that. Fourth bottom when I arrived, rock bottom at the end of the season. Not just bottom, either. Seven points adrift of Swansea City, who were second bottom. And back where I seemed to belong, in Division Four. Looked like I'd made a difference all right. Just not quite what Ron had been envisaging.

I actually played more games for Scunny than any other club, haring up and down the wing on that sloping pitch at the Old Show Ground. Perhaps seventy-two games doesn't quite qualify me as a Scunthorpe stalwart but it was the best I could do. I would have loved to have stayed longer at a club and really put down roots. Moving on every year, or every other year, played havoc with my life. I was always worried that the contract I was playing under would be my last. Because I wasn't good enough, I always thought that would happen. I wasn't a good enough player and I knew a club would always look to bring in two or three new players each year and the chances were I'd be asked to make way for one of them.

So I was always on edge. There was nothing else I could have done. I didn't have the ability to play at a higher level. My situation was different to, say, Gary Neville's. Everyone always talks about how he made himself the brilliant player he is through hard work but I just didn't have a cute enough football brain to be a top-class player. That's why I made a living out of moving round and that's what I did. I had a lot of different clubs but I made 300 and odd league appearances and that's not something to be sniffed at. I made it my ambition to play in the league for as long as I could but even though I knew I'd never be a top-class player, I didn't start thinking about management until the end of my career.

I made the best of what I had but I always felt under pressure because of the uncertainty of the occupation. The stress didn't help my personal life and it didn't do my first marriage any favours. You couldn't plan the things other people planned, like mortgages. I knew I probably wouldn't be in one place long enough to move into a house properly, let alone live in one. It was only when I got to Scunthorpe that I took the plunge and bought a house. It cost £4,620. It was a two-bedroomed detached at Carlton in Lindrick, about twenty miles east of Sheffield. We put £620 down and borrowed £4,000. I couldn't see how we were ever going to repay it. I used to talk to Sue about what would happen if it got repossessed. A £4,000 mortgage was a lot of money in those days and the level of the debt worried me.

I did okay at Scunthorpe once we were back in the Fourth

Division. That was the club's natural level, really. They had a reputation for uncovering good players and moving them on, particularly to Liverpool. Bill Shankly took Ray Clemence from the Old Show Ground in 1967 and went back for Kevin Keegan in 1971. They had got a bit above themselves when they got promoted to Division Three the year before I arrived. They had sneaked up in fourth place at the end of the 1971-72 season. Put it this way: it wasn't exactly a shock to anyone when they went straight back down. Ron Ashman moved on to Grimsby Town and his coach, Ron Bradley, took over. I suppose that really was the era of the Ron-manager.

Ron Ashman was from the old-fashioned brigade of put-the-ball down-and-play but Ron Bradley had much fancier ideas. He had been very taken by seeing Brazilians bending the ball around defensive walls in the 1970 World Cup so he had this bloody wall built for us to use at training. I know most Premiership clubs have walls like that now, so you might think Ron Bradley was ahead of his time. Except we didn't have Jairzinho or Rivelino in our squad at Scunthorpe. What Ron Bradley forgot was that we couldn't kick the ball straight, never mind bend it.

We finished eighteenth in that first season back in the Fourth but there were some decent players there. Some decent snooker players, too. There was a guy called Angus Davidson who was the best snooker player I've ever seen. Maybe that's because he spent more time in the snooker hall than he did on the football pitch. He was there every afternoon, all afternoon. But what a comedian. I could have laughed all day at him. Then there was the cabaret in training.

That consisted of our left back, John Barker, trying to break the leg of our left winger, Harry Kirk, every day. Barker had taken an extreme personal dislike to him for some reason. John became a gamekeeper after he stopped playing. A few years ago, I heard he'd shot himself. There was always something melancholy about him.

The second season I was there, we got to the fourth round of the FA Cup and drew Newcastle. That was the furthest I ever got in the FA Cup in my career. We were winning 1-0 at St James's Park before Terry McDermott got an equaliser ten minutes from the end. The replay would have been a belter under floodlights but there was an electricity strike going on so we played it at the Old Show Ground in the middle of the afternoon. I had to have a cortisone injection in my knee so that I could play but they injected you wherever and whenever you wanted it in those days and I was determined not to miss out. But because of the effects of the strike, the stadium was half empty and the atmosphere was flat. Malcolm Macdonald scored a couple and they killed us off easily.

It was while I was at Scunthorpe that I developed my interest in chiropody. Pre-season, I always got bad blisters on my feet, so I started looking after them myself. The physio, Charlie Strong, encouraged me to do a correspondence course in chiropody and I began to look after the feet of some of the other players, too. I enjoyed it. In fact, I enjoyed it so much that when my playing career finished, I was a practising chiropodist for six years. I had my own surgery.

The tap on the shoulder took longer than usual to arrive at Scunthorpe but I got it in the end in the spring of 1975. Tommy

McAnearney wanted me at Aldershot, who were in Division Three. They were the only southern club I ever played for and I noticed the difference in the culture at the club immediately. It was funny down south. If you nutmegged someone in training, they thought it was the world. They thought it was brilliant. They all clapped each other and collapsed laughing. But to me now, as a manager, if you nutmeg somebody and then lose the ball, I hate that. Down at Aldershot, if you nutmegged somebody, it didn't matter where the ball went. It was still an achievement. It was a learning curve for me. Wherever I had been before the emphasis was on not losing the ball and not making a mistake but at Aldershot it was different. I was used to hard work and now all they were concerned about was nutmegging and being flash.

For the first and last time in my career, I found it really difficult to settle. In fact, it wasn't long before I was desperate to get away. Tommy McAnearney might have been the manager but it was the centre forward, Jack Howarth, who ran the show really. He was an old pro who had been at Aldershot for donkey's years. He was like the guy in *Porridge*, Harry Grout, the villain who really runs Slade Prison. And Jack Howarth ran the club. He was the top scorer. The crowd loved him and the manager let him do what he wanted.

There were plenty of wide boys there, too. I mentioned to one of them once that I was thinking of buying a brown leather coat. Strange, I know, but they were all the rage in the seventies. 'Oh, don't buy one,' he said, 'I'll get you one.' A couple of days later, sure enough, he came into training with a brown leather coat. He wanted twenty quid for it. Which I gave him, because it was worth probably five times that much. I'd handed over the money when he winked at me. 'Just don't wear it in Guildford,' he said.

Part of the reason I found it difficult down there was that the year before I arrived, the whole area had been traumatised by the Guildford bomb blasts. Aldershot was a garrison town and everyone was jumpy. No one felt safe. Sue and I went to see *Jaws* and *One Flew Over the Cuckoo's Nest* on the same day and we were evacuated from both films halfway through because of bomb scares. Aldershot got relegated on the last day of the 1975-76 season, too, and it got to the point where I just felt thoroughly cheesed off with everything that year and so I decided to spend pretty much everything I had on a surprise lavish holiday for me and the wife to the Seychelles. I had to borrow some money to pay for it but I was feeling low and I just thought sod it.

We got three weeks for the price of two and then there was a catering strike on the airline and our return flight was cancelled so it turned into four weeks for the price of two. I learned to water ski in that last week and I also bumped into an ex-league referee, Bob Mathewson, who was helping to run a four-nation football tournament on the island that summer, some sort of Indian Ocean competition. He'd found out one of the match officials wasn't going to be able to make it and he knew I was a qualified referee, so he asked me if I'd help out.

I ran the line for him in a match between the Seychelles and the Republic of Somewhere or Other. Reunion, I think it was. Anyway, the Seychelles got a free kick outside the box, they floated the ball over the Reunion wall, a lad made a great run to get on to it and stuck it past the Reunion keeper. All the defenders put their hands up and claimed offside but it was never offside and I thought nothing more of it. Reunion lost the game and when the final whistle blew, I trotted on to the pitch towards Bob. As I jogged towards him, I noticed that he was sprinting towards me.

'Come with me,' he shouted as he ran past.

'Why, what's up?' I said, as I started to run with him.

'What's fucking up?' Bob said. 'Watch this.'

By then, we'd sprinted down the tunnel and through a gate. As soon as we went through it, a bloke locked it behind us. I turned round and about ten seconds later the entire Reunion team came flying into the tunnel and started clawing at the grille of this gate, trying to get at me. They wanted to kill me because they were so angry about me not giving the offside. I thought I'd had a good game but Bob had smelled it. It was quite frightening. That was the first time I thought, dear me, all that for a decision. Still, I got the use of a Mini for a week and they presented me with this double coconut called a Coco de Mar for my trouble. It all gave the holiday that little something extra.

It didn't make Aldershot any more appealing when I got back. The Recreation Ground was a picturesque little place and I scored two great goals that season but I was a bit out on a limb in terms of the other lads because there was already a strong group there when I arrived and I couldn't really infiltrate it. Sue was very unhappy down there, too, so she moved back up to Sheffield and we sold the house. But I couldn't get away from the club, so I bought a caravan, parked it up in Henley-on-Thames and lived in it with Dusty the

Labrador. They ran an article on me in the local paper under a section called 'Soccer at the Top'. I think they must have been taking the mickey. There was a picture of me and Dusty standing on the steps of the caravan. Six months I lived in that thing until, in the end, Tommy McAnearney let me go on the condition I paid back the £1,000 they'd given me for a signing-on fee.

I'd had an offer from Barnsley by then. Jim Iley was the manager and he wanted to take me back up to Yorkshire to add a bit of experience to his young squad. I soon realised why he had a young squad, too. He liked to bully his players. He ruled by fear and he knew the young lads wouldn't stand up to him. They came with the benefit of the fact that they ran all day and they were frightened to death of him. They were also in awe of Jim. Jim still thought he was the best player in the squad. We did a lot of ball work so he could show off all his tricks and his skills. One of his trademarks was that he used police cones as markers for us to dribble round. It was a standing joke that there were more cones at the training ground than there were on the M1.

You crossed him at your peril and if you weren't in the team, he didn't talk to you. You'd walk past him in the corridor and he'd ignore you totally, which I found strange. There was a lot about his man-management that I didn't agree with. On match days, if we were playing at Grimsby, say, and a couple of the lads lived in Rotherham or Scunthorpe, rather than let them hop on the bus on its route past their homes, he would make them come to Barnsley to get on the bus. Then, we'd drive back past their front door an hour later on the way to the game. It just seemed perverse to me. Didn't make sense. I didn't think it was good for morale.

But you know what, I enjoyed my football at Barnsley as much as I enjoyed it anywhere. We were in the Fourth Division but we played good football and if the football's good, you can forget about a lot of the stuff you don't agree with. We finished sixth in 1976-77 and seventh the next season, just a few points off promotion each time. I met a lad called Graham Pugh at Barnsley and we used to have so much fun. We laughed and laughed and laughed. And Graham Collier was my best mate and he was there, too. I loved the mickey-taking. You have got to be so much on top of your game to deal with all that and make sure you survive. We had a keeper called Peter Springett at Oakwell who was a bit tight with his money so he used to get plenty. Peter Price was the resident comedian in the side and whenever we got a win, he'd pretend to be Pete Springett calling his wife and lift an imaginary telephone receiver to his ear. 'Jane,' he'd say, 'great result, great result, another win bonus, get another fiver put in the Halifax straight away.' Peter didn't mind. He laughed it off. Sadly, he died a few years ago.

There were some good players there, too. Barry Murphy was the club captain. Luckily for me, he was right back and so having him behind me, covering me and yelling instructions at me, was fantastic. What a superb pro he was. He worked his socks off for years and years and he talked all day. I probably played as well as I played in my whole career at Barnsley. I had two and a half years there and really enjoyed it. I got one of my best goals there, too, a header in an FA Cup game against Huddersfield. Graham Collier took a corner and I came off the line and launched myself at it. I didn't get many like that and it felt even better to be getting it against one of our fiercest rivals.

But towards the end of my second season there, I found out from one of the girls in the office that the manager was planning to give me a free transfer. I'd been thinking it would be touch and go whether they were going to keep me on. If they released me, I thought I might not get another club. I was twenty-nine and I felt like I might be about to fall off the edge. So I devised a plan. The same day, I went in to see the manager, pretending I didn't know anything about his intention to release me. I told him I wanted to go part-time because I had the chance of a job in civvy street. I told him I'd play on for reduced wages and he asked for 24 hours to think about it. When he came back to me, he said he'd keep me on. Everyone was happy. He saw me as someone who would bolster his squad and be on cheaper wages. And as far as I was concerned, the arrangement kept me in the league and kept my career alive. The girl in the office got a box of chocolates.

The catch, of course, was that I actually did have to get another job to supplement my football income. So I worked for about six months for the Combined Insurance Company of America. They still do the accident and injury insurance for a lot of footballers now. We used to meet in the morning at the branch office in Barnsley and sing, 'If you're happy and you know it, clap your hands'. It was the manager's idea of motivation. The sales reps were drawn from all areas of society: well-to-do people, rough-as-houses people.

I knew it was good insurance and I used to tell people I got signed up how it was best to use it. But I didn't enjoy it. We had to go to people to renew policies. You'd focus on the Huddersfield area one day, then Lincoln, then Sheffield. All different areas. It was hard work. I would find myself sitting in the car, staring at the rain tipping down, dreading going into a shop or an office to try to flog them some new business. The company kept on and on about new business. Every renewal you got, you got a percentage but it was on new business where you really made your money. It was cold calling. Often, they'd seen you before and they didn't particularly want to see you again. We all had this company issue satchel and when they saw you come carrying that and they realised it was a salesman, their face fell. It was like the mark of Cain that satchel. You could see them thinking, oh no, not again. I hated it in the end.

I played in the first team for a lot of that season and then in the summer, just when I thought everything was coming to an end, York City came in for me out of the blue. Charlie Wright had got the York job and he had been allowed to go on a spending spree. He signed about seven or eight players, including me, and from Burnley a lad called David Loggie, who cost £20,000. That was an absolute fortune and this lad strutted in like I would imagine Ronaldo might do if he'd signed for Sheffield United. Boy, did he soon come back down to earth, particularly when his own team-mates were kicking him to kingdom come in training.

I could tell in pre-season that we weren't going to be a good team but I had a decent couple of weeks up to the start of the season and Charlie Wright told me I was going to be his captain. I was really pleased. But the first game of the season was away at Grimsby and on the Wednesday before the match, I developed flu symptoms. The next day, I couldn't get out of bed and I phoned the manager to tell him I wouldn't be able to play. He asked me to go and see the doctor on Friday and then come to the training ground to see him. The doctor said I wasn't strong enough to play and gave me some antibiotics but I went to the training ground, as arranged, to see Charlie, still in my shirt and tie. Charlie was panicking. He said I had to play. He said he wanted me for my influence. So that Friday afternoon, I ended up doing set pieces in training in my shirt and tie. We went to Grimsby and we lost 2-0. On Monday morning, Charlie called me in to the office.

He said, 'Neil, you've got critics in the boardroom, I'm going to have to strip you of the captaincy and leave you out.'

'Critics in the fucking boardroom?' I said. 'I've only played one game. And that was with flu.'

'Sorry, Neil,' he said. 'I feel bad about it but I'm under pressure here already and that's the way it's got to be.'

'I only did it for you, Charlie,' I said. Like Marlon Brando in *On the Waterfront*. Well almost.

Turned out two of the directors didn't like me and they wanted me out. I was amazed Charlie would be weak enough to be influenced by that but he was. I played four games for York City and then I was on my way. A few weeks before Christmas, Warwick Rimmer, the manager of Crewe Alexandra, got in touch. The journey was almost over.

5
PLAYTIME'S OVER

I THOUGHT THE JOURNEY from Yorkshire over the hills and through the Peak District to Crewe would be fine. When I went over to check it out before I'd signed, it was a lovely day. I drove down from Sheffield to Chesterfield, then across to Buxton, over to Congleton and on to Crewe. The sun was out, the sky was blue, the sheep were gambolling in the fields. I thought it was bloody beautiful. A drive made in heaven. It was a bit different when winter bit, though. It was so cold at Crewe one night before a match against Halifax that I wore a pair of women's tights and some black gloves. Thierry Henry eat your heart out. I scored after fifteen minutes, then pulled a hamstring after twenty-three minutes. Women's tights and me just didn't get along.

The drive got more and more difficult the deeper we got into the winter. Sometimes, I'd stop in a pub in the High Peak on the way home after training for a bite to eat and chat to the farmers. They were nonchalant about the weather. They said that if the lights were flashing on the signs that warned you whether the road was passable or not, just ignore them. They said the roads were always passable whatever the lights said. Don't take any notice, they said.

They scoffed about drivers being mollycoddled. They said it was just a precaution.

I drove over a couple of weeks later for a night game. It was snowing gently so I'd taken Sue's Austin A30 which was better in winter weather because it had a front wheel drive. When I got to Gresty Road, the game had been called off. So, after an hour or so in the bar, chatting with the other lads, I set off back home. I gave a lift to one of the lads, who'd had a few drinks. It was snowing more heavily now and, sure enough, when we got to the foot of the hills, we saw the yellow flashing lights telling us that the road was closed ahead.

I drove straight past them and on towards Buxton into deeper and deeper snow. When we'd gone past the lights, there was about an inch of snow on the road. Ten minutes further on, it was six inches and, soon after that, we started hitting drifts. We busted through a few of them but, as we got near the summit, we ran into drifts that were three or four feet high. We didn't know where we were by then. We'd got a bit disoriented and we were getting scared. We thought we weren't far from the Cat and Fiddle Road that joined from Macclesfield – as it turned out, we were only about 300 yards away – but then we came up against this ten-foot drift.

We knew that behind us the drifts would have got worse than they were when we came through them but we still thought we had no option but to turn around. We couldn't even see where the road was by that point because the snow had got so deep. We had no blankets, no warm clothes, no coffee in a thermos. We had nothing, really. We were like climbers going up Ben Nevis in a t-shirt and shorts. We hardly had any petrol left either, so we didn't have the option of sitting it out in the car with the heating on. We both realised we were in a lot of trouble at that point.

Anyway, I did a thirty-point turn on the road, inching the car back towards the opposite direction because I was petrified we might slide off the road into a ditch. We started back down towards Congleton and soon we were running into big drifts again. I thought we were going to get stuck for sure and my mate had to get out and dig through these drifts as best he could. It was a bloody frightening half an hour. We had to take a run at drifts and crash through them and then get out and wipe the snow away. It seemed to take an age as we crawled and crawled along but in the end, through the white stuff, we saw those yellow lights flashing and we knew we were safe.

None of that exactly endeared me to Crewe. But we were always struggling at Gresty Road. We only won three games there all season. We finished bottom of the Fourth Division with just twenty-six points and a goal difference of minus forty-seven. That takes some doing. Until Dario Gradi took over in 1983, they were always known for being at the bottom of the league. That was Crewe's sation in life.

At the end of the season, I had decided that the journey over from Yorkshire had become too much. Even though it was only sixty-five miles, it was two and a half hours. I was thinking about telling them I was going to pack it in, even though I still had a year left on my contract, but before I could talk to the club, I got a phone call from Tony Waddington, who'd taken over from Warwick

Rimmer. He told me he didn't want any travellers the next season, so I told him I'd move over to Crewe. I knew what he was thinking and he knew what I was thinking. It was like a game of chess. He wanted me out and I wanted out but I wanted my money, too. I went over to see him and he paid me in full. He gave me a year's salary just like that. It was the most money I'd ever made in my career.

That was the end of my life in league football but I kept on playing. I went to Burton Albion the next season and played up front with Kevin Hector. What a player he was. Even then at the end of his career, he was still class. Ian Storey-Moore was the player-manager and I had never seen a winger like him. He was magnificent, and a lovely man. On the odd occasions he played, he couldn't walk for days on end afterwards because he had dodgy ankles but when he did play, he was outstanding. I loved it there. Ben Robinson was the chairman then, and he's back as the chairman now. I learned a lot from him and that club about how to handle people. They respected people and they treated people well and that is why they always got the best in non-league.

I started really well at Burton and I thought I might be about to enjoy an Indian summer. But we played Marine early doors, some time in September, and I got badly injured. I was through on goal and one on one with the keeper but it was evens which of us was going to get to it first. I could have done him if I'd wanted to but I stopped at the last minute and raised my arm just as we were about to collide. The keeper just kept on coming, went right through me with his body and snapped my arm like a twig. I could have done him and he ended up doing me. It was agony. I held the arm for a minute then let it go and it just flopped in two places.

Then I made another mistake. I didn't insist on them calling an ambulance. They said Walton Hospital was only two minutes up the road and that we might as well drive. So I got in the back of a car and I was trying to support my arm and every bump in the road was agony. Because we hadn't gone in an ambulance, we had to sign in and wait in a queue at Accident and Emergency until we were called. And I waited for bloody hours. Everton were at home that day and there was all sorts of bother with the fans. As I was sitting there, a bloke came in with a knife stuck in the back of his head. Nice. There were all sorts coming in and there's me like a lemon in my football kit. Eventually, the pain got so bad I felt like I was about to throw up so they stuck me on a trolley for a while. I stayed in overnight in the end and got a plaster cast put on it. Sue came over and drove me home to Sheffield. I had to have a metal plate inserted in my arm with eight screws.

I still didn't want to pack football in but I took a job while I was trying to get fit. I worked for a mate of mine, Les Saxton, who managed a wholesale frozen food firm at Parkway Market in Sheffield. I played with Les at Rotherham and he knew I had a gift for words. So I used to sell packets of frozen food to shop-keepers, resting my bad arm on the till and yakking away to them at the same time. I did special offers, two for one, three for two, discounts, nods and winks, the whole lot. I could have sold ice to the eskimos at that time of my life. I worked there for six months and Les kept me going really. There was a lot of banter and we laughed all day.

I was fit by January and I got hold of a protective cast, like a corset, for my arm, which screwed on. We played away at Workington up in coal-mining country where Bill Shankly was once the manager, and I struck up the partnership with Kevin Hector again as if I'd never been away. But after half an hour, I got a whack on the same spot on my arm and I thought I'd broken it again. The pain was excruciating and I had to come off. The journey home was the worst journey ever. All the way from Workington on a bumpy bus, through the northern Lake District over to the M6 and then all the way back to Burton. I was destroyed mentally on that journey because I knew that meant I had to pack it in. I just wanted someone to put me to sleep.

I went to Sheffield Northern General when we got back that night. I had an x-ray and they said I hadn't actually broken it. One of the screws in my arm had fractured and made another hairline fracture. It wasn't completely gone but I had to have another plaster cast on it. I'd had enough then. I knew I had to pack up. Ben Robinson paid me every week for the rest of my contract. They didn't have to do that and I'll never forget him for that. Everybody said he was a man of his word and he is. It's not a coincidence that Nigel Clough has turned down a few offers to move because he knows you don't get treated like that everywhere. It was great for me to see him get a new stadium and then get Man United in the FA Cup in 2006. That cleared all their debts up. If anyone deserved a stroke of luck, it was Ben Robinson and his club.

But that was it for me. I was thirty-two and it was over. I made a couple of appearances as player-manager at Gainsborough Trinity and Burton, when I went back, but they were just an afterthought. Playing had been a difficult way of life while it lasted. Every Christmas, you didn't know whether you were going to get another contract at the end of the season. You were always very insecure and uncertain. You didn't know what was around the corner and the less secure you are, the harder it is to produce your best. The longest contract I ever had was two years. Barnsley was my happiest time, Rotherham was probably the best club and I loved Chester-field because that's where I started.

By the time I got injured again at Burton, I had started managing a Sunday league team in Todwick and enjoying it. I had been looking at management. I thought I would like to have a bash at it. There were so many things I thought other people were doing wrong and I thought I could do it better than them. There were so many things I wanted to try out. That is how it started. I didn't really feel any grief for the end of my playing career. I had just run out of places to play.

6

HAPPY FEET

W HEN I STOPPED making my living with my feet, I started making my living with other people's feet. I was a qualified chiropodist long before I stopped playing for Burton but when I damaged my arm a second time at Workington, I decided that was the right time for me to set up my own practice. So I rented some premises at 291A Sheffield Road in Tinsley for £25 a week. I had a little waiting room and a treatment room. That was my surgery. I had my name over the door: Neil Warnock, MSSCh. That's Member of the Surgical School of Chiropody, by the way.

For six years I divided my time between chiropody and football management. I got my first break as a boss when I took over at Gainsborough Trinity in the summer of 1980 and six months later I went back to Burton Albion as manager. I worked long days as a chiropodist so I could devote as much time as I possibly could to scouting opponents and looking for new players. And the press loved the idea of a football manager who was a foot doctor. At the first sniff of a decent game, a photographer would appear with one of those giant dinosaur's feet you sometimes still see in toy shops and they'd get pictures of me pretending to treat its toenails.

There had been a chiropody practice on the same site in Tinsley before I set up my practice but the previous guy had had it for donkey's years. He was in his eighties by the time he retired and he only charged a pound a foot. Well, I did the place up, decorated it and made it gleaming and spotless and beautiful and promised I'd give the patients twenty minutes each appointment. I put the price up to £5 a session which caused absolute uproar among the local old lady community.

'The previous man was so much cheaper,' they all said. 'I don't think I'll be coming again.'

But that was before I'd been to work on their feet. The previous guy, a lovely old bloke, had only spent five minutes on each pair of feet and I was taking four times that long. Once I had given those feet twenty minutes of the kind of attention they had never had before in their entire lives, every one of them came back for more. Not only that, they told their friends about me. They still gave me the same spiel about how expensive it was but I didn't mind as long as they kept coming back.

I loved my chiropody. I know most people would say, 'I don't want to be messing about with other people's feet', but I enjoyed it because I was good at it. If you're good at something, it's easier to do. I dealt with the usual range of foot problems: ingrowing toenails, soft corns between the toes, verrucas, fallen arches, you name it. You see a lot of problems before they develop if you are a good chiropodist.

I was very good at getting people to come in and then sending them out twenty minutes later feeling a million dollars. I did normal things like taking hard skin off the soles of their feet and smoothing rough skin down. I also developed a domiciliary practice going round to visit patients at their houses. Early on in the process of building the practice up, I still had three full days of spare capacity but I didn't want anyone to know that when I was starting out so I camouflaged my situation.

I wrote letters to British Home Stores, Debenhams, House of Fraser and GEC. I sent them to the personnel officers and said that I had found myself with half a day spare each fortnight and wondered if they would consider me coming in to do their staff. Four of them asked me in and I ended up doing two of them every week and the other two every fortnight. I go into the local Debenhams up on the moor sometimes and some of the ladies I treated are still working there.

The domiciliary practice was often more like social work than chiropody. Some of these ladies never saw anyone from day to day and week to week. Apart from me. There were some really lovely old ladies and they all looked forward to seeing me but there was one old dear who lived at Brinsworth, near Rotherham, who moaned from the start of my visit to the end of it. I had looked after her feet every month for about two years and she'd still give it the same patter every time I arrived.

'Oh, Mr Warnock,' she said, 'since you came the last time, my feet have been absolutely terrible. When you left, I couldn't walk. The pain was so bad I could hardly bear it.'

She went through the same routine every time, had her feet treated, paid me at the end of the visit, and then slaughtered me as soon as I walked through the door the next time.

Once I went round to her house the day after the Burton Albion team I was managing by then had lost a big game. I wasn't in a good mood. She started on her usual tack and I snapped.

'Listen,' I said, 'before I get my equipment out, could I just say that I think you should get somebody else. I've been treating you for a while and it's obviously not been helping you because you've told me every time I've come that you have been in agony with your feet. I don't want to take your money under false pretences, so I'm going to give you numbers for three or four people and I won't mind at all if you ring them up.'

She was horror-struck. 'Oh no, Mr Warnock,' she said. 'No, no, no, it wasn't as bad as that. You know what I'm like. Please forget I said anything.'

Well, what a change there was after that. There were no more complaints but that wasn't the half of it. Within a couple of weeks, I was sitting down having my lunch with her. Cup of tea, feet up, watching the *News at One* on the telly.

When I first started up the business, I was only taking £30 a week but it soon began to thrive. I was lucky because my first wife, Sue, was very supportive. She was a top-class secretary and she had a good job, so she paid all the bills while I was building the business. I branched out all the time. I got a contract with Leonard Cheshire Homes and the number of house visits grew and grew through word of mouth. I wasn't shy about touting for new business. In the early days, I looked after the feet of an old lady called Margaret Jones in Barlborough, near Chesterfield, and I asked her if any of her friends needed their feet doing. She was very enthusiastic.

Before long, she had organised a weekly social event around me treating all her friends' feet. She had them all round to her house like it was a Women's Institute meeting and they'd take it in turns to have their treatment.

I had the practice for six years, while I was managing Gainsborough Trinity and Burton Albion, but when I took over at Scarborough it got too much. I was charging £7 a session by then and £12 a visit. But I lost a bit of custom when the Midland Bank next door sold its premises and the place became a Thai massage parlour. Well, a brothel basically. Soon after it changed hands, water started seeping into my waiting room from the party wall. I knocked on the door and went in and there were a couple of women standing there in basques. 'This is a good massage parlour, this place,' I thought. I told them about the water and they apologised. Turns out it was coming from the showers, which seemed to be getting a lot of use. I sold the surgery in 1986 as a going concern. The building is still there but it's not a chiropodist's any more.

While I had been building up my practice, I was learning my trade as a manager, too. I was confident I could become a leader. I had always got an opinion when I was a player. Even if I wasn't the best player, I was always telling my teammates what to do on the pitch. I knew how it should be done; I just couldn't do it myself. Those first six years juggling chiropody and management were hectic because I was determined to have the success as a boss that I'd always known would elude me as a player. I was out every night, watching football for some reason or another at some level or another. Inevitably, my marriage began to suffer. But I knew what I wanted to be as a manager and I knew what I didn't want to be, too. I had taken something from all the bosses I had worked under and I had been to so many clubs that I'd already sifted through what to do and what not to do in my own mind.

From Jimmy McGuigan at Chesterfield, I'd learned that there was an art and a method to defending and attacking set pieces. Before anyone else was doing it, he was pioneering routines like the near post corner and the man coming in at the back to head in the flick-on. From Jimmy McAnearney at Rotherham, I'd come to appreciate the importance of a player's technical ability. Len Ashurst at Hartlepool probably taught me more than anybody, particularly about man-management. He showed me how you get blood out of a stone at a club with no money. He showed me about generating funds himself because he was so desperate to improve things. Some of the trips we did, he paid for out of his own pocket. When the chips were down, the way Len behaved taught me about being strong and having guts and believing in yourself and how far that could take you. I also took a lot from the training regime there and the short, sharp drills of our Commando trainer, Tony Toms. We did a lot of sprints and a lot of hurdling, too. Ask anyone who has ever played for me, to this day, what the main feature of pre-season training is and they'll tell you. 'Fuckin' 'urdles,' they'll say.

Ron Bradley at Scunthorpe showed me it doesn't matter how many qualifications and notepads you've got because if you can't handle players, you haven't got a chance in management. Tommy McAnearney at Aldershot was so obsessed with technical ability that his idea of training was a keepy-uppy competition. It was more like a social club than a football club. Nice man but he was not the type of manager I wanted to be. And from Jim Iley at Barnsley, I learned how not to man manage a group of players.

Because none of us had the ability Jim had, he wouldn't tolerate us. He bollocked me every single day of my stay at Oakwell. He was such a stickler for rules that he punished himself more than he punished us and the thing that used to bug me the most was that if you weren't in the first team, he wouldn't even look at you, let alone speak to you. Partly because of the effect that had on me, I have made a conscious effort since day one of my management career to spend more time with the players who weren't in the team than with the ones who were.

At York City, Charlie Wright thought he was going to change the world, but he didn't really know a player which was probably why he signed me. And he showed me how you can be manipulated as a manager if you're not strong enough. If you give directors an inch, they take a mile. I have tried to listen to directors, listen to their rubbish at times and bite my tongue. I have never really been confrontational with them. Everywhere I have gone, I have given them the same speech.

'If you have got anything to say about the players,' I tell them, 'keep it within these four walls and say it to me. Don't blab it to your friends or the gardener or the milkman or the press. Because if we are going to be a unit, we need to be together.'

Those were a few of the lessons I learned. They made me what I am today. They made me able to adapt to different situations. That's why I've always built a team around the players I've got. I was labelled a long ball manager when I had success at Notts County and there was no denying that. We did play the ball long: it's no good bullshitting, we couldn't pass the ball. We had one or two good players but you couldn't ask our defenders to be Rio Ferdinand. We were solid at the back and we broke and scored and we got two promotions with it. Nothing wrong with that.

Every team I have had, they have always worked their socks off. The minimum I have demanded is that even if they have a bad game on the ball, they can't have a bad game off it. I like creating a team that is hard to beat. The strikers have got to know their roles. If strikers want to stroll about in my teams, then I won't have them. Even when I watched Ian Rush in the great Liverpool team of the eighties, he worked his socks off. I have had strikers who wander round with their socks down and stroll about the penalty box but they don't last long with me. I don't want that type of striker. I want everybody to be together. Okay, perhaps I have missed out because some of those so-called flair players might have won me things. But with the dressing room spirit I have got, those types of players would antagonise the rest. They would undermine everything I was trying to preach to the other lads and a situation would develop where there was one rule for one and one rule for another and I won't have that.

While I was still playing for Burton, I had a little go at management with the local Sheffield and District Sunday League side in Todwick, the village where I lived. Dennis, the secretary, and I did everything. I collected the 50p subs after every game, I cleared the kit off the floor, I hauled it to the launderette. When I took over, I entered them in the National Sunday League competition and bought them all track suits. We drew a team in Stoke and I decided we'd prepare as if we were a professional club. We hired a coach, stayed overnight in a hotel and generally did things they'd never done before. I wanted to try it out. I wanted to make sure I made them feel right. We won the game but we didn't get much further.

I worked hard at it. Right from the start I was like that. We had one game deep into the winter that I was keen for us to get played but the snow started coming down on the Saturday night and I knew it was going to be touch and go. So the next morning, Dennis and I got up to the pitch at 6.30 and started trying to clear the lines and the two penalty areas before the referee arrived. We were clearing the lines with our shovels right up until kick-off. It nearly broke my bloody back. We even got an orange ball. The ref was impressed. 'Okay, we'll give it a go,' he said. Every other match in the league was off that Sunday but ours was on. We'd done it. And then we went and lost 1-0. After all that.

I loved it at Todwick. And it was valuable experience, too. Then, in the summer of 1980, I decided I was going to set my sights on getting a manager's job at a Northern Premier League club. I'd had a chat with a couple of lads I'd played with at Barnsley, one of whom played for Goole Town and the other for Gainsborough Trinity. The two teams were playing each other one Saturday and both had a vacancy for a manager. There was an opportunity there not to be missed. After the game, I spotted the Gainsborough chairman, John Davies, walking out of the ground. I went up to him and introduced myself. 'Chairman,' I said, 'I'm interested in going into management now and I was wondering how ambitious your club is because I want to get right to the top.' I interviewed him. Not the other way round. It worked, too. John Davies assured me Gainsborough were very ambitious and a couple of days later he invited me down to Gainsborough.

They interviewed me this time and it went well. John Davies was the chairman but the power behind the throne was the club secretary, Ken Marsden, who was also the league secretary. He was the Mr Big of the Northern Premier. I was worried about him because he had a reputation as a hirer and firer. But when I walked into the lovely old-fashioned boardroom at Northolme with its oak table and chairs and old ties pinned up on the wall, I was determined not to be intimidated by him, even though I'd been told he was impossible to work with and that he always wanted to pick the team. I had as many questions for them as they had for me and I got on very well with Ken at that interview. He seemed to know what he was doing and anyway he offered me the job. I took it. I said I'd play a bit for them, too.

When I started at Gainsborough I thought I would really go for it. Pour everything I had into it. Gainsborough drew an average attendance of about 300 and they had never done anything as a club so I made some changes. Pre-season, I bought all the players blue v-necked jumpers and made them wear a shirt and tie. Every Tuesday night, after we had finished training, I would arrange with the local pub that we'd go in and play pool and darts against the local team. We'd advertise in the local paper that we'd be there and we got involved in the local community which had never happened before. We trained at different places, too, mainly schools in the area. Of course, it wasn't long before Ken Marsden started talking about the players and asking who I'd be playing. I tried to keep him at arm's length as best I could. I realised that dealing with somebody like that was the grounding that I needed.

I improved the team, too. A lad was recommended to me from Blackburn Rovers called Andy Lodge. He had been released by Blackburn and he was thinking of going back to his old job as a clerk for a building society. He'd had a couple of offers from Boston United and Doncaster Rovers, too, but I was determined to get him. I went to see him and told him I wanted to build a team round him. I told him he'd be a big fish in a small pool. I gave him the full works. I sent flowers to his wedding in the summer and generally pestered him to death until he signed for me. He became the stalwart of the side. He was a good steady centre back. I took a lot of pride in the fact that I got him to sign for Gainsborough Trinity when there were so many people after him. He's a wonderful friend to me to this day.

Things soon started to get rocky, though. In September 1980, three or four weeks into the season, we played an FA Cup qualifying round tie at Corby Town and lost. I'd signed a six foot four inches lad called Stewart Evans, who had a real cannonball left foot. The trouble was, he was gangly and ungainly. He looked too big sometimes, like Peter Crouch can do. But he had a left foot like nothing else on earth and plenty of skill and I played him in the team that lost at Corby. They took that defeat badly at

Gainsborough because they desperately need the revenue from Cup runs at that level and when we had our next home game the following week, Ken Marsden caught my eye as I was walking out to have a look at the pitch and beckoned me over.

He said the directors had had a meeting and that they didn't think Stewart Evans was good enough.

'We hope you're not playing him today,' Ken Marsden said.

'Oh, right,' I said, looking at him.

He repeated himself. 'We hope that he's not going to be in the side.'

I thought to myself, well, boy, this is your first fucking challenge as a manager. Here goes. I put one hand behind my back and crossed my fingers.

'You can go back to your fucking meeting,' I said, 'and tell them that I'm picking the team and Stewart Evans will be playing centre forward alongside Neil Warnock and I'm not bothered what they say. He didn't have a good game last week but he's as good as we're going to get and he's in my team today.'

Ken Marsden still wasn't having it. 'I just thought you should know that that's what they said this morning,' he said.

'Well, we'll see what's what when the game's over,' I said. He went out and I took a big sigh. I knew it was a big bloody risk.

So Stewart Evans played and we won 2-0 and Stewart scored both goals. He had a great game. As we came off the pitch, Ken Marsden was waiting by the tunnel.

'Neil, come over here quickly,' he said, all urgent.

'I'm just walking off the fucking pitch,' I said.

'I know, but we've got a scout here from Sheffield United,' he said, 'he's in the boardroom now and they want to buy Stewart Evans.'

I laughed. 'You didn't think he was good enough to play for us ninety minutes ago, Ken,' I said, 'or was that the committee?'

'That was the committee,' he said. Thought it might have been.

Suddenly, he was saying that he had always wanted Stewart to play and it was just the other directors that were sceptical. I knew it was him. I told him to let me deal with it and I would get him more money. After all my time at the frozen food place, I knew I was a good salesman. I told him I would get them £10,000 for Stewart Evans but I could tell Ken Marsden didn't believe me. I spoke to the scout and told him what we would be looking for. He thought that was reasonable but then he went back into the boardroom and he told Ken that if they didn't accept four grand, Sheffield United would walk away. So Ken Marsden snapped his fingers off. I went in the boardroom an hour later and they told me what they had accepted. I was furious.

I stayed at Gainsborough for about twenty games. I got them organised on the pitch and off it. We were near the top of the Northern Premier when I left and when we played Worksop Town at Northolme around Christmas, we got more than 1,500 people there, which was unheard of. I left them with a set-up that would take them forwards but I knew that they couldn't really offer me what I wanted in terms of making a mark. When Ben Robinson asked if I would like to go back to Burton as manager, I jumped at it. I told Ken Marsden I wanted to go. I told him I'd got the team playing good football and made him some money through Stewart Evans. He said he wouldn't stand in my way. I think I must have been the only manager to leave Ken Marsden and Gainsborough Trinity of his own free will. Ever.

7

GOING FOR A BURTON

THE SEASON that made my name as a manager was 1984-85. That was when I got my first real taste of the limelight. My Burton Albion team made it through to the FA Cup third round and lost 6-1 to Leicester City and a hat-trick from Gary Lineker but not before our goalkeeper had been knocked out by a plank of wood thrown from the crowd. I played merry hell about it and, more importantly, so did a journalist called John Sadler from the *Sun*. Together we got the match replayed. Lineker's hat-trick was wiped from the records.

But it was a long road to that game, a long road for the club and for me. There was still an element of happy chaos about non-league football in those days and when we started that season's FA Cup campaign the previous September against a little village team called Wootton Blue Cross, the first qualifying round felt as if it was light years away from the kind of world Lineker would recognise.

Wootton's a lovely village near Bedford and most of us had got down there in good time. It was a glorious Saturday afternoon but I had a knot of tension in my stomach because I knew that our centre forward, Stewart Mell, who was one of our best players, had said he was going to get there a little while after the rest of us. He was a fireman and he had been on a late shift the night before. It was not the first time it had happened but I could never relax until all my players had arrived.

I had to put my teamsheet in an hour before the game. I stuck Stewart's name down because I was expecting him to turn up any minute and I was desperate for him to play. Time ticked on. It got to quarter past two and I began to get a bit worried. I thought he'd probably got stuck in traffic somewhere. Wootton's ground, Weston Park, was in the middle of a kind of housing estate, so I also began to think that he might have got lost trying to find it. I wandered outside and strolled towards the main road to see if I could find him.

While I was out looking for him, I walked past a wedding party who had just come out of the church. I always like to see a wedding before a game because it's lucky to see a bride. But as I was standing there, desperately looking around to see if I could see Stewart's car, the groom came up to me and asked if I wouldn't mind taking some photos for them. So there I was, twenty-five minutes before kick off, snapping away at the bride and groom, moving them all into their different family groups, friends of the bride, friends of the groom, and more and more starting to panic about my bloody fireman.

When it got to 2.45, I knew I was in trouble. I made my excuses to the grateful couple and left. I thought there was no chance Stewart was going to find it now. I realised I was going to have to get someone else on the teamsheet. I couldn't tell the referee that the centre forward had never been there all along so I put my thinking cap on. I told one of the other lads to get into one of the cubicles in the toilets and get his shorts round his ankles. I told him I'd cough when I walked in and on that signal he had to start retching and groaning for all he was worth.

'Heave like you've never heaved in your life,' I said to him, 'and no matter what anybody says, don't open the door whatever you do.'

Then I went and got the ref. I was terribly apologetic. I explained to him that Stewart Mell, my star striker, had come down with food poisoning and was puking in the toilet. I told him I didn't think he'd be able to start.

'I'm sure their lot won't mind,' I said, 'because he's my best player.'

'Oh, right,' the ref said. He looked a bit taken aback but he sent one of his linesmen up with me to the toilets.

I took him in there and gave a quick cough.

Well, this lad behind the door started off. 'Euggggggggh, euggggggggh,' he groaned, 'euggggggggggh.'

Bloody hell, that's enough, I said to myself. You'd have thought the kid was dying.

I turned to the linesman. 'That's how bad he is,' I said.

The linesman looked impressed.

'I'll come back with you to see the ref,' I said.

When he heard what the linesman had to say, the ref was sympathetic. He couldn't be much else after the report he'd heard of the events in that toilet. We agreed that I'd put Stewart Mell on the bench if he recovered sufficiently, which would allow me to get him on if he ever turned up. The ref said I could change the team and put one of the other lads in the starting line-up.

There were only five minutes to go until kick-off, so I dashed back into the changing room to try and give a very quick team talk before the lads went out.

And then Stewart ran in. Still in his fireman's uniform.

He started apologising to me. 'Gaffer, I'm terribly sorry,' he said, 'there were two accidents, I ran over a dog . . .'

'Just get changed,' I said, and set off back for the ref's room.

I knocked on the door. The ref opened it. He seemed surprised to see me.

'Listen, ref,' I said, 'I've decided it's just not fair. It's not fair on Wootton. I put Stewart Mell on my teamsheet in the first place so I'd rather start him. If I've got to bring him off after ten minutes, I will do.'

'Are you sure?' the ref said.

'I think it's only fair,' I said.

'Well that's fine then,' the ref said. 'It's very good of you.'

'Think nothing of it,' I said.

The bell went and Stewart Mell wasn't even changed but he made it out a minute or so after the rest of the lads. We won the game 4-0 and, yes, Stewart Mell scored. Course he did. I always knew he would. I still look for the Wootton Blue Cross result in the newspaper on a Sunday morning even now. What a bloody good grounding all that kind of madness was.

I learned other lessons at Burton, too. They had a lot of ex-professionals in the side when I first took over in January 1981. Ian Storey-Moore had brought quite a few in from Nottingham Forest, old mates of his or lads he had got through his contacts at the club. They were lads who had been top-class in their prime but now they were playing for pocket money. They didn't want somebody changing things and messing up their cosy little routine.

When I introduced myself to them in the dressing room before my first game in charge, which was away at Workington, it was as frightening an experience as I had had as a manager. I gave them my talk about how all I wanted from them was honesty and total commitment but, as I looked around, all the old pros had their heads down, staring at the floor. I could see one or two thinking 'we've heard this load of old shit before' and a couple of others glancing at each other with looks that said 'he'll not last long'.

The scariest thing about being a young manager is that often your players have seen more than you and achieved more than you. In my case, they had certainly played at a higher level than I had. Some of the players at Burton, men like Peter Winfield and Sammy Chapman, had played in very good Forest sides. I think they might even have played in Europe. I don't know. I never quite got round to asking them. Senior pros are as cruel as people can be if they don't fancy you. They can be like kids taunting a weak teacher at school. No one was openly confrontational with me until Seamus McDonagh gave me a dressing down a few years later at Scarborough, but often I've had whispers of dissent coming back to me through my coach or one of my assistants.

'Where's he ever played?' people have said. Stuff like that.

There was an easy answer to that when I was at Burton.

'Higher than the fucking Northern Premier League, pal,' I could say. 'We're not in Europe here, mate.'

I realised the kind of job I'd got on my hands when I went up to Workington. It was a Sunday game and, for some reason, they had played a match the day before as well. I went into the dressing room and saw all those old heads go down. Only the young lads looked straight at me. There was a left back called Clive Arthur and, as I looked around, it felt as though his was the only pair of bright eyes in a dark dressing room. I think most of the rest of them had been out on the piss on the Saturday night. They'd put a bit of weight on since their prime by the look of them and now they were struggling. There was no tackling or grafting. Workington battered us in the first half. To be honest, my lot never tried a leg.

'Listen, lads,' I said, when they wandered back in at half time, 'if that's what a new manager does for you, then we have got problems. If that's how you're going to show me that you want to play, then I think we'll be disagreeing.'

If they wanted to leave, I told them, they only had to ask. No wonder they brought me in there. That's where I got the Red Adair reputation from. When a chairman found himself with a club that was a gusher, he got me in to put a bloody cap on it. Every club I've been to since Burton, it's been a club that needed gutting or changing. It's been a club that has needed a fresh start and a bloody big clearout.

I've always packed my dressing room with lads who will lay down everything for me. I tried to do that right from my Sunday league days with Todwick. The only thing with Sunday league is that you have to resign yourself to the fact that at least one of your best players would have been out all night the night before the game. You have to tolerate that at Sunday league level but not higher up. At every club I've been at, if I could get nine players who were going to give me 90 per cent every week, I knew I had a chance. But the two players that you are not sure about are usually the ones that will win you the games. If you can get ten giving you 90 per cent, you've swum the Channel.

Burton might have been playing in the Northern Premier League but I thought they were southern softies. They were known as an easy touch in a hard league and I was determined to change that. I had a vision for them and the vision was to turn them into the new Mossley. That might not mean much to you now because Mossley are nothing like the club they used to be, but in those days they were the kings of non-league football. They were the Chelsea of non-league, in fact. They won everything and they were hard and relentless. They had real steel about them and their manager, Bob Murphy, had seen it all and done it all. I looked up to him the same way I look up to Sir Alex Ferguson now.

I was a bit in awe of him, really, and one day when we played at their place, Bob Murphy pulled me to one side.

'You know of all the success I've had, son,' he said, 'well let me give you a bit of advice. When you get success, they want more.'

He was right. Mossley had played above themselves for so long but, in the end, the board there thought success was their right, and when they slipped down the table they got fed up with Bob

Murphy. Now look at them. They got relegated from the Unibond Premier in 2007. They are way, way below where they were when Bob Murphy was in charge. They're in freefall.

Anyway, I wanted to get a team on the eastern side of the Pennines, tough as teak like Mossley. I wanted to compete with them. Burton Albion had got good facilities, a good pitch and a good crowd but you could kick them and then they wouldn't fancy it any more. When Ben Robinson got me in, part of the reason he did it was because he wanted a northern lad in charge. Until then Burton had usually recruited lads from the Midlands and Ben wanted to see if I could get access to a different group of lads from the north. At that level, you tend to recruit players from your own geographical base.

I agreed with that philosophy. I wanted to bring a bit more northern grit to Eton Park. I brought a lad from Mossley called David Vaughan who epitomised everything I wanted in a centre half. He lived in my village and I badgered him and badgered him to join us until I wore him down. He was my equivalent of John Terry. I made him my captain and he set the tone. He suffered no fools and he was as brave as hell. We became solid and not very nice to play against. I wanted to get a team as physically determined as Mossley were. I cleared a lot of the veterans out at the end of the season but there were still a lot of frustrations. I put my foot through the dressing room door at Mossley once after we lost there. Mossley sent the bill back to Burton and I had to pay for the damage.

If you think I get worked up at games now, you should have seen me back then when I was starting out in management. God, I used to get angry. I flew into one particularly spectacular rage after we had blown a lead against Macclesfield Town at their Moss Rose ground. We were winning 1-0 but it should have been at least 4 and, even though there hadn't been any injuries and very few stoppages, the referee took it into his head to play seven minutes of injury time at the end of the match. In the last minute of the seven, we gave the ball away in defence rather than booting it into the stand and Macclesfield equalised. I was absolutely disgusted. But rather than have a go at the referee, I walked into the dressing room and started having a go at the defenders.

I was extremely wound up and in the midst of going daft at my back four, I saw what I thought was a little cardboard box on the floor. It was quite dark in there and I was yelling about not pissing about in the seventh minute of injury time and I got myself so worked up that I took a run at this piece of cardboard and booted it as hard as I could. Only it wasn't cardboard. It was a scrap of cardboard that had accidentally fallen over one of those cast iron shoe-scrapers. That piece of iron beneath the cardboard weighed about two stone and I gave it a right whack.

I had had an operation to have a hammer toe straightened a couple of months earlier and been on crutches for a few weeks. I still had a pin in it. When I kicked that supposed cardboard box, I was expecting it to fly into the air and rebound in a gratifying way off the dressing room wall. Instead, it moved about a quarter of an inch and gave me the bloody shock of my life. In the seconds after I kicked that block of iron, I could feel the vibration going through the pin, right up my leg and almost to my brain. It absolutely killed me but it was early in my time as manager at Burton and I couldn't let the lads know what I had done. So I just gritted my teeth and I walked into a toilet a couple of strides away and bit into my hand to stop myself screaming. I bit so hard I drew blood but it was the only thing I could do. I couldn't let the players know.

Gradually, though, the frustrations began to ease. I moved some of the veteran players on and brought in plenty of my own. I knew Burton was a big opportunity for me. I knew the chairman was a football man who would back me and give me the support that I needed. I knew I had a chance of winning something and that I might be able to start earning a reputation as a manager who had something to offer. Someone who was going places at last.

When I was introduced as manager, I'd made a basic error at my press conference of guaranteeing that we would win something within two years. I've never done that again. The pressure weighed on me more and more the closer we got to the deadline I had imposed on myself and people took great delight in reminding me about it. As it happened, we won the Northern Premier League Cup in April 1983 by beating Macclesfield Town at Maine Road. It was two years, give or take a couple of months, since I had arrived. What a bloody relief that was.

The following season was when things really took off. We did okay in the league but we went on a great run in the FA Cup that really caught the imagination of the supporters. We beat a club called Rothwell Town in the first qualifying round, even though we were 1-0 down at half time. The away dressing room was in this little hut underneath the main stand and I gave my lads a fearful bollocking. I was effing and blinding and banging around and I think there may even have been a few sandwiches flying about. We turned it around and won 5-1 but after the match a few of the directors came up to me and said they'd heard every word at half time. I don't know if they expected me to be embarrassed but I wasn't. I wasn't really bothered who was listening, the way we'd been playing.

Next we won 2-1 away at Wednesfield in the West Midlands. Then we beat Oldbury United. In the fourth qualifying round, we drew 0-0 at Walthamstow Avenue on a bone-hard pitch where the ball was bouncing about twenty feet in the air every time either goalie kicked it out. We won the replay and we got more than 2,000 fans to Eton Park which was unheard of for Burton. Finally, we were in the first round proper.

We drew Windsor and Eton at home and I thought we could beat them easily. I went to watch them and they were poor but they came up to our place and battled for their lives. Late in the game, when we were 2-1 down, one of their players made a terrible tackle on Pat Lally and broke his leg. After that, I wasn't bothered about the result any more. I walked off with Pat down the side of the pitch and took him to the ambulance. He was coming to the end of his career so I knew that would probably finish him. That was the first of three broken legs we suffered at the club in the space of a couple of years. That's why I react so badly now when someone does an over-the-top tackle on one of my lads. I'll never forget the pain of losing those lads at Burton and the effect it had on their careers.

Even to this day, those tackles on Pat Lally, Mick Fletcher and Ian McLean still live with me. When I see an over-the-top tackle, and I know the refs don't see it because they don't know what they're looking for, it does my head in. The next minute somebody will bounce the ball away and the referee will book them for dissent. And yet you can break somebody's leg and not even get a yellow card.

That Cup run in 1983-84 was just the warm-up for what we did the season after, though. Our adventure might have had inauspicious beginnings with the anarchy at Wootton Blue Cross, but if I'd known what was at stake that 15 September, I probably wouldn't have spent ten minutes taking pictures for that bride and groom I happened upon while I was out looking for Stewart Mell. The victory that day launched us on a journey through the competition that eventually captured the imagination of the whole nation and established us for a short time as everyone's favourite underdogs.

We beat Stevenage Borough 2-0 in the second qualifying round on a pitch that was like a bowling green. Then we beat Willenhall Town. Then it was 1-1 at Wycombe Wanderers and a replay back at our place in front of 3,500. We had never had anywhere near that at Eton Park before. It was full. I could have painted a picture of it. When we came out of our dressing room, we could see all the faces of the supporters under the lights and the pitch there in the middle of it all like a little postage stamp. We couldn't go wrong in that atmosphere. We were walking on air before the kick-off and we swept past them. In the first round proper, we got Staines Town at home and everybody was gutted because we wanted league opposition. But we beat them with a forty-five-yard screamer from Dougie Newton. The reaction from the crowd felt like it was going to lift the roof off the old stand. We were in the second round for the second time in the club's history.

There was more disappointment among the fans and the lads when we drew Aldershot away. It wasn't the glamour tie everyone had wanted and because they were a half-decent Fourth Division side, most people assumed we were going to be knocked out. But I wasn't disappointed. I was thrilled to be drawn against one of my old clubs and I was relishing the trip from the moment the draw was made. I went down to watch them a couple of times and I knew we had a chance. We had a solid defence and Stewart Mell up front who was very quick. I told them before we got down there that we were going to win and that we didn't need to have any kind of inferiority complex.

It was another magical day. We arrived at the ground, got our bearings and then wandered out on to the pitch to have a look around. In those days, the railway ran along the side of the stand on the opposite side of the ground from where the dressing rooms were and as we stood there talking to each other, a procession of trains started approaching the station. They were the Football Specials that had been laid on for the Burton fans and all our supporters were leaning out of the windows, waving their yellow and black scarves and their flags. It seemed like a scene from the age of steam and, as soon as they saw us, all the fans started cheering and yelling out of the train windows. There were three trains full to the rafters of Burton Albion fans and what a noise they made inside that ground. We didn't let them down either. Stewart Mell scored and so did Nigel Simms, a lad who worked down the local pit. We won 2-0. We were in to the hat for the third round.

The dressing room was in uproar after the game. All the lads and everybody connected with the club was euphoric. And this time we got our glamour tie. They made us wait for it. In fact, our name was pretty much last out of the hat. Manchester United had come and gone, Arsenal had come and gone, Forest, Leeds, Liverpool, all of them. It got to the point where we couldn't think of anybody else that was left. But then they drew our name out as a home team. That got a cheer. When they drew Leicester City out as our opponents, there was absolute pandemonium. Leicester was about as local as it got for us and they were a top-flight team with big names like Gary Lineker and Alan Smith in the side.

We decided almost straight away that we wouldn't really be able to stage the tie at Eton Park so I asked the board to do everything they could to get it at the Baseball Ground. I loved the Baseball Ground because the crowd was so close to the pitch and I knew we could make it difficult for Leicester there. We got that sorted and then the build-up began in earnest. We were the biggest story in town for a few weeks because we were the most romantic bet to provide a giant-killing. Non-league against top-flight is as good as it gets in the third round of the FA Cup and the fact that I was a practising chiropodist ticked all the boxes for the media. I was mannah from heaven for them.

All the papers went mad on the chiropody angle in the week leading up to the match. There were pictures of me examining the players' feet. There were pictures of players wearing a giant furry animal foot with me inspecting their toe nails. It was great fun but in some ways the preparation was a nightmare. The problem was, I really was a chiropodist so I had my surgery to run too, and there was media mayhem ruling all around me. I worked it like this: I did a patient every twenty minutes and I worked eight hours non-stop so I could have a day clear for my football stuff. Even when I was working at the surgery, I took one phone call every twenty minutes and then I'd take it off the hook while I did my patient. Then I'd take another call. And so on.

There were more than 22,000 fans inside the Baseball Ground that January afternoon when we played Leicester. It was the biggest crowd they had there all season. Lineker put them in front after sixteen minutes, David Vaughan equalised after twenty-three minutes. It was an icy pitch. It felt to me like we were going to have a right good go at them. When we got that equaliser, I thought anything was possible. Leicester looked stunned. Then about ten minutes later, everything changed. A Leicester fan threw a block of wood from the crowd and it hit our goalkeeper, Paul Evans, who was standing on the edge of his six-yard box, on the back of the head and knocked him over. Brian Hill, the referee, stopped the game. He didn't have much choice. Our trainer went on and treated Evo and when he got back to the bench, he said Paul was not in a very good way. He thought he was concussed. We looked across a couple of minutes later and Paul was being physically sick. So we got the trainer back on and then half time came around. Evo didn't really know a lot about what was going on. He kept being sick. So during the interval, I went to see Brian Hill.

'I don't think our goalkeeper can go on, Brian,' I said.

Mr Hill was a fussy type. He looked flustered.

'Well, who are you going to put in goal then?' he said.

'Well, I don't think I should put anyone in goal,' I said. 'I think the game should be abandoned.'

He looked even more flustered. 'You can't abandon a game at this level,' he said. 'He'll be all right. I'll watch over him.'

It was quite obvious to us that Paul Evans was not right and that no amount of Mr Brian Hill watching over him was going to make him better. He went out for the second half and he didn't know what day it was. He made a few errors he wouldn't have made before. He flapped at a few. He was late down to shots. Basically, he was all over the place. Lineker got a hat-trick and Leicester beat us 6-1. Afterwards Gordon Milne, the Leicester manager, seemed to be pretending the injury to our goalkeeper had never happened. He had forgotten all about that piece of wood that smacked him on the back of the head and put him in la-la land. In the post-match interviews, he was condescending. He said what a valiant effort we had put up but that Leicester's class had told in the end. What a load of rubbish that was.

I saw him and Brian Hill talking to each other in a corner and they fobbed me off when I said there should be a replay.

'No chance,' Gordon Milne said. 'They don't do things like that in the FA Cup.'

But I was forthright about it. I didn't want to let it go. I said that at 1-1 we had a great chance and that if it had been a bigger team than Burton Albion that this injustice had affected, there would be a real controversy about the whole thing. It spoiled the whole day for me. I couldn't play the role of the gracious loser happy that his non-league team had had their day in the limelight and content to fade back into the shadows. I felt we had been stitched up and I didn't want to let it rest. But I didn't know how I could take it any further. I felt powerless. And then the next morning, I got a telephone call at home. It was John Sadler, the Chief Sports Writer of the *Sun*.

John was from the Midlands. As the *Sun*'s top man, he was one of the most powerful and influential men in sports journalism. He had been at the game and he said he had been thinking over what I said in my press conference about Burton being steamrollered because they were a small club. He said he agreed with me. He said it wouldn't have been allowed to happen to a bigger club. We had a chat and he wrote a big piece about it on Monday. It was strong stuff. It stressed the injustice that had been done to us and pointed out that the failure to act went against all the principles of the FA Cup. The lack of action punished the underdog, he wrote, and how was the spirit of the Cup to survive if nothing were done about it. And what would happen, he asked, if the FA did nothing. Did it mean that they were going to allow yobbos to dictate the results of football matches?

He was absolutely right, of course, and his article created bedlam. Burton v Leicester turned into a David and Goliath story. It went from strength to strength in the papers and on the television. It gathered momentum. By Tuesday afternoon the FA wanted to know more facts. They called a hearing that I had to attend. I went in to give evidence with Paul Evans. Ted Croker was chairing the meeting and he was very sympathetic. We were in the waiting room with Brian Hill and he was still saying there was no chance of a replay. But I spoke to the panel and reminded them the game was wide open at 1-1 and that our goalkeeper was so badly hurt he was violently sick. And after listening to both sides, they agreed with me. They agreed with Burton. They ordered that the game be replayed behind closed doors at Highfield Road, Coventry City's ground. Leicester were furious but I was elated. Justice had been done.

Paul Evans accompanied me to the hearing. Now he's my best mate and a solicitor. He's represented me more than a few times with the FA since then.

And we didn't waste our opportunity. We showed that we had been severely handicapped in the first game by what had happened to Paul Evans. We conceded a goal after four minutes at Highfield Road and everyone thought it was going to be a rout. But it wasn't. We were brilliant after that. They didn't score again and we came back into it. We even hit a post. And in the final stages of the game, Leicester were hanging on. We lost 1-0 but we went out with our heads held high. We had had a brilliant run and it had been a massive thing for me. We got a lot of publicity out of it and in the aftermath of the incident involving Paul Evans we routed Leicester in public relations terms at least.

I was hoping that the Cup run would give us the momentum to push on in the league, where we were mid-table, but just when we should have been grasping our opportunity, there was a change in the boardroom and suddenly things got a lot more difficult for me. Ben Robinson, the chairman who had given me so much support, left for a few years just before the Cup run began and a guy called Bill Royall, a decent bloke who was an architect, took over as chairman. As part of the change, the club secretary, Dave Mellor, took on more responsibility. He came on to the board of directors and brought another couple of blokes on with him. Dave was a schoolteacher and I had got on well with him when I first went there but his knowledge of the game was limited and now he was on the board, he thought he should start having opinions. We didn't begin too well in 1985-86. We weren't pulling up any trees and Dave Mellor was a changed person. He was an expert now. He wanted to flex his muscles.

There were a couple of niggles I was not happy about. I wanted to get a bit of extra money for one of our players, Jimmy Kabia. It amounted to £5 a week to help him with his travelling expenses. The board wouldn't have it. They vetoed it. Bill Royall told me what was going on in the boardroom and I didn't like the sound of it. People also started coming to me with stories about my assistant, Brian Fidler, who they said wasn't doing me any favours. Things were starting to go sour remarkably quickly given the heights we'd reached the previous season.

At the end of February, I wanted to sign a lad called Micky Gooding from Rotherham. A board meeting was called to discuss whether the directors would give me the £1,000 I needed to sign him. When they had had the meeting, Bill Royall rang me.

'Can you come and see me, Neil?' he said. 'Get in your car and come and see me.'

I thought it sounded ominous but I drove over to his house.

'We discussed Micky Gooding,' he said, 'and we put it to a vote and it was five votes to one.'

'Oh, that's great,' I said.

'No, Neil,' he said. 'I was the one. I was the only one who supported you.'

'It wasn't just about Micky Gooding then, was it really, Bill?' I said.

Bill nodded his head. 'That's what they're saying,' he said.

'Well, we can't go on like that,' I said. 'I can't carry on.'

My last game in charge of Burton Albion was against Oswestry Town at home on 1 March 1986. Then I was gone. Some people said I resigned. I reckon they sacked me. Like Bob Murphy said, when you get success, they want more.

8
UP AND AWAY AT SCARBOROUGH

I WAS OUT of football for a couple of months after I left Burton. Then I got word that Jimmy Holmes, the manager of Nuneaton Borough, fancied me as his assistant so I went to watch them play against Scarborough. I wandered into the bar after the game and spotted the Scarborough chairman, Barry Adamson, standing in the middle of a group of people. It would have been hard to miss Barry. He was six foot two and more than twenty stone. He was holding forth to anyone who would listen and I went over and joined in the conversation.

Barry was blustering on about how he would never have a manager who didn't live in Scarborough. And he didn't want players who wouldn't live in Scarborough either. I piped up then. I told him they'd never get anywhere with those rules. I told him Scarborough was too isolated to be able to attract a squad of players capable of winning things. I told him he needed to identify a training base somewhere close to, say, Leeds, so that there would be a far bigger catchment area for the club. That way you could get players from Sheffield and York and even further south into the Midlands if need be. I told him the players only needed to go to Scarborough on match days. It wasn't going to make any difference to the way they played football.

Well, the Nuneaton job never materialised but a couple of weeks later, I got a call from Barry Adamson. He wanted me to go for an interview. They had sacked the previous manager, Harry Dunn, after a struggle the season before when the club had flirted with relegation. What a man Harry Dunn was, by the way. He had played 901 times for Scarborough, 901 times for one club, one non-league club. Can you imagine that? I drove up there and stopped in a lay-by on the outskirts of town. Behind an AA box, I changed into my suit. I enjoyed the interview and they offered me the job. When I walked out into the stadium afterwards, I looked around at the Athletic Ground and to me it seemed like the Manchester United of non-league football. It was the crème de la crème. I thought I had just got the best job in the world.

It was a big year for non-league football. General Motors had just taken over from Gola as the sponsors of what used to be the Alliance and were paying £200,000 for a two-year deal, bigger money than the league had ever dreamed of, and from 1986 onwards the top tier of the non-league pyramid was known as the GM Vauxhall Conference. But the most radical and exciting change of all was that it was also to be the first season when the winners of the Conference would be automatically promoted to the Fourth Division, rather than having to rely on the Football League failing to re-elect one of their number, which was always about as likely as turkeys voting for Christmas.

I set about the job like a madman. I wheeled and dealed like Harry Redknapp with a rocket stuck up his backside. I talked to forty-seven players in the summer of 1986 and signed nineteen of them just by looking through the list of free transfers. My first signing was Cec Podd, who had become one of the first and most significant black players in English football when he made his debut for Bradford City in 1970. Cec made more than 550 appearances for Bradford and then went to Halifax Town for a couple of years and I was desperate to try and get him, not just for the benefit of all his experience but because I knew he had a reputation as a fantastic professional. I brought him up to the Athletic Ground and showed him around. I told him I could offer him £35 a week and that I wanted him to be my captain. He just said yes, okay. He never quibbled. He never asked for a pound or two more or talked about travelling expenses. He never wanted me to see his representative. I thought, this is going to be easy.

Others followed him. I got rid of all but two of the previous season's Scarborough side who had finished in fifteenth place, just four points clear of the drop zone. I got Mike Brolly and Tommy Graham from Scunthorpe. I got Cec, Barry Gallagher and Paul Kendall from Halifax. Then there was goalkeeper David Kaye from Chester City, Andy Harrison from Kettering Town and Steve Richards from Kettering Town. They were all free transfers. I did have a bit of money to spend so I blew £2,000 on Stewart Mell from Burton. When we made an average start to the season, I spent another £1,500 on Ian Bennyworth from Nuneaton and Mitch Cook from Middlesbrough.

All the lads were part-time so we still had some frantic juggling to do, making sure they got the necessary time off work to train and play. It never got quite as bad as the day at Wootton Blue Cross but there were some hairy moments. There were bound to be with such a range of professions in the side. Cec Podd was a social worker, Steve Richards was a policeman, Paul Kendall went working with relatives in a building firm. Neil Thompson was a nappy salesman, Andy Harrison was a brewery rep. Stewart Mell was still a fireman and Phil Walker, well, I can't remember what he did, but he didn't do it an awful lot.

Cec was a born-again Christian. He would chat to the most gorgeous girls on away trips and when he knew he had got them eating out of the palm of his hand, he would walk away and smile at the lads. 'I just needed to know I still had the magic touch,' Cec said. He found it hard to relinquish the vices of his former life. When he was playing for Bradford, he used to get an awful lot of racial abuse at away grounds but most of it had disappeared by the time he joined us. Anyway, he was the calmest man ever. He was an absolute gentleman and a great skipper.

There was nothing fancy about our training facilities. Sometimes we trained at Todwick, just off the M1 at junction 31 which was Sheffield South and Worksop. We had to train in the evenings because the lads had day jobs and there weren't any floodlights. But there was one security light that ran on a meter so we put 50p after 50p into the slot and trained partly by the light of that, partly by the glare from our car headlights which we left on when we parked our cars facing the pitch. Sometimes, when we wanted to treat ourselves, we got Worksop Leisure Centre, but that was usually only available between 10 and 11 at night. The rest of the time, it was booked out by lads who hit the phones about an hour before the leisure centre opened and rang and rang and rang until someone answered so they could grab all the prime times.

We didn't have a particularly smooth start that season. Most of the Scarborough fans had no idea who I was and their first impressions weren't good. We lost our first game 3-0 at Nuneaton, the club's heaviest opening day defeat since 1952, and in September we got knocked out of the FA Cup in the first qualifying round by Goole Town, who were a division below us in the Northern Premier. There was a lot of disquiet about that. We were the main subject in a weekly non-league column in the *Daily Express* that everyone connected with the Conference used to read. Barry Adamson was quoted in it. He said it was the worst Scarborough team he'd ever seen. He absolutely slaughtered us. I told him he was out of order and he put an apology in the programme the next week when we played Frickley Athletic. A few hundred people read that. A few million read the piece in the *Express*. Never mind.

We drew five games on the bounce in September and October, which was probably another record, and started to slip down the table. Maidstone United were one of the main candidates for promotion but the favourites were Barnet. They certainly had the highest profile which was hardly surprising with a chairman like Stan Flashman, who was a larger-than-life ticket tout, and a manager like Barry Fry, who's probably the most extrovert football manager there's ever been. And that's saying something.

We played Barnet a couple of games before our sequence of draws began. We drew with them, too, actually. But we did turn a corner that day. I was strolling about on the pitch before the game when I saw the Barnet goalkeeper, Kevin Blackwell, warming up at the other end. I had seen on the teamsheet that Barry had left him out. I walked over to him.

'What's going on, pal?' I said. 'I thought you'd be playing today.'

'So did fucking I,' he said. 'I'm the reason why this lot are doing so well in the first place.'

Blackie was a typical cocky cockney who loved himself. I didn't know then he'd be my trusted sidekick for sixteen years. He was a hell of a keeper and, a few weeks later, I managed to persuade Barry to let us take him on loan. A couple of other clubs had wanted him but Barry wouldn't let him go. The thing was, he didn't see Scarborough as any sort of threat to Barnet so he thought he had nothing to lose. We were slipping down towards mid-table and I felt that the next game at home to Kettering Town was shit or bust. We won it 1-0 and Blackie was magnificent. It was our first win in eight games.

Blackie was man of the match in the next game away at Stafford Rangers, which we drew 0-0. He was the star player again when we beat Sutton United a week later and a week after that he saved a penalty in the away win at Frickley. So I was pretty keen to hang on to him at the end of his month's loan and one of the directors, Alf Arton, dipped his hand in his pocket and we paid Barnet a couple of grand for him. He was worth every penny. He made a big difference to us and we started to climb back up the table.

We went to the top for the first time on 13 December when

Barnet lost at Maidstone and we beat Stafford, but a week after that, the club was knocked sideways when Barry Adamson died at an FA Trophy match against Morecambe. Barry was sitting with Don Robinson, the old Hull City chairman, when some Morecambe yobbos in the stand started acting up. Barry and Don tried to quieten it down and Barry got up and got amongst them and had a heart attack and died. He was only forty-seven. He was replaced by a smashing bloke called Terry Wood, who was a fish merchant.

As the season wore on, we kept seeing Barry Fry in the stands at our matches. He and Stan Flashman were there at Dagenham on 30 March to see us win 2-0 and go four points clear of Barnet at the top. They were desperate to see us get beaten but Barry had become our lucky mascot. Whenever he appeared, we won. If we found out he was in the stadium, all the lads used to wave to him up in the stands. Barry didn't look too bothered. Most people still assumed Barnet would go up, even though we started stretching our lead.

At the beginning of April, we went down to play Bath City at Twerton Park. There had been torrential rain the night before and they were talking about calling the game off. But we were desperate to play because we knew that if it was rescheduled for the following Tuesday night, a lot of our players wouldn't be able to make it. Neil Thompson had some sort of nappy presentation to do that Tuesday night. God knows what that involved. Luckily, Bath were keen to play, too, because they thought the conditions might even things up a bit. A young Paul Durkin was the ref and he told us that because we had come such a long way, he would try and leave it to the last minute to make a decision.

Eventually, he decided the match could go ahead. 'If I start it, I'm going to finish it,' he said. And he did. We scored two playing down the Twerton Park slope and won 3-0. Tommy Graham scored and did a run and a dive for a celebration. He slid about forty yards on the mud. I didn't think he was ever going to stop. After the game, a few of us drove straight down to London for the PFA dinner feeling pretty good about ourselves because we had just gone seven points clear. Ian St John and Jimmy Greaves were the compères and we were sitting at a table at the back. Ian St John said he'd like everybody to put their hands together for the chairman and manager of the team that was going to be the next members of the Football League. We were looking at each other and then Barry Fry and Stan Flashman stood up. Everybody clapped. It was good for us, that. It just made us more determined. It made us feel like nobody rated us.

We beat Welling United at home the week after that and then won at Kidderminster a week later. It was our twelfth away win in succession. Kidderminster were the top scorers in the league at that point and their fans spent most of the match dishing out stick to our striker, Phil Walker, who was having a terrible game. They were making braying noises at him and shouting 'donkey' and 'eee-ore' every time he touched it. Phil stuck it up them nicely when he lobbed their keeper for the winner. He ran the whole length of the pitch with his arms windmilling in the air, shouting 'Eee-ore, eee-ore' the whole way. He seemed quite pleased.

When we got to the end of April, we were three points ahead of Barnet with two games to play. We had an away match at Sutton

I went part-time while I was playing at Barnsley and set myself up as a greengrocer. My mother-in-law, Joan, a wonderful woman, ran the Orange Bowl while I was training. It's a Post Office now.

Another header, this time converting a corner from my mate Graham Collier to get the winner for Barnsley in an FA Cup tie against Huddersfield Town.

I won the first trophy of my managerial career in 1983 when Burton Albion lifted the Northern Premier League Challenge Cup at Maine Road. Ben Robinson, one of the best chairmen I ever worked for, is holding the cup with me.

I've been forced to take a few early baths as a manager. My eldest kids, James and Natalie, joined me for this one.

James and me at Scarborough's Athletic Ground in 1986 when he was six and I was guiding the club towards the Football League.

I thought I'd got the best job in football when I became manager of Scarborough. I took teams back to the town for weekends away long after I'd left.

Mitch Cook scores the second Scarborough goal against Sutton United in April 1987 that put us on the verge of promotion from the Conference.

The Scarborough team celebrate winning the Conference in 1986–87. It is still one of the proudest moments of my managerial career.

James and I spin a few discs for the Radio Nottingham Christmas Show in 1990.

I might have missed my vocation, judging by the elegance of this on-drive I played in a cricket benefit match for Kevin Cooper.

To commemorate the centenary of Notts County's appearance in their first FA Cup final, Phil Turner, me and goalkeeper Steve Cherry dressed up in Victorian gear in March 1991 as we prepared for the club's FA Cup quarter-final against Spurs.

I asked Derek Pavis, left, to sign Craig Short when I arrived at Notts County. He was one of the best professionals who ever played for me. We climbed plenty of ladders together.

I made sure other people's feet could do the walking. In this case, it was my Notts County centre half, Dean Yates, with Craig Short looking on.

Celebrating with my Notts County players after we beat Manchester City with a last-minute winner in the fifth round of the FA Cup in 1991.

Celebrating our victory to the top-flight with my son James, far right, who joined us as mascot.

Paul Evans, Dave Wilson and myself looking on anxiously during the play-off final against Brighton. Chris Short behind us looks worried too.

Notts County forward Kevin Bartlett was so fast he could catch pigeons so Arsenal's Lee Dixon had no chance of keeping up with him.

Brian Clough was a hero to me, and when we were both managers in Nottingham at the same time it was a privilege to get to know him. This photo shows him with me and my son James after a dinner he was speaking at in 2004.

United and Barnet had a blank weekend so we thought Barry would probably be in the crowd again. We drove down to London the day before the game and stayed over in a hotel. About 7.30, just as I was getting ready to go down to dinner, I got a phone call in my hotel room. I'd never heard the bloke's voice before.

'Hello, Neil mate,' he said. 'We've got mutual friends and I've got a nice little deal for you that's going to work for us all.'

'You're going to have to tell me a bit more than that,' I said.

'If Scarborough lose tomorrow,' he said, 'there's twenty grand in it for you. We'll work out the details of how to get the money to you later.'

I nearly shit myself. It really knocked me back. I thought the guy was probably mafia of some sort.

'Look, son,' I said, 'there's no way we'd do anything like that. I've got a genuine bunch of lads and they wouldn't know how to fix a fucking game even if they wanted to.'

He muttered something about it being a wasted opportunity for everybody and then the phone went dead. A few minutes later, it rang again.

'We'll give you fifteen grand if we can pick two players for you to leave out of your team tomorrow,' the same voice said.

I gave him the same answer and went downstairs for my evening meal. When I got back to my room, the phone rang again. This time, it was Kevin Blackwell. He said he had a problem and he wanted to come and see me.

He walked into my room looking edgy. 'Gaffer,' he said, 'I've had a phone call.'

'Fucking tell me about it,' I said, 'I've had two.'

They had offered Blackie £10,000 to let two soft goals in. I suppose it shows you the golden rule of match-fixing is nobbling either the boss or the goalie. But he'd told them he wasn't interested either. It would never have crossed our minds to do anything like that. It's the only time I've ever come across anything like that in my career and I don't think it is widespread by any means, even though there is more scope for it now that spread betting has come in.

If we had lost to Sutton, we would have been in trouble. Barnet had a better goal difference than us so two wins from their last two matches would have given them promotion. We were nervous when the game started. It wasn't just Stan and Barry in the stand this time either. It was the entire Barnet team and loads of Barnet supporters. Barry had made appeals for them to come down and cheer on Sutton. It was a dry, dusty pitch and Sutton attacked us from the start but Blackie played out of this world. Stewart Mell scored against the run of play ten minutes before half time and then they really did throw the kitchen sink at us.

Blackie defied them on his own. All you could see were clouds of dust every time he threw himself at the feet of a Sutton forward or dived to push a shot away. You'd have to wait for the dust to settle before you could tell what had happened. He made a few of the catches look like Gordon Banks's save against Pele but we could forgive him his showboating. Then Mitch Cook, who is still working for Scarborough now, won the ball on the half way line and went on a run and chipped the goalie from about thirty yards to put us two up. His mother was in the Kop and he ran across to her. I knew then that we had probably won the league. Geoff Bowman, the trainer, who was standing next to me in the dugout, gave me a handkerchief because I was crying my eyes out. Everything took over.

Barnet's next game was at home to Stafford Rangers and they had to win it to take the race for that priceless promotion spot down to the very last game. There was a commentary on Radio York so I settled myself down in the front room with my assistant, Paul Evans, at my house in Todwick. The Stafford boss, Ronnie Reid, had rung me earlier in the day apologising because his regular goalkeeper was injured and he was going to have to play a young lad. He was getting his excuses in early. On the commentary, it sounded as if Barnet were all over them, but somehow Stafford went a goal up against the run of play and at half time, it was 1-0.

But then Barnet equalised right after the interval and the tension got too much for me. Barnet were going down the slope in the second half and I knew it would be like the Alamo. I'd had enough. I couldn't stand it any more. I felt physically sick. So I left Paul downstairs and went up to bed and just curled up under the covers and crossed my fingers and my toes and my legs and everything. It went quiet for a while. Then I heard a scream from Evo with about five or six minutes to go. He was yelling out that Stafford had scored again from a breakaway. Evo came running upstairs saying someone called Phil Derbyshire had scored. I'll never forget that name. I shouted at him to go back downstairs so we didn't change the situation that had brought us luck. Me upstairs, him downstairs. I got back into bed and lay there again for what seemed like an hour. It was only eight minutes. When the final whistle went, Evo screamed the house down and we went mad.

It was emotional. It was the thought that a group of seventeen players that nobody had wanted, who were almost all free transfers and were 50–1 outsiders with the bookies, had come together and achieved what we had achieved. We had done it against the odds. Barnet were paying a lot of money and so were a lot of the other clubs. So to do it with our top earners on £35 a week was an absolute miracle. We were an isolated team, too, way out on the north-east coast. Nobody had expected us to have a chance. It was all about players coming together and showing incredible determination. One of the rival managers that season once said to me that the highest compliment he could pay me was that if you had asked the other managers who they would least like to play, nine out of ten of them would have put Scarborough top of the list. Some people would twist that but he meant it in the right way.

On the last weekend of the season, we beat Weymouth 2-1 at the Athletic Ground in front of a new record crowd for the Conference of 5,640. What a fantastic day that was. The crowd ran on to the pitch and Cec Podd lifted the championship trophy and we all started dreaming about the Football League. The next day we went on an open-top bus tour of the town and there were thousands on the streets. It finished at the town hall where they held a civic reception for us. It was the happiest time of my career up to that point. Even now, I still consider it my greatest achievement until the time I took Sheffield up to the Premiership. I got Notts County from the Third Division to the First in two years. I got Huddersfield Town up and Plymouth Argyle up, but Scarborough was special.

We had to spend about £200,000 on perimeter fencing in the close season to fulfil the league's ground requirements but we bloody needed it the first game we played in the Fourth Division. The fixture computer gave us Wolves at home for our league debut and they brought thousands up with them from the Midlands. It was a bank holiday as well, so they'd been on the beach all morning, drinking and having a laugh. They took over the town and then swarmed into the ground. It was a great atmosphere when the game started but it always felt like it had the capacity to get a bit tasty and, sure enough, when half time came around, it all kicked off.

We had gone ahead but they equalised and Steve Bull put them in front. During the interval, the Wolves fans set about destroying new toilets we had had put in for the away supporters. They were smashing the hell out of them. One bloke climbed up on to the corrugated iron roof of the stand and started jumping up and down on it. Next thing you know, the idiot's fallen straight through it. An ambulance crew swept him up off the floor, what was left him, and took him off to hospital. He discharged himself later, which amazed me. Because he was so pissed, the medical people said his body was relaxed when he hit the floor and it limited the damage. They patched the corrugated iron up where he'd fallen through it. You could see that patch for years to come.

The ref was talking about abandoning the game because of the crowd trouble so before the teams came out for the second half, they asked me and the Wolves boss, Graham Turner, to walk over to the away fans to try to pacify them. As I was walking over towards them, I could tell that a lot of them were pretty smashed. We got to within about thirty yards of where they were standing and suddenly this Coca-Cola can came flying through the air out of nowhere and just missed my head. I picked it up and it was full of sand. It was like a piece of concrete. I said to Graham, 'Feel that.' He was a bit timid, Graham, and he looked aghast. 'I think we'd better leave them to it,' he said. He turned on his heels and trotted off. He was one of the nicest people you could ever wish to meet in football so I trotted off after him.

They let the game continue eventually. It finished 2-2 after we equalised with a bullet of a shot from Ray McHale. He was a good player, Ray, and I'd wanted him to be my assistant as I started off on my managerial career. He had accepted the job but then, three days before the first game, he said Vic Hallam had offered him £50 a week more to be his assistant at Rochdale. I couldn't believe it. I was absolutely gutted. I told him he was making a mistake but he said he needed the money and he had made up his mind. It didn't work out for him at Rochdale, though, and I went back in for him and got him back as a player. But he had missed the chance of being my assistant by then. I often wonder if he regretted not coming with me for the sake of £50. I would have taken him with me everywhere over the course of my management career but he never seemed bitter about it.

The team developed well in the first season in the Fourth Division. Our first home victory, we beat Bolton Wanderers 4–0. I just have to reflect where both clubs are now plying their trade. Bolton are established in the Premiership and poor old Scarborough have reached the other end of the spectrum. In June 2007, with debts of £2.5 million, they went out of business and had to start again from scratch. We had a few reverses, of course, and one that stung me so much I was moved to seek revenge. One Saturday we got beaten 4-0 at Carlisle United and I was so angry with my team, I told them after the game that I wanted to see all of them at Todwick the next morning. There were a few of them who had weekends with relatives planned and all that kind of thing. Anyway they turned up at the appointed time and they were all sitting there in the poky little dressing room when I walked in.

'I'm glad you've all come today,' I said, 'because you ruined my weekend. Now I've ruined your fucking weekend. See you tomorrow.' And then I walked out.

Generally, though, things went well. I got particular satisfaction out of the emergence of a young lad called Craig Short, who I later took to Notts County and Sheffield with me. Shorty's the most genuine, honest professional I've ever met. If you wanted your son to grow up like somebody, it would be Craig Short. But when I first went to Scarborough, all I saw was a bloody six foot two inches lump who, for some reason, was playing as a right winger. Well he was useless there, so we tried him in the centre of midfield. Still useless. Tried him up front. Still useless. Tried him at full back. Still useless. We were about to give up on him when we had a reserve team game and the centre half went down. 'Put Shorty there,' I said, as a kind of last resort. He would do anything you told him, that was his main attribute at that stage, so I told him to stick to the opposition centre forward, who was renowned for being an aggressive, stroppy, muscular attacker. Well, Shorty stuck to him like a fly to a piece of shit. He never left him alone. The guy started moaning and groaning and basically gave up. It was the best game I had ever seen Shorty play.

The next week the reserves were playing against Birmingham and Peter Withe, who had scored the winner in a European Cup Final, was up front. I told Shorty I wanted to see if the previous week had been a fluke or whether he could actually play. I told him to do what he'd done against Jamie Lawrence. I said I wanted him to be all over Withe like a rash. 'In fact,' I said, 'if he has to go to the bog, I want you to follow him.' Within twenty minutes, he had kicked him a few times and after a bit Withe came to the bench and started moaning. 'Get a grip of this young kid, will you,' he said, 'it's only a bloody reserve match, you know. He's not playing for fucking England.' Before long, I had Shorty in the first team. He never looked back.

We had some good laughs that season, too. We had one lad called Steve Adams who was an absolute nut case and he got involved in some sort of disagreement in the dressing room with a couple of the other players. It was the kind of thing that was threatening to drive a bit of a wedge between the players so I organised a boxing match for the pair of them. We did it properly, too. We went to a gym that had a proper boxing ring in it and they each had seconds, dressing gowns, shorts, mouthguards, the whole lot. The rest of the lads loved it and Steve Adams and Steve

Richards got all their resentments out of their system. It turned something potentially divisive into something that brought us closer together.

We were still part-time so we still had some dodgy moments getting players to games. When I put my teamsheet in for the away game at Torquay United an hour before the match, I only had seven players at the stadium. The rest were still travelling down because it was a bloody long way. The nappy salesman had had to be in Preston at 1 p.m. Andy Harrison was in Hull. Fireman Mell was on a late watch or something. Steve Richards was working in the park. They turned up about fifteen minutes before kick-off. It was hardly surprising in those circumstances that Torquay expected to beat us. They had beaten Spurs in a Cup game and a win against us would have put them top of Division Four. We were so bad in the early stages they nearly had to abandon the game because we booted that many balls out of the ground, but somehow we scraped a 1-0 win out of it. After the game, a young lady came up to me and asked who my number twelve was. I told her his name was Stewart Mell and she said what lovely legs he had. So I said she had better meet him and I brought him outside and introduced them. Twenty years later, they're happily married with two kids.

We stayed down in Torquay that night and Cyril Knowles, the Torquay boss, was staying in the same hotel. We made such a bloody hullabaloo that night celebrating our win that he got all his lads in for extra training the next day. I knew one of the lads in their team and he told me what had happened. 'I've got you in today,' Cyril had told them, 'because all night I've had to listen to a rag tag and bobtail set of fucking amateurs running up and down corridors, pissed and laughing and joking until 5 a.m., women and all, so you are all going to pay for it this morning.' He ran them and ran them for two hours.

We started to climb the league, too, but I had lost a couple more chairmen and things weren't as straightforward as they had been before. Terry Wood had resigned. Then there was a bloke from the Scarborough Building Society. And then, at the start of that first season in Division Four, Geoffrey Richmond took over. Geoffrey was a big bloke with big ideas. I was told fairly early on that he wanted to get Billy Bremner in as his manager, even after everything we had achieved the year before. That didn't work out but then he called me into his office and gave me a list of four or five players he wanted me to sign.

One was Bernie Slaven at Middlesbrough. Another was Colin Clarke at Southampton. They were players we hadn't got a cat in hell's chance of signing. He might as well have asked me to go after Gazza. But Geoffrey Richmond was insistent. He told me I must do everything I could to bring them to Scarborough. So I rang Bruce Rioch, the Middlesbrough manager, and asked him about Bernie Slaven, who was a Republic of Ireland international at the time. He thought I was raving mad. 'That'll do his career no end of good, moving to fucking Scarborough,' he said. I muttered my apologies and rang off.

Richmond was naive. He had only just started in football and it was becoming difficult to work with him by Christmas. About that time, I wanted to sign a lad from Hull City on £80 a week and he was dismayed I wasn't going after bigger names. This lad from Hull played on New Year's Eve against Crewe Alexandra and scored. We won the game and went top of the table. Afterwards, I asked Geoffrey to come into my office and I told him I felt disappointed and that I didn't think I could be the manager he wanted me to be. I told him I wouldn't be talked to the way he talked to me. He tried to dominate me and patronise me. I told him I wouldn't have it, that he couldn't run a football club like that and that he could stuff his job up his backside. When we spoke years later, we agreed that we had both been inexperienced, and would have handled the situation differently with hindsight. Geoffrey had had his critics at Bradford but he only ever wanted to make their dreams come true, and I have a lot of time for him. The Scarborough adventure had been good while it lasted. In fact, it had been magic. But now it was over.

9
THE KING OF
THE PLAY-OFFS

W ALSALL HAD a job going when I left Scarborough so I applied for it. I didn't get a reply. John Barnwell had just left Notts County so I applied for that, too. Their chairman, Derek Pavis, invited me down to his house in Nottingham for an interview. I had a couple more meetings with club officials and they offered me the job. They were third from bottom of the old Division Three and Scarborough were at the top of Division Four so it didn't seem like a particularly upwardly mobile move at the time. But I knew Notts County had potential. They might be the oldest football club in the world but their history wasn't exactly littered with honours and I thought I could change that and give them something to shout about. Pavis promised that if I kept them up, he'd pay for the whole squad to go on an end of season holiday to Florida.

I was appointed the day before my first game in charge, which was at Swansea City in early January. I introduced myself to the players in the dressing room before the match and said I was looking forward to working with them. I told them if they gave me everything I would look after them but that if they wanted to fall out or if they wanted to go, they just had to ask me. I looked around the dressing room and, just like at Burton, all the older lads looked down at the floor and the younger ones looked up at me. There were a few old stagers there. Gary Mills and Garry Birtles had both been at Forest and Birtles had had an unproductive spell at Manchester United, too. Geoff Pike, the ex-West Ham midfielder, was on the books as well. Those three in particular gave every impression of thinking 'who the hell is this upstart?'.

We got beaten 2-0. Within about ten minutes Garry Birtles came off injured. I was puzzled. I asked the physio what the problem was and he said it was a hamstring. He said Birtles had been saying all week that it felt a bit tight. The whole thing seemed strange to me. Stranger still when I asked around a bit and found out the same thing had happened the week before. I had a bit of experience of the ruses that footballers can work by then. I'd been a bloody footballer myself. Anyway, I asked Derek Pavis if I could look at the wage bill. It turned out Garry Birtles was getting £1,000 appearance money every time he walked on the pitch, which was a fortune in those days.

I asked the physio on the Tuesday how Birtles was feeling. We had a home game against Blackpool the following Saturday.

'He thinks he's got a chance,' the physio said.

'Tell him he's got no fucking chance,' I said.

'What do you mean?' the physio said.

'Tell him he's going to have to play in the reserves for ninety minutes to prove to me he's fit,' I said.

'But Garry Birtles doesn't play in the reserves,' the physio said. 'Well, he does now,' I told him.

Garry and I still laugh about that episode now. He tried his hardest for me after that. He played centre half for me and all sorts. He went to Grimsby Town after he left us and had another couple of years at Blundell Park. But it was obvious to me that I had to clear out a lot of the deadwood and bring in new blood. I gave a lad called Tommy Johnson his debut when he was eighteen and when Geoff Pike got an injury during a match at Northampton Town a couple of weeks after I'd taken over, I stuck another young lad, Mark Draper, into the side and left him in for the rest of the season. We started putting a few results together and Derek Pavis started getting a bit ahead of himself.

'If you can get us into the play-offs,' Pavis said, 'I'll take the lot of you to America for free.'

'I think your memory's going a bit, chairman,' I said.

We finished ninth in the end, about five points shy of the play-offs. We never did get to America. All chairman are a little bit thrifty. Derek was bloody hard work like that. He looked after every penny and signed every cheque. Whenever we signed a player and the player, the chairman and I were in his office negotiating the lad's wages, Derek would lean back in his chair and say the famous words that I became so familiar with in my years at Meadow Lane.

'Neil,' he'd say, 'there's only so much meat on the bone.'

It got to the point where I would tell a player how much money I was going to try and get him and I'd warn him not to be disappointed with the chairman's opening gambit.

'And try not to laugh when he says "there's only so much meat on the bone",' I always told them.

Pavis was a character. He had made his money in plumbing and he'd been on the Forest board of directors. But Brian Clough disliked him intensely and forced him out. So he bought Notts County instead. A lot of people seemed to dislike him intensely, actually. Particularly managers who had worked for him. But I don't think anyone had ever tried with him before. I made up my mind that I'd have a real go at getting on with him. I used to take him to a lot of games with me and he'd drive me up to matches in his big Rolls-Royce.

Getting to know Cloughie was one of the real privileges of working in Nottingham. He was revered at Forest after everything he had achieved there and the teams he was still producing. I had a few private lunches with him while I was there. The first was at his local pub and I'd arranged to meet him at 12.30. I was nervous about meeting the great man so I got there fifteen minutes early. I waited for about an hour and there was no sign of him. I didn't know anyone in the pub so I felt like a spare part and eventually I went outside and rang Carol, Cloughie's lifelong secretary. She said she'd check on his whereabouts and she sounded very apologetic when she rang back. I think Cloughie had forgotten all about it. She said he'd be there in a couple of minutes. Ten minutes later, in comes Brian in his green sweater, looking freshly washed and shaved.

'Hello, young man,' he said, 'and what are you drinking?'

'I'll have an orange juice, Mr Clough,' I said.

'Will you?' he said. 'Well I'm having a bottle of pink champagne. Will you join me?'

We talked for two hours. At first, it was about Hartlepool where he'd managed and I'd played. We talked about some of the working men's clubs up there. And then he began to talk about how he didn't get on with Derek Pavis. 'I don't know how you've had any success working for him,' he said. He never called him by his name. He always called him 'him'. Actually, he used to call him worse than 'him'. I told Cloughie that, actually, I was getting on okay with Pavis. 'You're a fucking miracle-worker then,' he said.

I saw Cloughie now and again during my four years at Meadow Lane. From time to time, our paths crossed. We trained on a little scrap of land that was owned by Boots and Forest had an impressive facility next door to us on the banks of the River Trent that was luxurious in comparison. Their pitches were like velvet and they had brilliant changing rooms with lovely showers. Sometimes Cloughie walked past our pitch to get to Forest's training ground and, now and again, I saw him watching us flying into our tackles and squaring up to each other in training. It was the opposite of the more relaxed skill-based training sessions he oversaw. They were purists. We weren't. One morning, I saw him walking right across our pitch rather than around it. He was with his Labrador, Del Boy, and his assistant, Ronnie Fenton. He looked across the pitch towards us and just shook his head as he watched what we were doing.

Mick Jones, my assistant, who had played for him as a young reserve at Derby County, shouted across to him.

'Morning, gaffer,' he said.

'Call me Brian,' Cloughie shouted back.

I'd been talking on my mobile phone but I finished the call and shouted across to him, too.

'Morning Brian,' I yelled.

'Call me Mr Clough,' he shouted back.

I'd always liked Cloughie. Always respected him, too. Hero-worshipped him, really. I knew I wasn't going to get a top club job. I knew I was always going to get struggling clubs that needed Red Adair. That's why I liked what he did. He was the underdog a lot of the time but he showed that the underdog could still come out on top. That's why he was the best to me. I spent more time studying him and admiring him than anybody else because Sir Alex hadn't really come on the scene by then and I do regard Cloughie as the best of my era. I think he could have won even more if his lads had ever worked at defending free kicks or corners but then who am I to find fault with a bloke who won the European Cup twice. Watching them was like watching the modern Arsenal at their best. I could have listened to him talk all day and I tried to mould myself on him a little bit. What I liked about him was that he took vagabonds, he took rogues, and he made them into players. You look at men like Kenny Burns, Larry Lloyd, John McGovern and Archie Gemmill. Nobody wanted them and yet he made them fabulous players.

He could be a lovely bloke, too. You hear a lot of bad things about him and his drinking and his temper but he was an incredibly generous man. The first encounter I had with him was when I took Scarborough reserves down to Nottingham for a match against

Forest's third string at the City Ground one Sunday morning. I took my son, James, who was about five. Cloughie sat in the stand and I was on the bench. The referee made a cock up with something and Cloughie shouted down to me: 'You'd be having a go, wouldn't you young man, if that were your team with a decision like that.' He was shouting at the top of his voice.

At half time we went down to the tunnel and I told James to stand outside the dressing room door for a couple of minutes while I gave a quick team talk. I told him not to move until I came out. But when I got out, he wasn't there. He was only a little boy and the stewards didn't know where he'd gone so I started to panic. Eventually, the chief steward told me he'd gone down the corridor towards the home dressing room and that he'd be back in a minute. Sure enough, he soon appeared, laden with presents. He was like one of the contestants on *Crackerjack* who had to carry as many prizes as they could under their arms without dropping them. He had about six Easter eggs in boxes, a toy fire engine and all manner of other things.

I asked him where he'd been.

'I've only been with Brian, dad,' he said.

'Brian?' I said. 'You mean Mr Clough.'

'No, dad, he told me to call him Brian,' James said.

I had never called him Brian. Except for that one time at the training ground. He had a big heart, though, Cloughie. He did a lot of good things people never knew about. He taught me a few useful lessons, too. He told me once how much he regretted falling out with his great friend and assistant, Peter Taylor, and not making it up with him before Taylor died. I had a similar kind of disagreement with Mick Jones when he stayed on at Plymouth Argyle after I got the sack. We didn't speak for a few years but after a while I thought about what Cloughie had said to me and decided that life was too short. I gave Mick a ring and he was on the staff with me at Bramall Lane and remains a great friend.

I would love to have seen Cloughie get the England job but he just upset too many important people. That was another thing I liked about him: he didn't mind upsetting people. I did a sportsman's dinner with him once a few weeks after he'd got into trouble for giving a Forest fan a cuff for invading the pitch at the City Ground. I got up to give my speech and he started heckling me from the floor. He was full of it that night.

'It's all right for some,' I said, pointing at him. 'He can clip one of these fans round the ear, give them a kiss and get away with it. You can't do that if you're me.'

I saw him a few weeks before his death, too, at a dinner for about thirty people somewhere in the Midlands. I got up and said a few words about how so many people wished he had been England manager but that he had left an incredible legacy at Derby and Forest and that he had been a hero to countless managers like me. His reign at Forest was on its downslope by the time I arrived at Notts County but it still felt like an impossible dream to try and match them. When we drew 1-1 with them at the City Ground in our year in the top flight, it was one of my proudest achievements. He was very magnanimous towards me afterwards and I'll always treasure those words.

Days like that seemed a long way away in the spring of 1989, though. I had my clear-out in the summer and brought some new lads in. I signed Phil Turner from Leicester and made him my captain and I got a lad called Dean Thomas from Northampton Town who had a sweet left foot. I brought Craig Short over from Scarborough and put him in the centre of defence with a great young player called Dean Yates who had come up through the ranks at Notts County. Then I paid £23,000 to Hull City for a right back called Charlie Palmer who, pound for pound, must be just about the best signing I ever made. Nothing fancy about him but he was incredibly consistent and he always gave 100 per cent. His eyes always lit up the dressing room.

'What are you looking at, Charlie?' I used to say to him whenever I caught him staring at me expectantly.

'Nothing, gaffer, nothing,' he'd say. And then, when he realised I was joking, he'd light the place up with this great big smile.

I had a defence of Charlie, Shorty, Yates and Nicky Platnauer at left back. All great lads but none of them very good on the ball. When people asked why we played long ball at Notts County, the answer was simple. It was because we couldn't pass water. We had to play to our strengths and passing definitely wasn't one of them. We had Steve Cherry in goal. He was a little overweight but what a goalie. He hardly ever made mistakes and he went right through with us to the top flight. Don O'Riordan was the sweeper and he could put a sixty-yard ball on a sixpence. He was about the only one who could, though. We usually played a five at the back. Sometimes Don would play in front of the four, sometimes behind. Then we played two in midfield and three up front with Tommy Johnson roving. Tommy was the kind of player who could always win you a game out of nothing.

I had a big lumbering lad called Gary Lund up front and I wanted Kevin Bartlett from Cardiff to play with him and Johnson up front. But Bartlett went to West Brom with Bobby Gould instead. Then, within two weeks, I noticed Bobby Gould had dropped him. They had lost a couple of games and it seemed like Bobby Gould might be having second thoughts. People had told me he was already having doubts. So I thought I'd try and rescue it. I went on to Bobby Gould on the pretext of talking about something else and mentioned as casually as I could that I would give him his money back for Bartlett. It worked a bloody treat and he rang me back and said he'd like to do a deal. I liked Bartlett. He was so fast he could catch pigeons.

By the start of my first full season in charge, I felt we were in a good position to move forward. I was working hard at getting on well with the chairman, I was putting my own stamp on the team and I was happy with my backroom staff. I had Mick Jones as my assistant and a bloke called Dave Wilson as physio. They say there's a fine line between insanity and genius and Dave Wilson walked that line. He had been at Arsenal at some point in the past and when we played at Highbury a couple of years later, one of their directors told me Dave would have had his own Harley Street practice if he hadn't been such an antagonistic so-and-so.

But Dave didn't care about money. He was a true eccentric. I played badminton with him every lunchtime and I always just beat him. We both got a good sweat on but he would never wash his kit. He just put it on the radiator and dried it. Then, on a Friday afternoon, after all the players had gone, Dave would lower himself into the bath in the dressing room, still wearing that kit. He'd scrub the kit with soap while he was still wearing it, then get out, take it off and put it on the bloody drier. He was a right character.

I went round to his house once and I was sitting on the settee with Shorty, talking to Dave, when Dave's dog, Bessie, limped in to the room. She looked awfully sorry for herself and so without breaking off from his conversation to us, Dave grabbed hold of her and got her on her side. He manipulated her back for a minute and then did something to her sacroiliac joint at the base of her spine just like he would to a human patient. The dog let out this yelp and then shot off towards the garden with her tail between her legs. It seemed to have cured her limp, though. Dave just carried on with the conversation as if nothing had happened.

He'd been with me at Scarborough for a while and when I got the Notts County job, I tracked him down to somewhere in Hong Kong and asked him if he'd come and join up with me again. Dave had a bad stammer and, because it was a big decision for him, he started stuttering twenty to the dozen. I was in a rush for some reason and I'm afraid I wasn't very patient.

'Look, Dave,' I said, as he tried to get his answer out, 'I haven't got time for this. Is it yes or no?'

'Y-y-y-y-y-y-y-es,' Dave said from Hong Kong.

With everything in place, we were vastly improved in 1989-90. We still had a few uneven patches of form but we went ten games unbeaten in November and December and twelve games unbeaten at the end of the season. We finished third and missed out on automatic promotion by four points to Bristol City. That meant the play-offs. It also meant that even though Bolton Wanderers had finished eighteen points below us in Division Three, they had a shot at us in the play-off semi-finals. It didn't seem very fair but there was nothing we could do about it. The sense of injustice got worse when we went to Burnden Park for the first leg and within fifteen minutes of the start, the ref had given them a penalty. What a shock. It was rubbish. It was never a penalty but Gary Lund equalised and we went back to Meadow Lane and beat them 2-0 in the return.

That was when it was worth being in the play-offs. Because for the first time, they were holding the play-off finals at Wembley. It was the first time Notts County had been to Wembley in their entire 128-year history. Somehow, even though they'd been formed in 1862, they had always avoided the place up until then. We were up against Tranmere Rovers in the final that would decide whether we secured the promotion spot to Division Two that should have been ours anyway. The week before the game, Tranmere already had a Wembley date. They were playing Bristol Rovers in the Leyland DAF Trophy and I decided to take my team down there to watch them and soak up a bit of the atmosphere at the same time.

We had booked the top floor of the Hilton across the road from the stadium for the play-off final the following week so we stayed there when we were just spectators as well. It was like a dry run.

That was what I intended it to be. We wandered over to the ground an hour or so before the kick off and discovered we were in the same section as the Tranmere supporters. They recognised us and there was a lot of good-natured banter about how badly they were going to beat us the next time we met. Underneath the joviality, though, we all sensed they thought the game against us the next weekend was already won. They were all a bit complacent. And their confidence grew when they beat Bristol Rovers and got a taste of Wembley glory.

On the day of our final, we went across to Wembley in the bus early in the morning to lay the kit out in our dressing room and I took the players on the pitch. We weren't supposed to be allowed to do that but I wanted them to see the stadium early and nobody stopped us. I wanted them to get an idea of the angles and the size of the pitch and the feel of the grass. I wanted to do anything that might give us the smallest edge over Tranmere. We wandered back over to the Hilton and by then the fans were turning up and the atmosphere was beginning to build. By the time we hopped on our coach for the short journey back with our police escort, the place was awash with fans in black and white.

I needn't have bothered too much about trying to gain an edge. Tranmere provided one for us. When we wandered up the tunnel an hour or so before the game, the Tranmere centre half came past us going the other way. He had these super-cool fancy sunglasses on, and the whisper went round among the lads that Tranmere were playing it flash. They thought he was trying to be Mr Big Time, looking down on us like he was some sort of Hollywood film star. It wound them up nicely. They thought Tranmere were being arrogant. 'Let's sort these fuckers out,' one of our lads said.

I fulfilled one of my greatest ambitions by leading a side out at Wembley and as I was walking out of the tunnel at the head of my team alongside the Tranmere boss, John King, I couldn't believe I had realised that dream so early in my managerial career. We were brilliant that day, too. Tommy Johnson put us ahead midway through the first half with his twentieth goal of the season and, after Steve Cherry had made a brilliant save early in the second half, Craig Short headed home our second after sixty-two minutes. There was no way back for Tranmere after that and Phil Turner went up to the Royal Box to collect a special trophy containing an illuminated scroll. I stayed on the pitch, clapping the players up, and applauding the 15,000 County fans who had travelled down from Nottingham.

I have never experienced anything like the journey back up to Nottingham that evening. The M1 seemed to have been painted in black and white. We let the cameras on the bus for a little while and then spent the rest of the journey waving at the supporters who were heading back north with black and white scarves flying out of their car windows. On the outskirts of Nottingham, there's a pub by the Clifton Island called the Crusader. There were hundreds of Notts County fans outside with their pints and I told the coach driver to go round the roundabout three times. We went on the balcony at the Town Hall the following day. The club had been so starved of success that it made the supporters appreciate it even more. They were great times.

And they kept rolling. I signed a couple of lads from Barnet, Dave Regis and Paul Harding, in the close season and we started our campaign in Division Two the same way we'd finished off in Division Three. We beat Newcastle 2-0 at St James's Park, we beat Blackburn at Ewood Park and we beat Wolves at Molineux. We were starting to feel comfortable among the big boys so it wasn't quite as big a surprise as it was during my days at Burton to find myself in the middle of another great run in the FA Cup.

I didn't have the inconvenience of the qualifying rounds to worry about any more and it seemed like quite a luxury to be entering the competition in the third round proper. We beat Hull City 5-2 away, then won 2-0 at Oldham in the fourth round. In the fifth round, we drew Manchester City at Meadow Lane and Cup fever took hold. I always tried to do something different for Cup ties in terms of the team's preparation and, because City were a good top-flight side, I decided I wouldn't train the lads too hard in the week leading up to the game. The snow had been coming down hard as well, so I organised a dozen sledges, tipped off the television cameras and took the lads down to Wollaton Park in Nottingham for a bit of fun.

We sledged for two and a half hours and the media turned up in their droves. I wanted it to come over that we were all light-hearted and that we were enjoying the Cup and that we weren't going to let a big game unnerve us. As I was doing the interviews, the lads were all throwing snowballs at me and whacking me on the back of the head with them. What I didn't realise was that, as I was speaking, both my goalkeepers, Steve Cherry and Kevin Blackwell, were on the same sledge going down this hill at about 100 miles an hour and weaving in and out of bloody big trees. One of the journalists mentioned it to me afterwards and I laughed it off.

'Course I knew about it,' I said. 'We don't worry about things like that at this club.'

Inside I was full of relief. If those two bloody idiots had crashed their sledge and wiped themselves out and we'd have been without a goalie for our biggest match in years, I would have looked like a right idiot. But they didn't crash and we got volunteers down to Meadow Lane early on the morning of the game to sweep the snow off it and try and get the match on. We knew the conditions would be a leveller and so did Man City. Their manager, Peter Reid, and his assistant, Sam Ellis, arrived a couple of hours before kick-off and said there was no way the pitch was fit for play. The referee disagreed and the game went ahead. It was end to end stuff and both goalkeepers made fantastic saves. Then, just when it looked as if it was going to a replay, Gary Lund scored the winner in the ninetieth minute and we were in the quarter-finals.

We played Spurs at White Hart Lane in the last eight. It was the first time Notts County had ever been featured on live television. The oldest club in the world was racking up a lot of firsts all of a sudden. We were starting to feel like we could beat anybody and we took the lead when Don O'Riordan cracked in a beauty from about thirty-five yards. I had put Paul Harding on Paul Gascoigne to do a man-marking job on him and it had been working a treat. Harding was a hard case. He'd man mark anyone. He didn't give a toss who they were. And he got to Gazza early on. Gazza reacted, as he often did, by swinging an elbow and pole-axing him. The referee was in a good position but he didn't send him off. A couple of minutes later, he had a quick chat with Phil Turner.

'That probably should have been a red, shouldn't it?' he said.

'You know it should, ref,' Phil Turner said.

It was too late by then, though. Gazza made one and scored one and we lost 2-1. Harding had a horrendous black eye after the game which made it even more obvious that Gazza shouldn't have stayed on the pitch. In the modern game, he would have been done by video replay and banned. The sad thing is if he'd been sent off and Spurs had lost, he wouldn't have done his knee with that tackle on Gary Charles in the final against Nottingham Forest. I know that logic is warped by my Notts County allegiance that day, but Gazza's whole career might have been different. The history of English football might have been different. And Notts County might have made it to Wembley again.

But at least getting knocked out of the cup let us pour all our energies into the league for the last six weeks of the season. We missed out on automatic promotion to the top flight by a few points but we knew by the last game that we were already guaranteed a play-off spot. So we went into that final match, against West Ham at Upton Park, with nothing particularly at stake. It was different for West Ham. They were vying with Oldham for the Division Two title and if they beat us or got the same result as Oldham, they would go up as champions.

I've always liked playing at West Ham because the atmosphere's usually fantastic and my sides always gave them a good game. We got there that day and all the balloons were out and we found out that the Football League had arranged for the Second Division trophy to be there ready to be presented to West Ham. The celebrations were all ready to go. They were trying to tell us that we were supposed to be spectators at a coronation. It really wound me up.

I'll show this bloody lot, I thought.

I really got in to the players in the dressing room. I was determined not to finish the regular season with an anticlimax. Mark Draper scored two fantastic twenty-five-yarders and we won 2-1. With about five minutes to go, word went round that Sheffield Wednesday had gone 2-1 up at Oldham and the crowd went wild. As long as Oldham didn't win, it didn't matter to West Ham that they had lost to us. Then there was word that Oldham had equalised but it was quickly followed by a massive roar. Everyone was saying the final whistle had gone at Boundary Park and West Ham were champions.

We looked over at Billy Bonds and everyone was patting him on the back so I went across to him.

'Congratulations, mate,' I said. 'Sorry about today but delighted for you.'

At the end of the game, we went over to thank our supporters and then we heard this gasp going round the ground. It was like a prolonged murmur of horror. It turned out that in the fourth minute of injury time, Oldham had got a penalty and they'd won. So the only time Joe Royle ever won anything at Oldham, it was me that bloody won it for him. Nobody else would have beaten West

Ham on that day. His title was down to me, nobody else, and I have told him a few times since.

We played Middlesbrough in the play-off semi-finals. The first leg was at Ayresome Park and we absolutely pasted them for the first forty-five minutes. We scored one goal but it should have been three or four. We wasted a hatful of chances and then on the stroke of full time, they equalised. It stayed that way to the end and we knew that we had missed a brilliant opportunity. We knew they'd have Stuart Ripley back for the second leg at Meadow Lane and he was their best player. And that second leg was unbelievably tight. It was difficult for us because we went into it knowing we should have finished things up in the north-east and when we came out for the second half and it was still 0-0, I felt physically sick with nerves. Suddenly, it was end to end and it was anybody's game. Thankfully, Paul Harding scored twenty minutes from the end and we squeaked through into the final.

So we were at Wembley again. We followed the same routine as the previous year. We stayed at the same Hilton Hotel, in the same rooms. We got the bus over in the morning and had our clandestine walk around the pitch. Then we walked back over to the hotel and got the bus back to the Twin Towers with our police escort. Our line-up was similar to the year before, too. We had seven of the eleven players who had faced Tranmere twelve months earlier. Don O'Riordan had come in, Dave Regis was up front, Mark Draper was in the starting line up and Alan Paris had replaced Nicky Platnauer at left back. Most of them were familiar with the routine.

This time, we were up against Brighton and Hove Albion. This time, the stakes were higher than they had been before. This was for the right to play in the top flight of English football. We all knew what was resting on it but we felt confident nonetheless. Brighton had played Millwall in the other play-off semi-final and we had all assumed Millwall would win because they were a better, harder side. But Brighton beat them heavily in the first leg and killed the tie off. I thought that was a bit of a fluke. I knew we were better than Brighton if we could only play to our potential.

But Brighton started off better than us and when Tommy Johnson scored after half an hour, it was against the run of play. We had a real alarm when Clive Walker, the former Chelsea winger, hit the post for them with a header, but then Tommy scored again after an hour and Dave Regis got a third ten minutes later. It was like being in a dream. Dean Wilkins got one back for them in the last minute but it was too late for us to have to worry about it. What a feeling it was when the final whistle went. I hugged Paul Evans on the touchline. I hardly knew where I was but I knew we were both in tears. We had made history again, the first team ever to win promotion two years on the run in the play-offs. I could hardly believe it. I'd been managing a non-league club three years earlier. Now I was going to be a boss in the top flight.

10
REGRETS – ONE OR TWO

T HERE WAS another reason why I was desperate to win the play-off final against Brighton. Towards the end of the 1990-91 season I had been offered the manager's job at Chelsea and I was agonising about whether to join them. I'd been to meet Ken Bates, the Chelsea chairman, and I knew that the chance to become the manager at Stamford Bridge was a shot at the football big time for me. They were offering me a four-year deal that would have set me up for life.

The whole issue was hanging over me like a bloody dark cloud during the climax of the season and I was determined to get Notts County up so that no one could accuse me of derailing our promotion push if the news came out that I had been talking to another club. The situation played havoc with my mind. I'm an ambitious man but I'm loyal, too. I was on the horns of a dilemma.

I met Ken Bates at his farm in Beaconsfield in Buckinghamshire. Later, I had a meeting with him at Stamford Bridge, too. Bobby Campbell was the manager at the time and Bates said he would be moving upstairs. The club had a very strong dressing room with some powerful characters but they were locked in a cycle of mediocrity and Bates wanted someone to shake them out of it.

Bates took me out on to the pitch at Stamford Bridge and we walked across to the centre circle. I think I was supposed to be impressed but I wasn't. The stadium wasn't the way it is now. It was falling to pieces. There were bits hanging off it everywhere. It needed a hell of a lot of work doing to it. It seemed like quite an eerie place to me. I'd already seen the training ground at Harlington, near Heathrow. That was dilapidated, too. Chelsea didn't even own it. It just didn't feel right. None of it. Then Ken got out all these plans of the way the stadium was going to be when all the renovations were done. It was all hotels, restaurants, corporate boxes, new West Stand, the whole works.

'These are the outlines of how it's going to look in six years,' Ken said proudly.

'Why are you showing them to me then, Ken?' I said.

He laughed.

'When have you ever kept a fucking manager for six years?' I said.

He laughed again and we had a good joke about it all. But then, as we were talking, he turned to Colin Hutchinson, who was his right-hand man.

'Right,' Bates said, 'I'll leave you in Colin's capable hands. Nice to see you, Neil, and see you again soon, I'm sure.'

I thought what a strange thing for a chairman to leave when I hadn't agreed anything. That's not how I work. I wanted to talk everything through with him. I wanted more discussion than that. I wanted to know that we could have a good working relationship. My relationship with a club chairman is always key to me. I know I need their support if I'm going to have a chance. So I wanted him to agree everything with me and it seemed odd he was leaving it to somebody else. I thought he couldn't want me one hundred per cent if he wasn't prepared to see it out. That's what went through my mind.

I had other doubts, too. Both times I went to meet Ken, at his farm and then at the ground, I got stuck in horrendous traffic on the M25. The first time it was an hour and a quarter, the second time fifty-five minutes. Bloody gridlock both times. I hate traffic. It's the one thing I hate. I won't leave my house in Sheffield in the morning until 9.15. I'll do all my phone calls at home before I set off just so I can avoid the rush hour. I hate being still and not being in control of how quickly I can get somewhere. That's why I want to live in Cornwall when I'm finished in management. The only traffic you get in Cornwall is if a tractor pulls up at the post office.

When the season was over, the news began to seep out that I was considering an offer from Chelsea. Dean Thomas, Phil Turner, Craig Short and a few of the other Notts County lads came to see me at my house in West Bridgford, near Nottingham, and pleaded with me to stay. They said they had been faithful to me and that their families had stood by me. They said I owed them one year in the top flight. It was emotional blackmail really, but I understood their point of view. I would probably have tried the same tactics if one of them had wanted to leave. They were all great lads, too, and they had given me everything. I didn't want to turn my back on them.

I was on about £60,000 at Notts County and Chelsea were offering me three times that. But I was beginning to feel morally obliged to stay. I knew all my lads at Notts County well. They weren't the most gifted squad technically, so I knew that if a new manager came in, everything we had built would soon get dismantled. I knew their best chance of avoiding the drop would be if I stayed. After we had won promotion, the squad had flown out to Spain for a post-season tour of some sort, so I went out to join them. I had another chat with them out there. I was quite confident I could keep them up in the top flight for at least a season and I thought that, if I did that, I'd be able to get any job I wanted. So I decided to give them a year. I went to see Colin Hutchinson, who was also in Spain at the time, and told him I was going to stay put.

He still didn't give up. During the meeting, Mick Jones went to the toilet and Colin took his chance.

'Listen, Neil,' he said. 'I'll give you Mick Jones's salary on top of what we've offered you and I'll get you a number two.'

'Who will you get as a number two?' I said.

'Ian Porterfield,' he said.

I had recommended a young player called Richard Jobson to Ian Porterfield when I was at Burton and he was manager of Sheffield United. He'd never even got back to me. I always remembered that.

'I'm not really a big fan of Ian's, if I'm honest,' I said, 'and I don't think I'd want to work with him. It's not about money anyway.'

The meeting didn't last for long after that. Colin Hutchinson kept saying how surprised he was that I wasn't taking the job but I'd made up my mind. They gave the job to Porterfield in the end. That

153

guy must have thought all his Christmases had come together but he only lasted eighteen months. Even now, each time I bump into Bates, he bangs on about how I should have gone with him all those years ago. 'I know, I know,' I say, 'don't tell me.'

I like Ken Bates, me. Can you imagine what it would have been like, me and him together at Chelsea. It would have been lively, for a start. But I think he would have supported me. He had the vision to build Chelsea into what it is today and even though he ran up debts and got lucky with Roman Abramovich, he still got the job done. I admire him for that and sometimes I think that I should have accepted his offer, just like he says. Sometimes I regret not going to Chelsea that summer.

I don't have a lot of regrets about my past but I do have a chip on my shoulder about the fact that I never got a shot at another big job after that. It bugs me when I see other managers getting top jobs and I know they're not as good as me. The way I am, the way I say it as it is, I don't help myself and I suppose I put a lot of chairmen off. But if you look at my record, it's nearly as good as anybody's. I'm proud of that but, yes, I do regret not having had a go at a bigger club in the Premiership.

That was my hot spell then. That year when I took Notts County to the quarter-finals of the FA Cup and got them promoted to the top flight was when I was flavour of the month. That was when a lot of people were considering me for the top jobs. That was my time, I suppose, and because I felt this loyalty to my lads at Notts County, I never quite seized the opportunity to move on.

Sunderland came in for me around that time, too. Their interest came to a head in February 1992 while I was trying to keep Notts County in the top flight. My relationship with Derek Pavis had soured by then and I met the Sunderland chairman, Bob Murray, and liked him and thought the club were great. They had sacked Denis Smith a couple of months earlier and given the job to Malcolm Crosby on a caretaker basis. Even though they were struggling near the foot of Division Two, Malcolm had got them going on a bit of a run in the FA Cup but Bob Murray said that the Cup didn't matter and he wanted me to take over.

I wavered about it. It would have meant walking out on Notts County while we were in the middle of a relegation fight. There was the issue of Malcolm Crosby, too. Malcolm and I had played together at Aldershot and I didn't want to step on his toes while they were still in the FA Cup. I didn't want to do anything behind his back and ruin that Cup run so I struck an informal deal with Bob Murray.

'I tell you what, Bob,' I said, 'I'll come when you get knocked out of the Cup.'

Everybody was happy with that. The club wouldn't have anything to play for once they had been eliminated and I could have a couple of months up at Roker Park at the end of the season to assess the squad and plan for the following campaign. There was only one problem: Sunderland never did get knocked out of the Cup. They went all the way to the final. How unlucky can you get? When they beat Norwich City in the semi-finals at the beginning of April 1992, I knew they would have to give Malcolm another year. So I had let another chance of managing a big club slip away.

But I was happy at Notts County when the 1991-92 season began. That was part of the problem, I suppose. I didn't have a great hunger to get away because, at that stage, I was still enjoying being at Meadow Lane. Until things changed in January 1992, I still had a good relationship with Pavis and I had a great bunch of lads. I thought that with the spirit we had, we would give a few teams a run for their money in the top flight. I thought we had enough to avoid the drop. I was looking forward to the challenge, even when the fixture computer sent us to Old Trafford to play Manchester United for our opening game.

United might not have won the title since 1967 but Alex Ferguson was putting the finishing touches to the side that was going to end that barren spell the following season. They might not have been champions when we arrived in Division One but it was still a fairly humbling experience for us to play at a stadium like Old Trafford. The press asked me afterwards if there was one thing that had brought it home to me that I'd arrived in the big time.

'Yes,' I said, 'when I walked out on to the pitch before the game and saw a warning sign that had been put up for the supporters.'

'What sign?' they said.

'Keep Off the Grass,' I said.

'What was so strange about that?' one of the press lads asked.

'It was in fifteen different languages,' I said.

I hate to admit it but there was one other thing that gave me an almighty shock that day. Nothing to do with my team. My line up went like this: Cherry, Palmer, Paris, Short, Yates, O'Riordan, Thomas, Turner, Regis, Draper, Johnson. The nucleus of the side was still drawn from the team that had won promotion from Division Three in 1989-90. But an hour or so before the kick off, we got the United teamsheet and there was a name on it that I didn't recognise.

'Who the fuck is Andrei Kanchelskis?' I said.

I was met by a row of blank faces. None of my staff knew either. I was mortified. In fact, I was in a blind panic.

'Well who the hell is he?' I kept saying. 'Who is he?'

I was livid. Steam was coming out of my ears. Here were we, new to the big time, and there was some player in their team we'd never heard of, let alone done our homework about. We'd been so occupied with the play-offs at the back end of the previous season that it had passed unnoticed that Kanchelskis had made his debut for United in their penultimate league game, against Crystal Palace. I didn't even know which position he played.

I went into damage limitation mode. I told someone to go and try and find out who he was without giving too much away. That is, without letting United know we had no idea who one of their players was. All we got before the kick-off was that he was a right winger from Russia.

Alan Paris was our left back. He was going to be marking Kanchelskis.

'Stick tight to him,' I said.

In the first two minutes, United knocked a ball over the top and Kanchelskis went past Alan Paris like a whiff of wind. He left him about thirty yards behind, crossed it and they nearly scored.

Alan looked over at me pleadingly. I rushed out into my technical area at the side of the pitch.

'Drop off him, drop off him if he's that quick,' I screamed at him.

Next thing, Kanchelskis gets the ball in acres of space, turns, plays a one-two with Mark Hughes, whips in another cross and they nearly scored again.

Well Alan Paris got absolutely battered that day. It must have been one of the most torrid ninety minutes of his whole career. He couldn't get anywhere near Kanchelskis all afternoon. It was a miracle we only lost 2-0.

At the end of the game, I was standing by the tunnel when Alan walked off the pitch.

He looked at me, half ruefully, half accusingly.

'Well, gaffer, we know who he fucking is now,' he said.

Despite that slightly chaotic start, some of our players began to get international recognition, although it often needed a bit of prompting from me to get their names in the frame. When Tommy Johnson got called up to the England Under-21s, I rang their manager, Lawrie McMenemy, and told him we had another young lad I thought he should consider. I told him his name was Mark Draper but I could tell that Big Lawrie had never even heard of him. He was asking me what position he played in and everything. The next week, though, Drapes was in the squad.

I made sure I kept their feet on the ground. Some time after they had both made their debuts for the Under-21s, I took the Notts County lads away to Scarborough for a short break. We didn't stay in hotels. We stayed in a couple of guest houses. Johnson and Draper thought they were the king bees by then because they were with the Under-21s. It turned out that the guest houses didn't have quite enough rooms to accommodate us and that two lads were going to have to sleep in a kids' room that had a pair of bunk beds in it. I stuck Draper and Johnson in that room.

Derek Pavis did his best to keep our feet on the ground, too. When we got to the top flight, he came up with the brilliant idea of not staying at a hotel overnight before away games. It was a cost-cutting measure. So we had to eat our pre-match meal when we were on the coach travelling. We had this aircraft catering system set up on the bus, all pre-cooked and heated up in containers covered with tin foil. When you put them on your lap, it felt like you were on a package holiday to Malaga.

When it was time to eat, we had to pull off the motorway and heat the meals up. We were on our way down to West Ham at the end of August and, when it was time for the pre-match meal, we came off the M1 at one of the Luton exits and parked up on this industrial estate to eat our food. Loads of people were coming out of this factory and staring at this First Division football team eating its lunch on the bus. We felt like exhibits in a museum.

'Is this soccer at the top, gaffer?' one of the lads said.

We didn't do too badly at the start of the season, though. We beat Southampton in our first home game and we drew 2-2 with Chelsea at Stamford Bridge, having been two goals up. We should have been three up but Dave Regis went round the goalkeeper and then rolled his shot against the post when he had an open goal. Still, that result gave me some small vindication for rejecting Chelsea's overtures the previous summer. I got plenty of stick from the

Chelsea fans because they knew that I'd knocked them back but my players did me proud that night.

They were brilliant in the next game against Liverpool at Meadow Lane, too. But not quite good enough to cope with the Liverpool manager, Graeme Souness. We outplayed them for a lot of the first half and Souness was going nuts at the referee, Alf Buksh, from the touchline. At half time, he got stuck into him again as Alf walked down the tunnel, ranting and raving about some of the decisions he said had gone against Liverpool.

As I went into the tunnel, I saw Souness disappearing into the referee's room, so I told one of my staff to go and have a listen at the door. Souness was slaughtering Alf Buksh about giving us more decisions than we deserved. I told the lads straight away that we were going to have to be very careful in the second half. Tommy Johnson put us ahead but they equalised and then Ronny Rosenthal took a dive in the box that was worthy of a ballet dancer in *Swan Lake*. To me it was obscene but Alf Buksh gave it. They slotted it away and beat us 2-1.

A couple of years ago, I read an interview with him in a magazine. It was all about his heart operation and his life and times as a player and as a boss, but in the middle of it somewhere, he said the only time he ever influenced a referee was at Notts County. Out of all the hundreds of games he played in and managed, that was the game he picked out.

We didn't have any complaints when we played them at Anfield, though. They didn't need any dodgy penalties that night. They battered us. We never had a kick. Watching Liverpool play that day was like watching poetry in motion. Steve McManaman, Robbie Fowler, John Barnes, Michael Thomas and Ian Rush were all superb. They beat us 4-0 and I did the press conference saying how proud I was to have lost only by four. I meant it.

When I went into our dressing room, I could see my lads were shattered by the way they'd just been taken apart. I was racking my brains about how I could lift them and, in the end, I pointed at Charlie Palmer, Mr Reliable at the back.

'Charlie,' I said, 'if I ever hear you saying that to me again on a football pitch, I will fine you more money than you have ever earned in your whole fucking life.'

'What do you mean, gaffer?' he said, looking alarmed.

'You know what you said,' I told him.

'No, gaffer,' he said.

'If you ever repeat that to me on the field of play, I've done with you,' I said. 'I've finished with you.'

'What, gaffer?' he said, pleading with me.

'You fucking know,' I said.

'I don't, gaffer,' he said.

'I heard you say it,' I said.

'What, what?' he said.

I made my voice a little bit more high-pitched to imitate Charlie's and said it quietly.

' "Help",' I said.

All the lads cracked up. It broke the mood. They took their heads out of their hands and laughed. Then I reminded them all how far they had come and told them how proud I was of them. If they hadn't had the spirit and the commitment of a proper team, we would have been beaten by ten that night.

We didn't cave in that season. We kept fighting. We had some really good results. We beat Sheffield United 3-1 at Bramall Lane, which was special for me because it was the first time I had ever been involved in a competitive match there. The Kop kept singing about me being a Blade and it didn't bother me in the slightest. Because I was a Blade. We still beat them, though. We beat Sheffield Wednesday, too, which gave me a lot more pleasure.

We lost at Villa in November but I still got a laugh out of that game. Cyrille Regis clattered one of our players near the touchline and I leapt up and started yelling at him, saying what a disgraceful tackle it was as usual and all that. Ron Atkinson was the Villa manager and he got up, too, and started walking over towards me with his swanky overcoat, his lovely tan and his designer shoes.

I looked over at him and he was waving his programme at me. He was getting closer and closer, still jabbing his programme in my direction and getting really worked up. Then, just as he was getting near to me, he turned away, sort of sheepishly. I was puzzled. I didn't know why. Months later, I found out that he had put his foot right in the bucket of cold water that was behind the wall separating our seats. Those lovely designer shoes were ruined by the physio's bucket. He turned right round and looked at Jim Walker, the Villa physio. He had a fixed grin on his face. 'If anybody ever finds out about this, you're sacked,' he said to Jim.

We beat Chelsea at Meadow Lane on Boxing Day. We drew with Manchester United there a few weeks later. And we drew with

Forest at the City Ground which was a massive boost for our fans, particularly as we'd been battered 4-0 at home by them earlier in the season in what was the first Trent derby for a long time.

But a couple of days before the game against Forest, everything changed for the worse for me at Notts County when Derek Pavis sold our main striker, Paul Rideout, behind my back. I had bought Rideout from Southampton for £250,000 a month into the season. The chairman didn't rate him very highly but I didn't care about that. I rated him. That's why I bought him. He scored a few goals for us in the short time he was there and I considered him a valuable member of our squad.

One day in January, I was away from the club and, while I was gone, the chairman agreed to sell Rideout to Glasgow Rangers for £500,000. Just like that. Unbelievable. He said he tried to contact me but I never got any messages. I just couldn't believe it. He was my starting striker and we were playing Forest the next day.

He said it was too good an offer to turn down. But that was rubbish. It was a crap offer. I didn't want to sell him anyway. We should have been buying players, not selling them, because we were fighting for our lives at the bottom. I lost all my trust in the chairman from that day onwards. Our relationship was gone after that. I think that relegated us more than anything else. We weren't a unit any more. We weren't united any more.

It was too late for me to talk Rideout out of it, too, because the chairman had told him Rangers were in for him. When he heard that, he wanted to go. I didn't blame him for that. But it should never ever have got to that stage. Derek apologised to me about it but not until years later and I never forgave him. I felt bitter about what he had done and the bitterness ate away at me for the rest of the time I was at Meadow Lane. It didn't seem like much of a way to repay me for everything I had done for the club.

We went fourteen league games without a win in the aftermath of Rideout's transfer. It was as if it had sapped the club of its will and its spirit. We never recovered from that run. We tried to rally in the last weeks of the season but it was too late. We were relegated at the end of April with one match still to play when we lost against Manchester City at Maine Road. We finished the campaign four points adrift of Coventry City and safety.

Things didn't get any better the next season. I'd agreed a new contract with Notts County when Chelsea were trying to lure me away but I was so naive that I had agreed that, if we got relegated, I would go back to my old contract. Why I should have done that when every bloody club was after me, I will never know. I was an idiot. I was on a six-figure salary while we were in the top flight. But it went down 50 per cent when we were relegated.

I didn't need to agree to that clause going into my contract because the chairman was desperate for me to stay when Chelsea came in for me. So not only were we relegated but I was suddenly taking a 50 per cent pay cut. Everything deteriorated and there was a real malaise at the club at the start of the 1992-93 season. We had only won four games by the beginning of January. We were selling our best players and falling fast.

In fact, just about the only thing that gave me any real pleasure that season was wreaking revenge on that miserable man, Arthur

Cox, who was manager of Derby County at the time. Even in the midst of all Notts County's problems, screwing Arthur over a couple of my players gave me an inordinate amount of pleasure and acted as something of a consolation for me in the dark days at Meadow Lane.

The story of me and Arthur Cox had started way back when I was at Scarborough and we had gained promotion to the Football League in 1987. I'd had a lad called Paul Richardson in the side who had once been on Derby's books but had been forced to retire from professional football because of some sort of problem with his lungs. He'd got an insurance pay-out of £24,000 and started playing a bit of non-league football for his local amateur village side somewhere near Nottingham.

I picked him up from there but when we got promoted to the Football League, we knew that if we wanted him to play for us, we would have to pay back his £24,000 insurance. We were willing to do that and so I phoned Arthur Cox at Derby because they still held his registration. I assumed it would just be a formality that they would release him but Cox said they wanted a transfer fee for him. I couldn't believe it.

'How can you demand that, Arthur?' I said.

'That's just how it is, Neil,' he said.

I went back to him soon afterwards. I told him about the £24,000 and made it clear that we couldn't afford any more. I told him that we hadn't got that kind of money. I said we could offer them a percentage of any fee we got if we sold the player to someone else.

'I think that's a good deal, Arthur,' I said. 'That's the best that we can offer.'

'You can't have him then, Neil,' Arthur Cox said.

It was unusual for a league club to be as miserly as that but then Arthur Cox was an unusual man. So poor Paul Richardson said he would stop where he was and play local league football in Nottingham. He was upset about it and so was I.

I rang Arthur Cox one more time. I still thought he might relent. I thought he must have a human side somewhere.

'I can't believe what you're doing to a non-league club,' I said. 'You know how hard up we are.'

'That's just the way it is, Neil,' he said again, like a robot.

I snapped then. I'd had enough.

'Well let me tell you now, Arthur,' I said, 'one day you'll want one of my players and it'll fucking cost you. And I mean more than twenty-four fucking grand.'

'Sorry about that, Neil,' he said. And then he rang off.

Five years later, in September 1992, my assistant, Mick Jones, walked into my office at Meadow Lane and said he had taken a phone call from Roy McFarland. Arthur was still Derby manager and Roy McFarland was his deputy. Roy had told Mick that Arthur wanted to sign Craig Short.

'You tell Arthur Cox to ring me direct,' I said to Mick, 'because this is the fucking day I've been waiting for.'

Within half an hour, Arthur rang me. I was beaming when I heard his voice.

'Hello, Arthur,' I said.

'Craig Short,' he said. 'I'll give you £750,000 going up to one million.'

'No chance, Arthur,' I said. 'You're joking, aren't you?'

'I'll give you a million cash but you've got to make your mind up by five o'clock,' he said.

'I don't need to make my mind up, Arthur,' I said. 'There's no chance.'

I told Pavis about it. He liked the sound of a million quid. He liked it a lot. But I told him I had to deal with this one. It was important to me.

Next day, Arthur Cox rang again.

'Ill go up to one and a quarter,' he said. 'I'll give you cash up front and we'll do the deal tomorrow.'

'I'm sorry, Arthur,' I said. 'It's still no chance. That's not good enough.'

'Well you sleep on it,' he said.

Pavis was really starting to sweat now. I told him the people at Derby would try and put the heat on him and ring him direct.

There were numerous calls over the next few days. The price kept going up. It went to £1.5 million, then £1.75 million and then Cox rang the chairman. He wanted to know if Pavis was aware of the bids. He wanted to know if I was trying to run the show by myself. He was trying to drive a wedge between me and the chairman. He was almost succeeding. Pavis came back on to me, panicking.

'We can't turn this kind of money down,' he said, 'we just can't.'

'Derek, you promised,' I said. 'Just stay calm and let me deal with it.'

Craig Short's price went up to £2 million and then £2.25 milion.

Then Blackburn came in for him. I spoke to Kenny Dalglish, who was the manager at Ewood Park then. He said he'd give us £2.5 million.

'That'll do for me, my son,' I said to him. 'I'll get him right over.'

Craig went over to Blackburn and spoke to Kenny but his agent got into his head about how he wouldn't have to move house if he went to Derby. I thought it was a mistake. I thought he would have played for England if he'd gone to Blackburn.

But I didn't think the transfer fee was a mistake. In the end, Derby County and Arthur Cox paid £2.6 million for Craig Short. That was probably about £1.5 million more than they would have done if Cox hadn't tried to screw Scarborough for a few grand over a decent lad called Paul Richardson. If you screw people, they'll screw you back. Oh, and I nearly forgot. We got £1.3 million out of him for Tommy Johnson, too, another fee that was well over the odds. I couldn't have too much of a good thing when it came to Arthur Cox.

But as far as enjoyment went, that was probably about as good as it got in the first half of the 1992-93 season. By Christmas, I could tell that Pavis was losing patience. My loyalty to him when Chelsea came in for me didn't seem to count for much now. Early in the New Year, we lost to Millwall at home in the league and then played an FA Cup third round tie at home to Sunderland. We lost that, too. Pavis called me and Mick Jones into his office the following Monday.

'I never thought it would come to this, Neil,' Pavis said. 'You're like family to me and we've done so much together but we've come to the end of the road.'

It was the usual bollocks.

'This will be the biggest mistake you'll ever make, Derek,' I said to him.

Mick Jones got up to leave. 'You won't realise how good Neil is until you've lost him,' he said.

We went back to our office and called the *Nottingham Evening Post*. They sent a couple of photographers round and Mick and I cracked open a bottle of champagne and toasted everything we had achieved at the club. They had built a whole new stadium on the back of our promotions and Cup runs. There were three new sides to the ground since I arrived. There was a Derek Pavis Stand, of course. There was a Jimmy Sirrell Stand, too, named after one of the club's best former managers.

'Which one's going to be the Neil Warnock Stand?' I said to the chairman once.

He just laughed awkwardly.

In one way, I was relieved when he sacked me. I still think we could have turned things around but we weren't pulling any trees up and the whole thing had been blown apart a year earlier when he sold Paul Rideout. But I was also very hurt. I'd never been sacked before, not as a manager anyway, and after I'd been so loyal to them and achieved so much at Meadow Lane, it felt unjust to be fired so quickly.

Pavis had an itchy trigger finger all of a sudden but when Sunderland had come in for me, he had chased Bob Murray away. He took his wife up to Roker Park to watch a match and confronted

Bob Murray in the directors' lounge and told him to stay away from his manager. And when Chelsea were interested in me, he pleaded with me to stay. He talked about our families and how, morally, it would be wrong for me to go to Stamford Bridge.

I had turned down two top jobs and now, little over a year later, I was being kicked out of the door. Goes back to the old football saying, doesn't it: loyalty's the thing they screw you with. When Portsmouth came in for me while I was at Sheffield United during the 2005-06 season and offered me a king's ransom to go to Fratton Park, Craig Short, who had I brought to Bramall Lane, came to speak to me.

'I don't want you to go, gaffer,' he said, 'but I'd never tell you not to take it. Not after what happened at Notts County. Do what's best for you.'

I stayed at Sheffield, partly because I loved the club, partly because we were on the brink of a promotion that was my greatest ambition and partly because I had a good relationship with my chairman, Kevin McCabe. But that was one of the lessons I learned from the way everything at Notts County fell apart: your best time as a manager is when you have got a relationship with your chairman.

I have found that I am only successful in the times that I have had a good chairman. Although I didn't like a lot of things Derek Pavis did at the club, I got on well with him. I made myself get on well with him. I enjoyed his company and I enjoyed his family's company. When that relationship broke down, everything else broke down, too.

That applies at every club. If Jose Mourinho does not have a cordial relationship with Roman Abramovich, that's bound to have an impact on things. Every manager needs that relationship. Otherwise, who motivates the motivator? You need somebody. Everybody thinks managers are impregnable because of the bravado we put on for the cameras but we all need a pat on the back. We all need a text message or a conversation.

When Sheffield United lost to Newcastle United at home in April 2007, I felt terribly despondent. I texted Kevin McCabe to say I had not felt as low as that for many years. He texted me back and said we had three more home games and that I could motivate the lads and that I'd be back up by Monday and then we'd get going again. You need messages like that. Everybody needs loving. People tend to forget that. All the love had gone at Notts County, that's for sure.

It was sad the way it all ended at Notts County after so many good times. Pavis appointed a guy called Mick Walker after me and they avoided relegation by the skin of their teeth. But towards the end of the 2006-07 season, I went down to Meadow Lane to watch them. They had to win their last game to be sure of avoiding relegation to the Conference. That's how far they've fallen. I hope I'm wrong but I suspect they'll never have the same success that they had with me.

A few years ago, Pavis admitted he should never have sacked me. Bit late by then but we're on good terms again now. That's the thing with me, though: I've had success at every club I've been to and yet, maybe because I've had more publicity than the chairmen, it has always soured.

Perhaps that's just a law of football. Perhaps it's always destined to end in tears for all of us. I get on fine with all my old chairmen now. I just couldn't keep the relationship going when we were at the various clubs together.

But even though I've got my regrets about not going to Chelsea or Sunderland, I often think that it all worked out for the best in the end. I was starting a new relationship with my second wife, Sharon, around that time and I'm not sure if we'd have been comfortable with the scrutiny that the Chelsea job, for instance, might have brought us. She and I are still incredibly happy and we've got two wonderful kids, Amy and William. That's the most important thing.

And in the spring of 2007, I went to a Notts County reunion at Meadow Lane. I met up with a lot of my old players and we laughed and laughed. About Alan Paris and Andrei Kanchelskis, about the time Phil Turner and Phil Stant let down the tyres on Derek Pavis's Rolls-Royce, about Tommy and Drapes and the bunk beds in Scarborough and about Dave Wilson clicking Bessie's sacroiliac joint back into place.

Maybe if I'd walked out on Notts County to go to Chelsea, I wouldn't have gone to that reunion. Maybe I wouldn't have been welcome. Maybe I would have felt I'd betrayed myself as well as them. So I'm glad I did what I did, even if it took me an awfully long time to get back to the top.

11

FROM THE BOTTOM UP

MY LIFE was in turmoil in the weeks after I was sacked by Notts County. Being fired hurt. Of course it did. But the turmoil was about more than that. My marriage to Sue, which had lasted for twenty years, had been falling apart for some time and the stress of everything that had happened in my last few months at Meadow Lane increased the strain we were under.

Sue and I had got married in 1972 while I was at Hartlepool. So I can hardly accuse her of marrying me for the glamour of the game. We had two lovely kids, James and Natalie, who are grown up now and who I love to bits. But when I became a manager, I spent every hour God sent working at trying to make my teams better, whether that meant supervising extra training, going off on missions to watch our opponents or scouting new players.

I was away from home a lot. If I wasn't actually away, I was out most nights. And that began to put a lot of pressure on my marriage to Sue. Gradually our relationship changed to the point where we were more like brother and sister than husband and wife. And by the early nineties, it was really only a matter of time until we split up. I met Sharon around that time as well and then things accelerated.

I suppose they'd call the reasons for our divorce 'pressures of work'. That usually covers it, doesn't it? Sue might say different, I don't know. But I do know that when we divorced, I wanted her to have our house. I felt an obligation to her and I was determined that it wouldn't get bitter. She was a terrific mum, for a start, and I'm glad there wasn't a lot of acrimony in the split because James and Natalie have been able to have a situation where Sue and I get on better since our divorce than we did before at times.

My younger kids, Amy and William, think the world of James and Natalie and that means an awful lot to me. It's worth more than any amount of money. Sue's got another partner now, a lovely bloke, and when the initial hurt had gone from our separation, we shared our Christmases together for a while. Sharon and I, Sue and her mum sat round the same table, together with the kids.

Sue and I had just drifted apart, I suppose, but the way it all happened has made me feel that I won't be in management too much longer. When James and Natalie were growing up, I didn't see nearly as much of them as I should have done. With William and Amy, I'm determined that that doesn't happen. These days, I don't let football overtake my family responsibilities. I still work too hard but I've got a better balance in my life. I'm very lucky to have the family that I've got.

A few weeks after I was fired by Notts County I got a call from Kevin Blackwell. He was goalkeeping at Torquay United and they were in desperate trouble down at the bottom of the old Fourth Division. They were in danger of going out of the league, the fate that finally befell them in 2007, and Blackie wanted to know if I'd think about going down to Plainmoor until the end of the season to help them out.

The boss down there was a young lad called Paul Compton, who had been promoted from the youth team set up and was happy for someone else to come in to give him a hand. The club was in almost as big a mess as I was. They had become a bit of a soap opera really. Ivan Golac, the former Southampton player, had been the manager for a few months the season before and Justin Fashanu had played out some of his last sad days in English football at Plainmoor during the season that I arrived.

In many ways, moving down to the south-west to help out a club that was as low as you could get on the professional ladder didn't really make sense. A lot of my friends told me it was professional suicide. They told me I was mad even to think about going down there. They asked me to think about the damage it would do to my reputation if I went from being the boss of a top-flight side one year to presiding over a team that lost its league status the next.

They were worried I'd never get another job in football and I have to admit I could understand their point. I knew it was a risk but I'd always loved Torquay as a place when I'd visited there with football in the past and I was desperate to get as far away as possible from all the troubles that seemed to be ganging up on me. Torquay fitted the bill.

I took up my post at the beginning of February 1993. I was the manager in everything but name. I was still fighting for my pay-off from Derek Pavis and it was hard enough getting the money out of him without giving him another excuse. So I told the Torquay chairman, Mike Bateson, that I didn't want to be paid to be boss at Plainmoor. I just wanted my expenses and a place to stay for a few months. Instead of manager, I was called a consultant.

They had lost eight games on the trot when I got there and most of the lads were on £100 a week. They had no training facilities to speak of, just a pitch on top of a hill in Torquay that was one of the windiest places to play football I've ever come across. The people at Plainmoor were lovely, but in football terms it felt as though I'd arrived at a club that was about to fall off the edge of the world.

Torquay's fans hadn't exactly been raised on success. They were used to fairly frequent applications for re-election when they finished at the bottom of the old Division Four. But now that relegation to the Conference was automatic, there was a greater urgency about trying to beat the drop.

It didn't start too smoothly for me at Plainmoor. Then again, Torquay were the kind of team where nothing ever started smoothly. We lost the first couple of games after I took charge. First to Crewe Alexandra and then a 4-0 spanking at Ninian Park against Cardiff City. We got a win against York City, who were one of the better sides in the division, but then we lost the next game to Chesterfield. I had been intending to stay up in Yorkshire for the rest of the weekend but, the morning after the game, I got a call saying I was needed back in Torquay on Monday morning for an urgent meeting with Mike Bateson.

Bateson was a decent enough bloke with a lovely wife, Sue. Bit eccentric at times. He had a system where we'd have our pre-match meals on away trips from sandwiches that had been packed in

Tupperware boxes. He was a ventriloquist, too, and he had this dummy called Algernon that he used to put on his arm. He'd get Algernon to talk to visiting directors, apparently. He had him dressed up in a tie, a blazer and a smart shirt. Rumour said Algernon had head-butted a fan once. Who knows? Anyway, Mike Bateson never got Algernon out for me, I'll tell you that.

Anyway, after that defeat at Chesterfield, Mike Bateson started getting jumpy. He got me and Don O'Riordan, the player-coach I'd had with me at Notts County, and Paul Compton into the office. He went through the four games that had taken place since I'd been in charge and said that he had worked out that if this carried on until the end of the season, we would be relegated. He asked Don what he thought and then Paul, who had gone back to being youth coach. He gave his own opinion as well. I just sat back and kept out of it. I let them get on with it. Then he turned to me.

'What do you think, Neil?' he said.

'Chairman,' I said, 'if you don't want me here, I won't be here, simple as that. But how much have you got invested in the club?'

'Over a million quid,' he said.

'All I'd say to you,' I told him, 'is that if I had over a million quid invested in Torquay United and I had got the chance of Neil Warnock managing my fucking team for the last ten games in this league, I would snap his hand off.'

Bateson smiled at me uneasily.

'Don't make a decision now,' I said. 'Ring me at nine o'clock in the morning and if you don't want me to come in again, there's no hard feelings.'

I left the meeting. Next morning, at nine o'clock sharp, my phone rang.

'I've been thinking about what you said,' Bateson said. 'I'd like you to stay.'

'Fine, chairman,' I said. 'Now we know where we stand.'

The next day, I told all the players to assemble at 9 p.m. outside a nightclub in Torquay. We went in and I told them that if I caught anyone leaving before 1 a.m. they would be fined a week's wages. It did wonders for team spirit, that night. One of the lads told me afterwards that it was the first time he had been threatened with a fine for not being in a nightclub at 1 a.m.

Things picked up a bit. We drew at Lincoln City and beat Halifax Town in early March. We got three 2-2 draws on the spin against Scunthorpe, Colchester and Walsall and, even though we lost our next three, we embarked on the long trip north to Carlisle United for our penultimate game of the season knowing that if we got a win, we'd be safe and out of the reach of the bottom two clubs, Gillingham and Halifax, who were playing each other.

We took thousands up there with us. Torquay to Carlisle has got to be just about the longest trip you can make in league football and it was inspiring to have that kind of support. We won the game 1-0 and Torquay's league status was secure for another year. I felt incredibly moved by the scenes of celebration up there in Carlisle.

In the dressing room afterwards, I told the players they would always remember what they had achieved that day. And I told them that, even though they were on peanuts for wages, they had restored my faith in football. They had me given me back my love for the game. They were bloody good lads and they had given me all the effort I could wish for. I'd had good times but that day in Carlisle was as good as anything. As I was talking to them, I had a bloody tear in my eye.

I had been planning to drive back to my place in Nottingham but I couldn't miss out on the celebrations. So I got on the bus with the chairman after the game for the long journey back to the West Country. There was an electric atmosphere on that coach. The players were dancing up and down the aisles all the way down the M6. I wanted us to have a celebration of some sort, so we pulled off the motorway at Lancaster and went to a Chinese restaurant. The lads loved it. You would have thought we had won the World Cup with all the singing and dancing.

I felt so pleased because I knew that my presence and my organisation and drive had kept them up. It was good to feel good again. The months of adversity at Notts County had taken it out of me. Everybody might have said I would regret going to Torquay but those people didn't know what I would get out of it. I got my belief back about motivating players. I made them feel important, even though everything around them was poor, the pitch was a paddy field and the dressing rooms were poky. I got my confidence back, too. In both my professional life and my personal life, I felt like I was putting the bad times behind me. I was ready to move on.

I had loved it at Torquay but it was never suggested to me that I stayed on after the end of the season so I never considered it. Don O'Riordan took over at Plainmoor and did a tremendous job and I moved back north. I spoke to the Huddersfield Town chairman,

Terry Fisher, who had parted company with the previous manager, Ian Ross, and he had a vacancy. He asked me over to Leeds Road for an interview and he offered me the job.

Moving back into the area made the split with Sue final and brought it home to James and Natalie that we were going to be living separately. It was hard to tell them I wasn't going to be there. I made a pact with myself that I would speak to Natalie every night and I did. It must have been so boring and monotonous for her to have me on the line asking her about school and stuff but I suppose it made me feel better. Although it was hurtful at the time, it was best for all of us.

Things didn't start brilliantly for me at Huddersfield in the 1993-94 season. It was the club's last season at Leeds Road and there was a feeling of something coming to an end rather than a new beginning. The club had spent much of the previous season in what is now League One flirting with relegation (they won eight of their last ten games and still only finished in mid-table) and we were too close to the bottom for my peace of mind in the first few months of my time in charge too. I can't claim that I had an immediate impact. We only won one of the first eight games and we were hovering above the drop zone for most of the period up until Christmas.

Leeds Road was getting rough round the edges by then and there were these old iron gates just behind the dugouts that the fans used to cling to and peer through. They used to rattle the gates as if they were prisoners trying to get free. They always made me feel slightly uncomfortable for some reason. Particularly when things weren't going well, the bars on those gates made me feel like I was in prison myself.

But for the first and last time in my career, I was saved by the Autoglass Trophy. We went on a bit of a run in the competition and it deflected attention away from our poor league form and gave everyone a bit of a lift. We got through to the Northern Area Final against Carlisle and battered them 4-1 in the first leg at Leeds Road. The day after, I went into the secretary's office and they were on the phone booking coaches for Wembley.

'What the hell's going on here?' I said. 'We haven't even played the second leg yet.'

'Oh, we'll be all right now,' one of the club officials said, 'don't be so silly.'

'Don't you know it's bad luck to do something like that?' I said. 'It's tempting fate. And if you have to do it, never, ever do it in front of the manager or any of the players. It's the kiss of death.'

They looked at me like I was being barmy, as if I was being incredibly over-cautious. But when we went up to Brunton Park the following week, their attitude soon changed. We had a torrid time at Carlisle. We were 2-0 down after twenty-five minutes. One more goal and Carlisle were through. I had to bring off Peter Jackson, one of our best players, at half time because of an injury. We were so threadbare that I had to bring on a lad called John Dyson, who was a student. In the second half it could have gone either way. They missed chances and so did we. The referee played eleven minutes of injury time and I felt so nervous I wanted to be sick.

I knew that my whole career rested on those last few minutes. Everything I had worked for and hoped for in the future was hanging in the balance in that added time at Brunton Park. I had been to Torquay, which was the back of beyond, football-wise. I had come to Huddersfield and I hadn't been able to lift them away from the relegation zone and now we had a chance of throwing a 4-1 lead away. I knew that this result could once again give my career an upward curve. If we could get to Wembley, the club could take off.

This is it, I thought, as I stood in the dugout that night.

We just hung on. What a feeling it was when the final whistle went. When we got to the final, I knew it would keep the buzzards off the flesh at least until the following season. Huddersfield hadn't been to Wembley since 1938 so it was a big deal and a huge boost to everyone at the club. We played Swansea City in the final but I knew the crisis had passed. We lost on penalties after a 1-1 draw but I didn't watch the shoot out. I couldn't stand it. I walked off into the dressing room and waited for the lads to wander back in.

The next season, we moved to the McAlpine Stadium and the whole mood lifted. It changed a lot of things. Leeds Road was a fine old stadium but this place was brand spanking new with a lovely sweeping design and it made it easier for me to sign players. It was a stadium that we could all be proud of and the club was a lot more attractive all of a sudden. The stadium sent out a message we were an ambitious, forward-looking club who wanted to improve. We weren't stuck in the past any more.

I was lucky that I had a good strike force. I had Ronnie Jepson and Andy Booth up front and they were good for plenty of goals between them. Jepson got two goals on the opening day of the 1994-95 season and we got off to a flier by beating Blackpool 4-1 at Bloomfield Road. And Andy Booth was a class act too. He was probably the best header of the ball that has ever played for me.

I got a bit worried about his fitness at the start of that season though. One Monday in August he complained that his back was hurting him and that he wouldn't be able to train. I was a bit puzzled because he hadn't mentioned anything when we'd been in on the Friday. I asked the physio about it and he was mystified, too. He said Boothy had told him the pains had crept up on him on Sunday night.

A couple of nights later, I was out at a presentation dinner at Hall Bower Cricket Club. I was there to hand out the prizes. An old fella who was one of the club officials came up to me and started chatting away.

'Eee, that Andy Booth, eh,' he said, 'what a bloody good innings.'

I tried not to let him see that I didn't know what the hell he was talking about.

'Oh, aye,' I said.

But there must have been something in my expression that told him he needed to give me more details.

'165 not out for us on Sunday,' he said.

'Oh, I know, it was fantastic,' I said.

I was fuming inside.

You'll have a different kind of fucking knock tomorrow, Boothy, I thought to myself.

No wonder he had a bloody bad back. He'd been out at the crease for about four hours. I gave him a right going over the following day.

Boothy's mum worked at Leeds Road. She did the teas or the cleaning or something. During one of the games, Andy got pole-axed by a defender and they had to bring a stretcher on for him. Suddenly there's this woman rushing past the dugout, heading for the pitch and she had to be stopped and ushered away by security.

'Who the hell's that?' I said.

'It's Andy's mum,' one of the lads said.

It wasn't a kickabout we were at. It was a bloody Second Division game and we've got a player's mum on the pitch.

I went to Boothy's testimonial for Huddersfield a couple of years ago and he hasn't changed at all. He's a lovely bloke. After I left, I recommended him to Sheffield Wednesday, of all clubs, when David Pleat was there and they paid £2.7 million for him. They were doing well at that time with a core of English lads and then all of a sudden they go and sign loads of foreigners and end up bankrupting the club and getting relegated. I thought that was a good lesson. You've got to keep a certain amount of English players.

Andy Booth scored twenty-seven league goals for us that season. He was phenomenal. Jepson wasn't bad either. A few tensions were developing off the pitch in the 1994-95 season, but on it everything went well. I had my enthusiasm back now and I set my stall out again. We had played Arsenal at Highbury the season before in the League Cup and I went up to George Graham's office afterwards and looked round at the leather sofas and the nice desk. I knew my time had gone for that size of club but I wanted at least to rub shoulders again with the rich clubs . We spent most of the 1994-95 season right near the top of the table and, although we missed out on automatic promotion, we qualified comfortably for the play-offs, albeit in the last of the four places.

We had finished fifth, so we had to play Brentford, who had finished second, four points above us. We drew 1-1 at the McAl-pine and their striker missed three golden opportunities to put the tie out of our reach. We hung on and drew. When we went down to Griffin Park, I went up to the directors' box before the game with Mick Jones and spotted two dozen bottles of champagne they had got ready for the celebrations afterwards. They were that sure they were going to finish us off. So, obviously, I mentioned that in my team talk.

They scored first through a lad called Martin Grainger and then Boothy equalised and it went to extra time and penalties. It all came down to a spot kick from Darren Bullock, a lad I had signed from Nuneaton Borough for £35,000. I went to watch him play against West Midlands Police in a Birmingham Senior Cup tie one night. I knew after five or six minutes that I was going to sign him. He was everywhere, tackling and heading and dashing about as if his life depended on it. He was a window cleaner by trade. He had a bit of a nutcase reputation and I thought we'll have some of that. He was a likable rogue, always in trouble, but a good lad basically. And there he was at the end of that game at Brentford with a penalty that would take us into the Division Two play-off final.

When I saw him walking up to take it, I said to Mick Jones, 'Oh my God, what's he taking a penalty for?' He was a cocky little lad and he placed the ball on the spot and then strutted back to take his run up. He hit it and the goalie dived and it must have bobbled about seven times before it crept over the line in the middle of the goal. It took an eternity to get in but eventually it made it. We were going to Wembley.

So I was in another final, this time against Bristol Rovers. Having them as the opponents gave the game a bit of extra edge for me because since the day we had played them at Twerton Park in Bath the season before, I had been getting hate-mail. There had been an incident after the game when I was walking down the tunnel. It was covered with a metal mesh and the Bristol Rovers fans were having a go at me. When I looked up at them, someone spat in my face. I mentioned this at the Saturday night press conference afterwards and was critical of the incident. The following Tuesday morning, a letter was delivered to the house in Holmfirth that I was sharing with Sharon. It mentioned Sharon's name and made it very plain that we ought to start watching our backs from now on.

I didn't think too much about it initially but we got two letters a week every week after that. The police took it very, very seriously and suggested we install a panic button. The letters kept coming. 'ACCIDENTS HAPPEN' one of them said. That was all. We had a special alarm system fitted as well. We didn't lose sleep over it but it wasn't very pleasant. It made us fairly vigilant when we were out.

One night in the winter of 1995, the snow started coming down and Holmfirth was cut off. It was about 10 p.m. and cars were stuck and all sorts. So we got our wellies on and went down to help the people stranded in their cars. It was like the old war days. The cafe had stayed open and the owner was giving cups of tea out to people who were stuck. The fish and chip shop was the same. By the time we went back up to the house, we had helped dig a couple of cars out of drifts and we felt good.

It was about 1 a.m. by then and all the power was off because one of the lines had been brought down by the snow. Some time in the middle of the night, the lights came back on and I staggered out of bed and turned them off. About three minutes later, there was this thunderous banging at the front door. It was hammering like you'd never heard. I looked out of the window and all I could see was these dark shapes in the night. We wondered what the hell was going on. It was frightening.

I went downstairs and peered out and there were two policemen there with guns in their hands. I opened the door and there were three more police in armour-plated vests. It turned out the power cut had triggered the alarm and because the roads were blocked, the officers had had to run up from the police station. That's when we realised how seriously the police must have been taking our hate-mail.

It's not the only time I've had threats. When I was at Bury some vicious stuff was posted on the fans' website. Even at Sheffield United I had poisonous letters, but a more old-fashioned variety made up of words cut out of newspapers – though the sender was clued up enough to use water not spit to seal the envelope, so the police could never have got him on DNA testing. This sort of attention is what football managers, like others in the public eye, have to put up with. It's the way football's going. Nobody who has threatened me has ever been caught. That's why Sharon won't be disappointed when I retire and we go to Cornwall.

Anyway, my unfortunate history with Bristol Rovers made me especially keen to put one over on them at Wembley that day in May 1995. I had my play-off final routine off pat by then. It had always worked for me so I stuck to it. We stayed in the Hilton again, in the same rooms we had stayed in when I was with Notts County, and took the bus over on the morning of the game to do the private tour.

Bristol Rovers were the favourites, I suppose, given that they had finished just behind Birmingham, who were the only side that went up automatically that season. They had Marcus Stewart and Gareth Taylor up front who were dangerous. They had other good players, too. But we absolutely battered them in the first half. It got to injury time and I was thinking we would never score. Then we scored. Then, deeper into injury time, they scored, too. When the half time whistle finally blew, I walked off chuntering to the referee about why there had been so much added time but all the time I was jabbering, I knew I had a hell of a job on my hands to lift my players.

That was one of the most difficult half time tasks I'd ever had. We had played well and we had had the euphoria of scoring the goal and then all of a sudden we had been kicked in the face.

Instead of being on a high, we were on a low in the space of thirty seconds. If you didn't know what the score was and you had gone into our dressing room and looked at the players' faces, you would have thought we were losing 3-0. Mick Jones was worried. He said I better do something because they were so flat. I went back in and tried to get them off the floor. I reminded them how much we had dominated Bristol Rovers and that we could do it again.

We went back out and it was obvious the effects of conceding the equaliser were still lingering. Bristol Rovers were on a high and Marcus Stewart had two great chances which our goal-keeper, Steve Francis, kept out with two superb saves. We were very fortunate, but after about twenty minutes of the second half we stopped feeling sorry for ourselves at last and began to play again.

Ten minutes from the end, I took Gary Crosby off. He was disgusted with me but I knew it was the right thing. I brought on a lad called Ian Dunn, who was bald as a badger.

The fans had a song for him that helped make him a cult hero way beyond Huddersfield. It went like this:

> Iain Dunn
> Iain Dunn
> Iain, Iain Dunn
> he's got no hair
> but we don't care
> Iain, Iain Dunn

He was a lovely lad, Iain. There was no malice in him. I put him on the left wing and the first time he got the ball, he went past his full back and whipped in a cross. A local Huddersfield lad called Chris Billy came flying into the centre and threw himself at the ball. It whizzed like a bullet off his head and nestled right in the bottom corner. What a moment that was. We hung on and hung on for those last agonising minutes and when the final whistle went, the celebrations were fantastic. We got back up to Huddersfield and the town was going mad.

It should have been plain sailing from then on. I could have turned Huddersfield into another Notts County and taken them up to the Premiership. But it wasn't plain sailing. In fact, by the time I won that play-off final, I had made up my mind I wanted to leave. It was the same old thing: falling out with the chairman.

About February of the promotion season, I had a disagreement with Terry Fisher. He promised me certain things and then a few weeks later, he reneged on them. I wasn't on a lot of money at Huddersfield so I had asked him if I could supplement my wages by opening a club souvenir shop in town and running it. I was willing to spend the money on the shop to do it and I would give the club a percentage of the takings.

Terry seemed to be in favour of the idea and he said he would get back to me. A few weeks after the conversation, the club decided to open a shop of their own. I felt let down by that. Terry Fisher just said that was business. But our relationship broke down after that.

I realised after the play-offs that I wanted to leave. Some of the Huddersfield directors came to see me when they heard I was intending to leave and asked me if I would consider changing my mind. I told them it had gone too far. It had got to the stage where I didn't want to stay. I'd had enough.

I was in demand again. I had an interview with Lionel Pickering at Derby County and took great pleasure in telling him how Arthur Cox had cost him a couple of million quid. And Derek Pavis met me at The Belfry and asked me to go back to Notts County. I knocked them both back. I took the option no one expected me to take, dropped down a couple of divisions and accepted the manager's job at Plymouth Argyle.

12
THE LONG ROAD TO A DREAM

I DIDN'T JUST want a job in Plymouth. I wanted a lifestyle. I wanted somewhere idyllic to live with Sharon. We could afford that down in the West Country. I wanted a house in the middle of nowhere. Somewhere to start again. When we were driving down there, it felt like a new beginning all round. My career was starting again as well. Plymouth were newly relegated to the old Fourth Division but I thought they had masses of potential. It was just that no one had realised it yet. I thought I could change that. I thought I could turn them around.

I knew that the chairman might be a bit unpredictable. Dan McCauley had a reputation as a difficult man to work for. There was talk of interference in team affairs, refusal to release funds and an itchy trigger finger when things got tough. On top of that, he was a publicity-seeker who liked being in the papers and spouting off about his manager. I didn't see anything unusual in any of those things. Par for the course for a football chairman, as far as I was concerned. His reputation didn't faze me one bit. I thought that once he saw how I ran the club, he would let me get on with it. I saw Dan McCauley as part of the challenge.

I had a busy time in the transfer market that summer of 1995. We sold about £1.5 million worth of players and brought a few in. The chairman let me spend about £500,000, which was a lot of money for the bottom division. I got Adrian Littlejohn from Sheffield United because he was quick and I thought pace would get a player a long way at that level. And I signed a new goalkeeper, Nicky Hammond, from Swindon Town, too. I was pleased when I got him but, when the season started, I soon realised he was paralysed by nerves. He was more nervous than any lad who had ever played for me. His confidence started off low, he made a few mistakes and it quickly got to the point where he would have been struggling even if he'd been trying to save a toe poke from his granny.

We lost the first four league games on the spin that season so by the end of August, middle of September, we were rock bottom of the old Fourth Division, We were ninety-second out of ninety-two league clubs, having spent 500 grand on players. By the fourth game, I knew Nicky Hammond had gone. His confidence was absolutely shot. We played Hereford United at Home Park at a time when they couldn't buy a goal either. They were right down there in the mire with us and that match should have been a home banker. We played well enough. Going forward, we were fine, but I was nervous every time they got near our goal. Not as nervous as Nicky Hammond, unfortunately. Late in the game Hereford got a long throw and Nicky told the defence he was going to claim it, come what may. You can't do that. Not before you know where it's going. Anyway, he came for it, got nowhere near it, someone flicked it on and a lad called Steve White scored the winner.

So there we were: four games, four defeats, no points. We had lost in the League Cup home and away to Birmingham for good measure. I knew I had to do something about Nicky Hammond. It was awkward for me because I had signed him on a two-year deal and paid £40,000 for him and here I was dropping him after five games. But I had to do it. I couldn't let it go on any longer, hoping that he was going to get his confidence back. Much more of that and I wouldn't have a job. There were one or two murmurs about me by that stage. A lot of the fans were beginning to think the club had done the wrong thing and I suspect a few of the directors were having second thoughts, too. I apologised to Nicky and told him I was going to leave him out for the next game. I couldn't see us getting a point with him in nets. I brought Kevin Blackwell back in his place.

The fifth game was away at Bury. Dan McCauley called me in a couple of days before we travelled and said he was still fully behind me. I made a couple of other changes. I had Blackie in nets and a striker called Micky Evans, who had never been given a proper run in the side before, up front. Things improved spectacularly. We won 5-0 and suddenly it wasn't me who was in trouble but poor Mike Walsh, the Bury manager. He got the sack two days after that. I looked back at the pictures of that game a few months later and who was sitting behind him in the dugout but Stan Ternent. Ternent was the assistant boss there and he got the job when

Mike Walsh got fired. You wouldn't want a man like Ternent behind you. Ever.

After that, it was like a dam had burst for us at Bury. We got a huge confidence surge and set off on a run. We only lost twice in the next 18 league games. But then I started having problems with the chairman. I had noticed a change in his attitude towards me around the turn of the year. Even though we were going from strength to strength, he had become very distant. I had no idea what I had done wrong. Not a clue. I couldn't fathom it. He stopped ringing me and started communicating with me through his secretary. Either that, or by fax. It started to do my head in. The relationship was breaking down. In the end, some time in March, I couldn't stand it any longer and I rang him up to have it out with him.

'Dan, tell me why you are not supporting me now when we are so close to the play-offs,' I said.

'No, there's nothing wrong,' he said.

'Listen,' I said, 'I know there's something wrong. Just tell me.'

After a few minutes of going round the houses and him denying anything was wrong, he blurted it out. It went back to the previous December. We had played at Lincoln City and I had had a suite at the hotel where we were staying. I always had a nice room. I was the manager. Well, a couple of months later, we stayed at the same hotel because we were playing at Scunthorpe. I had the same room. We were having a meeting with some people from Huddersfield Town, getting their advice on building a new stadium at Plymouth after the work they had done with the McAlpine. My room had a table and chairs in it so it was the obvious place to meet. The Huddersfield lads came and met Dan in my room and they had their talks there.

'Well if you must know,' he said, 'if you worked for my company, and you, as an employee, had a bigger room than me on company business, I would have dismissed you.'

'Dan,' I said, 'I only had that room because I was superstitious and we'd got a decent result at Lincoln and I wanted the same one. I wasn't aware you wanted the main room.'

People must have been winding him up. But it seemed ridiculous to me that our relationship had been soured because I had a bigger room than him at a hotel. It was so petty. But it had been soured. The job became an uphill struggle. In March, I wanted to buy a couple of new players to strengthen the side but he didn't want to know. We still won five of our last six games and finished fourth, one point off the last automatic promotion spot. I was in the play-offs again but we lost the away leg of our semi-final against Colchester United 1-0 at Layer Road. That was the first time I had ever lost a play-off game and I wasn't particularly optimistic about the return. I knew how pressurised second legs could be. I knew how precious a one-goal lead was.

But we played superbly in the second leg. We were winning 2-0 when Adrian Littlejohn got chopped down outside the box by Mark Kinsella when he was clean through on goal. It should have been a straight red and that would have sealed the tie for us. There would have been no way back for them with ten men. But the referee, John Kirby, only gave Kinsella a yellow. A few minutes later,

Kinsella whacked in a goal from thirty-five yards which dragged them back to 2-1 and would have put them through on away goals. I went ballistic on the bench. I was disgusted at the injustice of it. I couldn't believe it. I suppose I've thought that a few times during my career but I was so incensed that the ref sent me off. There were only eight minutes to go and I thought it was over. I vaulted over the side of the dugout and stood with the crowd.

Then in the eighty-eighth minute we broke away down the right wing and the ball came over into the centre. No one could believe it when they saw who was there but suddenly our left back, Paul Williams, who had never been in an opponent's box in his life, popped up from nowhere and headed our third goal. The whole place went nuts. That put us through to the final. What a turnaround in fortunes and emotions. That's how it is in football, particularly in the play-offs. Things can change so quickly. I went to see the ref afterwards to have it out with him but when I saw him, I couldn't be bothered. He was the most relieved man in Plymouth that night, that ref. We'd got him out of jail.

We played Darlington in the final. They had beaten us home and away during the course of the season so they fancied themselves. But I knew we were the better team. We did the same preparation again. My tried and trusted play-off routine. Same Hilton Hotel, same rooms, same morning bus trip across to the stadium for a walk around, same walking back to the hotel. We took 35,000 people from Plymouth to Wembley that day. They closed the town, they said. Wembley was full of green and white scarves. It was the first time Plymouth had ever played at Wembley and it was as if the West Country had been moved to north-west London.

We went in at half time 0-0. We were whacking everything long into the box and their big lads were gobbling everything up. So I told the full back, Mark Patterson, to make a late run the next time we got a corner. I wanted the corner played short to him so he could cross it from a different angle and shake their defenders out of their comfort zone. So the first corner we got, Patterson came short and crossed it and Ronnie Mauge met it with a header about eight or nine yards out and scored. All the staff looked over at me because it was exactly as I had said it would be. I felt like a prophet. And that was enough for us. Darlington had a few near misses but they couldn't get an equaliser. We were up.

The celebrations were magnificent. Everyone was hugging and as the lads went up the steps to get the acclaim of the crowd, Dan McCauley came and stood by my side. I put my arm around him and we looked around Wembley at the hordes of Plymouth fans and the sea of green scarves and delirious happiness.

'Chairman,' I said, 'if you just support me now, we can take this club and you can have the best chairmanship in the world. Look around you at all these fans. That's us. We've done that.'

'I know, I know,' he said.

'We can have more of this,' I said to him. 'This should just be the start. This could be a big club. Look at these fans. And there are plenty more where they came from.'

He nodded his head again. I thought perhaps the message was getting through to him. I thought that maybe that Wembley victory could wash away the petty bitterness of the grievance he felt about me having a bigger room than him in the hotel. That feeling only increased when we got back to Devon. Plymouth was going mad. We had a civic reception the following day and took an open-top bus from Home Park to the Town Hall. Roy Keane might not have approved but we had a great day. We all said a few words to the crowds and it was just fantastic.

Later that day, we took Natalie and James up to Scotland for a holiday. I was looking forward to getting away from it all, spending some time with them and regrouping. I had told the chairman the names of a few players I would like for the next season but that was it. I thought I would have a quiet few weeks with nothing to worry about. Then, on the Monday morning, I got a phone call from the local press guy asking if I was aware of the statement the chairman had put out. My heart sank. He had laid down an ultimatum, the journalist said. He had warned that if the lads did not return the shirts they had worn at Wembley to the club, he would sue them because they belonged to Plymouth Argyle.

I was dismayed. Again, it seemed awfully petty. And anyway, a lot of the players had already given their shirts away. One had promised his to a dying relative, another had already given it away to charity. But Dan wasn't having it. He went on the television next, demanding these shirts back. He made national headlines. I just banged my head against a wall. I had thought the Saturday at Wembley was a turning point and everything was going to be great. Two days later and he's talking about suing the players for their shirts.

Things deteriorated from there. I wanted to sign Dean Kiely from Bury for £175,000 and Kinsella from Colchester for £100,000 and Barry Hayles from Stevenage for about £200,000. I went for these players pre-season and we didn't get any of them. We never offered enough. I could tell the chairman didn't want to sign them. He was still banging on about me getting the shirts back from the final. He seemed to want to downgrade everything now that we had got promoted. The team had taken a step forward but he was intent on taking a couple of steps back. His investment in the team dwindled.

In the Third Division, for instance, we had played at Rochdale and stayed the night before the game at the Copthorne Hotel in Salford Quays. It wasn't the lap of luxury but it was a decent enough hotel in terms of our preparation. Now, all of a sudden, we were playing at Stockport County in the Second Division and the chairman didn't want us to stay overnight. He wanted us to get from Plymouth to Stockport and back in a day on the team coach. The Copthorne was too expensive, we were told. We could only stay at places where we were paying a maximum of £25 a night per head. It was ridiculous. There was no way we were going to stay in some fleapit so we all drove up in cars. The lads who were based in the north stopped up with their families the night before. We just met up for a pre-match meal. That was it. Funnily enough, we got beaten 3-1. Dave Jones, the Stockport manager, was on his uppers at that point and there was a lot of talk about how he was going to get the sack if they lost to us. They won and his career took off. He can thank Dan McCauley for that.

The mood at the club plummeted. We started to struggle in the league and, at the beginning of January 1997, we lost in the FA Cup third round at home to Peterborough. I had got Bruce Grobbelaar playing for us by then, even though he was in the middle of his court case surrounding allegations of match-fixing. He was a great guy and a good character to have around and to have someone of his stature at the club was terrific. He was a great influence in the dressing room. Okay, he made mistakes but then he always had done. Anyway, against Peterborough, he made another one. He came out and dropped one and big Ken Charlery knocked it in. We tried to claw our way back into the game but we couldn't. And that's when I got the sack.

Dan McCauley didn't tell me. The vice-chairman phoned me. After the play-off final, we had reverted to the system where the only communication I had with the chairman was by fax. So I suppose it was obvious I wasn't going to hear it from him. I got the message while I was driving to another game to watch some opponents and then reporters started ringing me and I had to tell them I didn't know about it yet. It was a bit embarrassing. For me and the chairman. Not a particularly classy way of going about things. But that was his prerogative. He owned the club. There was nothing I could do about it. It was an old-fashioned personality clash. I think he was jealous of all the publicity I got and he felt that I had been given too much credit for what Plymouth had achieved. I could understand that. It was his intervention that had saved Plymouth.

He had put his money in when nobody else would and I wouldn't have been there in the first place if it hadn't been for him. I wished it could have been different because Sharon and I had some great times with him and his wife, Anne, and I was convinced that together we could have taken the club forward. Still, looking back, we have so much to thank him for because we would not have found our little piece of heaven in Cornwall which we call home if it hadn't been for him.

Out of a job, I felt isolated living in Cornwall. Out of sight, out of mind down there. I didn't want to be stuck out on a limb moping about. I had a look around at which clubs were without a manager and I rang Ian Stott, the chairman at Oldham. They had just parted with Graeme Sharp and I asked him if he would consider taking me until the summer and then we would take it from there. So I went up for an interview and they offered me the job until the end of the season and asked me to take Andy Ritchie as my assistant.

That's when I fell out with Mick Jones. Dan McCauley had kept Mick on as caretaker manager at Plymouth after he'd fired me. Mick had been my assistant for a long time and we were very close. We had spoken about the move to Oldham and Mick had told me he was coming with me. He came everywhere with me. I trusted him. But a couple of days before I took over at Boundary Park, he rang to tell me he was staying put. That was one of the most disappointing moments in my football career because I trusted him with my life. The parting was made more bitter by the knowledge that Dan would have been pleased as punch to split us up. I asked Mick how long he thought he would last. Perhaps that wasn't fair but I knew that even though he was a brilliant number two to me, a great bloke and a good friend, he wasn't cut out to be a manager in his own right. Sure enough, Dan McCauley sacked him at the end of the following season when they got relegated.

I didn't talk to Mick for a number of years after that. But after a while, I got to thinking about what Cloughie had told me about wishing he'd made it up with Peter Taylor. So I spoke to a mate of his, who told me Mick would love to speak with me again. I began to think life was too short to harbour grudges. I called him. He was glad to hear from me and I brought him to Bramall Lane with me soon after I got the Sheffield job. I think he knew he had made a mistake and he regretted it. You know, when you analyse it, there are not many people who have left me and prospered. Something bad always seems to happen to people that let me down.

I wasn't a great success at Oldham but I don't think anybody could have been. The club was in a bit of a mess in general. We were second from bottom of what is now the Championship when I arrived there in February and not much changed. We were relegated by five points in the end but I don't class that as a relegation against my name really because, effectively, they were already down when I arrived.

Despite our relegation, they gave me another year's contract to take charge of the team for the 1997-98 season. We never challenged the leaders but we more than held our own. As the season began to approach its end, I started to fret a bit about whether they were going to offer me another contract. It never pays to plan too far ahead in football but Sharon was heavily pregnant with our daughter Amy by then and we were trying to think about things like whether we should buy a house or continue renting.

I had had my vasectomy reversed and the doctor told me I would have a few years before Sharon had a chance of getting pregnant but she caught the first month. I was going to sue that bastard. He had told me there was only a 40 per cent chance of getting pregnant that early. Sharon says I'm only mentioning all this so we can call this chapter 'Superstud'. Anyway, we were renting a house and I wanted to try and get an idea of my job prospects before we decided whether to buy one instead. We were friendly with the club secretary, Alan Hardy, and he was very reassuring about it all. He said we should go ahead and buy. He even arranged a few property viewings and came with us to look at them. We put an offer in for one but I was nervous about it. I went to see Alan Hardy again and reminded him that my contract was up at the end of the season.

'You'll be fine, Neil,' he said.

Amy was born on 17 April 1998. The last game of the season was two weeks later against Grimsby Town at Blundell Park. The managers' dugouts are on the opposite side of the ground to the directors' box there so I could see all our lot from across the pitch. We had nothing to play for but Ronnie Jepson put us ahead midway through the second half. All our fans went mad but I looked across to the directors' box and not one of our lot had moved. Not one of them had jumped up or waved his arms or pumped his fist. Nothing. In fact, one of them had his head in his hands.

That's funny, I thought.

Three minutes later, Ronnie Jepson scored again. The same thing happened in the directors' box. Not one of the Oldham contingent moved.

Oh shit, I thought.

I got home to Sharon and the baby that night and told her about it.

'Listen, darling,' I said, 'I'm not going to get a contract.'

'Of course you are,' she said, 'Alan Hardy's told you. He's told you to buy the house.'

'Darling,' I said, 'let me tell you, I know I will not get a contract.'

I told her about the directors at Blundell Park.

'If I was getting a contract,' I said, 'those directors would have been standing up and clapping those goals and at least making it look as if they were enjoying it.'

'Well, I don't believe you,' Sharon said.

The next day, I got a phone call from Ian Stott. He wanted me to go and see him at the ground. I knew what was coming.

Lovely bloke, Ian. Lovely voice, too. One of the old brigade with eyebrows like Jimmy Edwards. Very knowledgable as well.

He sat me down in his office.

'Well, Neil,' he said, 'I've asked you to come in because I've got some sad news for you. We're not going to renew your contract. I have to say that I didn't want you to come in the first place but I don't want you to go now. I wasn't your biggest fan but I am now.'

'Don't you worry about it, chairman,' I said. 'I knew things were happening behind the scenes. And I know from your point of view it's got to be a cheap option having Andy Ritchie as manager next year. But you know and I know that it's a mistake.'

'Yes,' he said, 'I know.'

I went home and walked through the door.

'Shaz,' I said, 'we're leaving.'

She burst into tears. We rang the vendors to tell them we wouldn't be buying their house after all.

That summer, a couple of jobs came up. Sheffield United was one. Bury was the other. I'd known Kevin McCabe, who was an influential director at Bramall Lane at that point, for a number of years, so I made contact with him and he agreed to interview me. I was pleased with the way it went but what I didn't know was that, at the same time I was being interviewed in the south, Steve Bruce was being interviewed in the north. For the same job. And his interviewer was Mike McDonald, the Sheffield chairman, and the man who still held the power at the club.

I met the Bury owner, Hugh Eaves, in London on the same day I had the Sheffield interview. He wore a wig. I couldn't take my eyes off it. At one point, he slid down on the sofa a little bit and it knocked the wig about six inches lower on his forehead. He moved it back as casually as he could. I was biting my bloody lip for most of the time we were talking. I wasn't over keen on the job, really, because my mind was on Sheffield and Bury was never going to be a life-changing option for me but I told him I would think it over. When Steve Bruce got the Sheffield job, I didn't want to be without work so I went to Bury.

Terry Robinson, the Bury chairman who I really liked, showed how much he wanted me. Which was nice. That was the start of a long working relationship between me and Terry which continued when he became chief executive at Sheffield United after I had become manager. I was instrumental in getting him that position and Terry later went on to become chairman at Bramall Lane.

At Bury it was even tougher than I had imagined it would be. Stan Ternent had been the manager at Gigg Lane and he had got them promoted to the Championship and kept them up for a season by the skin of their teeth before he left for Burnley. There was no way they were going any higher than that. In fact, there was no way they could sustain a Championship level club. They had reached their ceiling and I knew it would be a difficult act to follow. Difficult wasn't the half of it. A few months after I took charge, Mr Eaves, who was a stockbroker, confessed to having embezzled money from his partners to pay for Bury. He had lent the club £750,000 and guaranteed a larger loan from Lloyds TSB, mortgaged on the ground at Gigg Lane. It was a right bloody mess.

It wasn't helped by Ternent. He was trying to screw Bury as well, just in a different way. I had taken an instant dislike to him when he was the manager of Hull City and, now that I had his old job, he did everything in his power to try to destroy what I was doing. He talked to Terry Robinson a lot. A few months after I arrived, they bought one of our best players, Lenny Johnrose, from us for a few grand because they had already tapped him up. They took a lad called Dean West, too. I wanted him to stay but we couldn't match the money Burnley were offering. Then Ternent started with my big hitters, Chris Lucketti, the centre half, and the goalkeeper, Dean Kiely, the best two players in the team.

I got a phone call one night from Dean Kiely. He didn't like Ternent.

'I've had Ternent on,' he said. 'He'd had a few drinks but he says he wants me to sign for him.'

'Go on,' I said.

'He said he wants to get Lucketti away from the club as well and I think it's out of order,' he said.

'Look, Dean,' I said, 'I know you and Chris Lucketti can get more money elsewhere, but by God you can do better than Burnley and fucking Stan Ternent. Would you want to work for him again?'

The next day, I spoke to Lucketti and it turned out Ternent had been on to him, too. Never off the phone to them both. Pestering them and all sorts. I put a marker down early with Ternent. We got Burnley in the Worthington Cup, drew 1-1 at Gigg Lane and battered them 4-1 at Turf Moor. We dumped them out in the first round. That was nice.

But Ternent wouldn't leave the club alone. I wanted to tell the local papers about everything he was doing to try to ruin Bury but Terry Robinson wouldn't let me. I thought that would show the fans what their hero was trying to do to the club but I had to let it go. I asked Lucketti and Kiely to give me one more season and they did, but we lost Johnrose and Dean West and gradually our results began to suffer.

We started off all right. We only lost once in our first nine league games but we couldn't sustain it. The club just wasn't set up for that level of football. All the way round, the facilities at Bury were a joke. We trained at a place called Goshen Park and in the morning we had to go and clear the dog shit up before we could start training. We had people checking for dog shit every morning but we'd always miss some and one poor bugger or another would land in it. We are talking about Championship level, don't forget.

One week, we were due to play a televised game against Sheffield United so Sky came down to do some interviews a couple of days before the game. The training pitch was that badly flooded, a flock of ducks landed on it while I was doing the interview. We hadn't got fuck all. We didn't have bibs and what stuff we did have, we used to leave in this derelict house that had been burned down. We had a key to it and we tried locking it up but it got pinched regularly. In the winter, when the pitch was frozen, we had to travel miles to train on an all-weather pitch.

The best thing about Bury was living in Ramsbottom, which was a lovely village. That and Jill Neville, the club secretary and the mother of Gary and Phil Neville. She was the best person ever. She doesn't need to work but she was absolutely spot on. She was brilliant at her job. Nothing phased her. She's a wonderful woman. You look at her lads and they are a credit to her but she is a credit to them, too. She was one of the highlights of Bury for me. And believe me, there weren't many.

The money problems were always in the background and problems started mounting on the pitch, too. We weren't helped by some outrageous decisions. We played Bristol City in October of that season and Alan Wiley, the referee, was about forty yards behind the play when one of the Bristol forwards, Colin Cramb, was chopped down by one of our lads about five yards outside the box. No exaggeration. Five yards. Maybe more. But Wiley blew and pointed to the spot. I couldn't believe it. They scored the penalty and we lost the game 1-0. I sent him a video and he wrote back and apologised but it was a bit late.

We were in trouble for most of the season after that. We were in and around the relegation zone. It was incredibly tight in what was then the First Division. Oxford United and Bristol City were below us but there were four clubs scrapping for their lives above that. Bury, Port Vale, QPR and Portsmouth. We all finished on forty-seven points and we had a better goal difference than Port Vale. But this was during a period when the Football League decided it would be a bright idea if promotion and relegation was decided on goals scored not goal difference. We hadn't scored as many as Port Vale and so we went down.

That was cruel. Not unlike what happened on the last day of Sheffield's Premiership season in May 2007 really. It just seemed like there were a lot of things working against us. By late in my first season at Bury, that included the Bury fans, too. They didn't like me very much and in some ways I couldn't blame them. They associated me with failure after a decent period of success and it wasn't long before they started making their feelings known.

We had played Bradford City at Gigg Lane in April 1999 and it was not a comfortable experience. Bury fans didn't like me by then because we were heading back towards the Second Division and the club's finances were in turmoil. And the Bradford fans hated me because I had once been manager at their hated rivals, Hudders-field. We went 2-0 down and a chant went round the ground of 'We Want Warnock Out'. The whole bloody ground was singing it in unison. I looked up and all four sides of the ground were singing it. That was a first, even for me.

By that time, it was absolutely terrible for me going into work. I had kept my promise to Lucketti and Kiely and sold them in the summer, so the team was even weaker. Although we won 5-0 at Blackpool early in my second season, we weren't pulling up any trees in the Second Division. I didn't enjoy going into work. Sharon was unhappy, too. She didn't want to go out. We felt like we were under siege. Then Neville Neville, who was the commercial director at the club, came into my office one morning.

He was a terrific bloke, Nev, and he looked at me with a grim smile on his face.

'We're getting down to the nitty-gritty now, Neil,' he said.

'What's up?' I asked him.

'Have you not seen the website?' he said.

I hadn't seen the website but I was soon looking at it. It was a Bury fans' website of some sort and one of the messages on it said that the best way of getting rid of me would be to set Sharon on fire while she was out shopping. Lovely. It was copycat stuff, apparently, because something similar had been said about Jimmy Mullen's wife when he was manager at Burnley. But that pretty much tipped me over the edge. I'd had enough. I went back home and told Sharon about what had happened. I decided I wanted to get out.

'Listen, darling,' I said, 'let's go. I'm not enjoying it. And the fans aren't happy anyway.'

I started talking to John Russell who was the chairman of

Scarborough. He knew I was really low and he wanted me to go back up to Yorkshire.

'Why don't you come back here?' he said. 'Everybody loves you. You know the place.'

It sounded good to me. Anything would have sounded good at that stage of my career as long as it didn't involve Bury. It would have meant dropping back down to the bottom tier again but we would get our lives back at least. We could take Amy on the beach, enjoy the town and try and rebuild. It would have been a lot better than the situation we found ourselves in. I arranged to go and meet John Russell for lunch.

As I was mulling over the old adage about never going back, a set of events began to unfold on the other side of the Pennines. On 23 November 1999, Sheffield United lost 3-1 at home to Port Vale in front of 8,965 fans, and the manager, Adrian Heath, quit. They made Russell Slade the caretaker and drew away at West Brom on the Saturday and lost at QPR the following Tuesday. They were deep in relegation trouble.

The same night that they were losing at QPR, I took my Bury team to Ninian Park for an FA Cup second round replay against Cardiff City. I threw a few kids in and we played ever so well and only lost in the very last minute of extra time to a goal from Mike Ford. We had been superb. I saw the Sheffield result and even though I only got back home in the early hours of Wednesday morning, I got up at 7 a.m. and rang Kevin McCabe, who held all the power by then, in his office.

'What's happened to the club, Kev?' I said.

'I don't know, Neil,' he said. 'When can you start?'

'Yesterday,' I said.

'Leave it with me,' he said.

I didn't tell him I had this meeting in Scarborough because I didn't want to do anything to spoil whatever chance I had of getting the Sheffield job. In fact, I rang John Russell and told him I wouldn't be able to come up for a few days. All sorts of names were being mentioned in connection with Bramall Lane but at least I knew Bury wouldn't stand in my way. Terry Robinson knew I was desperate to go and he was happy for me to go and talk to Sheffield.

I was interviewed by Derek Dooley, a hero to both United and Wednesday fans in Sheffield, who was the chairman of the football club board, and by Bernard Procter. I loved every minute of it. They could tell I was enthusiastic and I told them everything I would do, all the plans I had and the changes I would make. I didn't leave them in any doubt that I had the drive to rebuild the club. I told them everything they wanted to hear.

They said they would let me know within twenty-four hours. They were interviewing me and Gary Megson and I made sure I dropped it in that Unitedites would be dismayed if a man with such strong Wednesday connections as Megson got the job. I went home to Ramsbottom and waited for the call to come. I was that bloody nervous I could barely sit still.

The next night, which was my birthday, I was in a Chinese takeaway in the village picking up my order with my son James when my mobile rang. It was Derek Dooley.

'Can you speak?' he said.

'Not really, Derek,' I said. 'I'm in a Chinese takeaway. I'll be home in five minutes.'

'I'll ring you in fifteen minutes, Neil,' he said.

I put the phone away. Then I thought, oh my God, why didn't I just ask him?

Those fifteen minutes seemed the longest fifteen minutes ever. We got the Chinese home but we didn't eat it. I couldn't eat anything. I had butterflies like you wouldn't believe waiting for that call. I had my fingers crossed, willing the phone to ring and thinking, please let me get the job. Sharon and James were just as nervous as I was.

The phone went and we all looked at each other. I picked it up.

'Neil,' he said, 'it's Derek Dooley.'

'Hi Derek,' I said, trying to sound casual.

'Well, son,' he said, 'Happy Birthday. Your dream's come true.'

13
THE BATTLE OF BRAMALL LANE

I TOOK CHARGE of Sheffield United on a Thursday. I sat at my introductory press conference with a Blades scarf round my neck talking about the journey from Frecheville to Bramall Lane I took every other Saturday of my childhood with my dad. I talked about the last-minute rush into the ground and being passed down over the heads of the men on the Kop. The memories flooded over me as I stared at that Kop again, covered these days with banks of seats. I was on the other side of the fence now. The dreams of these supporters were in my hands.

I wanted to take charge on Thursday so I could get the press stuff out of the way and have a training session with the lads on Friday. We had Portsmouth at home on Saturday. We were next to bottom but Portsmouth were struggling down near the foot of the table with us. I knew it was a game we had to win to start the process of getting out of trouble. I needed that training session. I needed to know what kind of men I had got in my squad. I told the kit man to make sure the players brought their shinpads.

It was chucking it down with rain on Friday. The groundsman at the club's old training ground said there was nowhere fit for us to play because it was all flooded. I told him I was having a training session whether it was flooded or not. All I wanted was a patch of land forty yards by forty yards. I told him to do the best he could for us and he managed to make a square of grass just about playable. So we put the nets up and had a ten-a-side match.

We had two goalies in and the players all had their pads on. If they didn't tackle, I gave a penalty. If someone didn't head a ball when I thought they could have headed it, I gave a penalty. If anybody shirked a challenge, I gave a penalty. By the time they had played four or five minutes, it was brilliant: they were kicking lumps out of each other. They were battling. You could smell the defeatism drifting away. They had not won for ten games but you could see the fear disappearing. In a game like that, I get an idea of who's with me and who isn't.

There were a few scrappers in the squad. Paul Devlin was there for a start. I had signed him from Stafford Rangers when I was manager of Notts County. He had thirty-nine disciplinary points by Christmas that season at Stafford but he was a likeable rogue. In fact a super lad. That is, until he had had a drink. He had been slipping out of favour under Adrian Heath but I brought him straight back in. We needed his type at that time.

My Sheffield United team in the first of my 339 league games in charge of the club went like this: Tracey, Murphy, Quinn, Sandford, Derry, Ford, Gysbrechts, Devlin, Ribeiro, Marcus Bent, Smith. We won it 1-0 and Devlin got the winner. He picked the ball up way out, went on a dribble and whacked it into the top corner. That was after twenty minutes and we hung on and won. That gave us new belief and the platform for what anyone would call a dream start. We didn't lose a game that month. We won four in December 1999 and moved away from the relegation zone. I even got the Manager of the Month award.

A few players surprised me. There was a lad at the club called Shaun Murphy who I had seen when he was playing for Australia at the 1992 Olympics in Barcelona. I signed him for Notts County after that but we fell out because he saw himself as a fancy Dan centre half and I flogged him to West Brom. He had only been at Sheffield for a few months when I arrived and the other lads told me he'd been praying I wasn't going to get the job when I was being linked with it. The first day I was in charge, he came to see me and wanted to know what his position was.

'Everyone's got a clean slate,' I said to him. 'What's gone on in the past is finished. If you are good enough to be in the team, you'll be in the team.'

I was actually thinking, there's not a fucking chance of you being in my team. But he proved me wrong. He was a super player for me. The first game he played for me, which was at home to Rushden and Diamonds in the FA Cup, he let a ball bounce instead of heading it and they nearly scored. He tried to dribble when he should have whacked it clear. At half time, I went ballistic at him.

'I expect you to be my centre half,' I said, 'and I want centre halves to head it and kick it. That's all. Head it and fucking kick it.'

Rob Kozluk, who's one of the best lads I've ever had at a football club, a man whose humour makes it impossible for anybody to be down for too long, used to take the micky out of me for that in later years. If a defender made a mess of something in training, he put on his thick Yorkshire accent and did his best impersonation of me.

'What do I want you to do?' he'd say to the offending player. 'Head it and fucking kick it.'

Kozzie was one of the secrets of my success at Bramall Lane. He wasn't a bad player. Almost every year he was at the club I thought he might be coming to the end of his time with us, but he always did enough to earn a new contract. Most of all, he was a great lad. He was the life and soul. One of his party pieces was stealing the mobile phones of the other players and sending me texts pretending to be from them.

'Please play me, gaffer,' they'd read, 'I'm begging you. I'll never forget it if you can just play me this one time.'

He would hide cars, he'd fill other players' boots with yoghurt. Once he rugby-tackled our press guy, Andy Pack, on a muddy training pitch when Andy was wearing his suit. The next day, Kozluk drove all the way to Nottingham without realising that an obscenity had been scrawled in big capital letters across his back numberplates in reprisal.

Every club needs a Kozzie. I don't think chairmen and directors realise how big a part people like him play. I love that lad. He has given me so much pleasure over the years and he can play a bit, too.

Anyway, from that match against Rushden and Diamonds onwards, Murphy headed it and kicked it and he was in my team on merit. He had been too lethargic for me at Notts County but he changed his ways at Sheffield. He started defending properly and he played for me for another three seasons. It reminded me not to pre-judge people. They have a habit of surprising you.

The club was big in debt when I arrived. It was about £20 million Something like that. Maybe a bit more. So in the early days, part of my task was reducing the wage bill. The crowds were low and the fans were despondent. They weren't sure about me, either. Me being a fan and a local lad didn't seem to hold much sway with them.

I didn't get a bad reception but I was hardly coming to them on a high. I had bombed a bit at Oldham and Bury. The glory days at Notts County were ancient history. And of course there was an element of fans who wanted a big name. But I knew the only reason I had got the job was that they couldn't afford big names. Anyway, it would be fair to say there was some scepticism. One of the television stations interviewed a guy called Andy Nicholson who's head of the Blades Independent Fans Association. There are only about four people in it besides him but it still gave him a platform.

'It's no good being a fan if you can't be a manager,' Nicholson said when they interviewed him in the car park. 'Warnock wouldn't have been my choice.'

But when the majority of supporters saw that the lads had started battling and that they were showing their fighting qualities, they knew it was better than what had gone before. I didn't have a lot of money to play with. Like I said, my brief was to lower the wage bill. Michael Brown was my first signing and what a player he was for me. He was playing for Portsmouth in that first game of mine at

Bramall Lane but he was on loan from Manchester City and the word was Portsmouth wanted shut of him.

I thought he was a smashing player and when Portsmouth sent him back to Maine Road, I got him on loan for a month from Joe Royle. Joe thought Brown was trouble. He had a reputation as a big-time Charlie and there was talk he had refused to play in the reserves at Portsmouth when they'd asked him to. Joe was desperate to get rid of him so we paid £400,000 for him and he became one of the best players I had at Sheffield United. Joe was that keen on selling him to me that they let us pay the fee over three years.

I liked Brownie. He was my favourite. I always have a favourite. Whoever it was, the lads called him my son. Craig Short was my favourite at Notts County. At Plymouth, it was Adrian Littlejohn. In my later days at Bramall Lane, it was Phil Jagielka. I would make a joke of it. If it was raining when I was doing a team talk, I'd take my brolly out and hold it over Brownie's head and give him a piece of chewing gum. He was a bit of a rogue, Brownie. I thought it might make him think twice about telling me to fuck off if he was my favourite. I like likable rogues. I like the challenge of straightening out a player that no one else wants.

When I first got to Bramall Lane, the directors told me that our centre forward, Marcus Bent, was a disaster. They had paid £300,000 for him at the beginning of 1999 and they wanted me to offload him for whatever I could get. But I saw something in him and I liked him as a lad. They were playing him right wing, which was never his position, but I told him I was going to play him up front and stick with him. He got me the goals, too. He scored a great hat-trick against West Brom in a 6-0 win that was my biggest victory at Sheffield. I had him for one year and then I sold him to Blackburn for £2.1 million. I made him a millionaire.

But Bent and Paul Devlin didn't get on. They didn't get on at all. There was one match where Devlin was in space and screaming at Bent to give him the ball. Bent was more interested in doing a few tricks and in the end he got tackled and we lost possession. Devlin didn't like that. If you didn't give him the ball, he would go bananas. They had a confrontation on the pitch and, at the end of the game, they went into the dressing room and they were still at it, slagging each other off. Marcus stripped his shirt off and went over to Paul's peg and started shouting at him again. Marcus put his face next to Devlin's and started to yell right at him from close range.

Unh-oh, I thought, shouldn't do that.

But it was too late.

Straight away, Devlin tilted his head back and head-butted him. Smashed his nose. Blood everywhere. It was brilliant.

'Will we be taking any disciplinary action?' one of our press people asked me later on.

'Disciplinary action?' I said. 'Don't be silly. I bloody love it. Just what we need.'

Michael Brown really improved us in my first season in charge and we were safe by the end of February. We even got as high as twelfth. At that stage I brought a few younger players in to try them out and give them a bit of experience and we finished the season in sixteenth, eight points clear of the bottom three.

I fixed up a tour at the end of the season to Trinidad and Tobago.

I allowed Bobby Ford and Shaun Murphy to miss it. Bobby Ford was getting married and Shaun Murphy was going back to Australia to see his family but there were no other exceptions. Before the last game of the season, one of the lads walked in to the dressing room and mentioned that he wasn't aware that Bruno Ribeiro, a Portuguese lad who was one of the crowd favourites, wasn't going either. I told him it was news to me, too. I got Bruno in.

'They tell me you're not going to Trinidad, Bruno,' I said.

'I no go, gaffer,' he said.

'Well, I want you to go,' I told him.

'Ford and Murphy no go,' he said in his Portuguese accent, 'so I no go.'

'If you don't go, I'm going to fine you two weeks' wages,' I told him.

'You no do that, gaffer,' he said.

'I'm telling you that's what I'm going to do,' I said.

He didn't turn up. So I fined him two weeks' wages. And he just paid it. It was £12,000. That was a lot of money in 1999. Twelve grand not to go to Trinidad and Tobago. That brought it home to me that he wasn't at Sheffield for the right reasons. I didn't want players like that. I got rid of him. It took me a while but I flogged him back to Portugal.

Having said that, the trip to Trinidad and Tobago was not a total success. I was sitting at the front of the plane on the journey out there and all the lads were at the back. We were somewhere out over the middle of the Atlantic when someone came down and said to me that Paul Devlin was a bit high. All the players had got these little miniatures and given them to Dev who'd drunk the lot. The chief steward said to me that, if he kept misbehaving, they were going to put him in a straitjacket, lock him in the toilet and then hand him over to the police when we landed in the Caribbean.

I walked to the back and sat down next to him.

'All right, gaffer,' he mumbled.

'All right, Dev,' I said. 'What's going on?'

'Nowt going on, gaffer,' he said.

Michael Brown was sitting just in front and Devlin didn't get on with him, either. Brownie started laughing about something else with whoever he was sitting next to and Dev went all rigid.

'Look at him, fucking laughing,' he said fiercely.

He wanted to get up to chin him. I got my hand through his arm to hold him down. I was stuck there then for about three hours. None of the rest of the staff were around. I spent the whole time trying to talk him out of chinning Brownie.

When we landed, I had to be introduced to the Trinidad and Tobago government hierarchy and there was a steel band welcoming us. Devlin could hardly walk. Dean Riddle, the fitness guy, had to hold him up.

'Whenever the next flight back to England leaves, make sure he's on it,' I told him.

As if we didn't have enough scrappers in the team already, we even had a bloke who ended up becoming a professional boxer. Curtis Woodhouse used to get into some right scrapes when he was at Bramall Lane. He was as good as gold in the dressing room and out on the pitch but he always seemed to get into trouble when he went home to Goole. We were on first name terms with the coppers who used to come round asking questions about his latest bout of fisticuffs.

We got a bit of a result when we sold him to Birmingham City in February 2001. We got £1 million plus Peter Ndlovu for him. I wasn't surprised when I heard a few years later that he had quit football and that Frank Warren had taken him into his boxing stable. Curtis always liked a scrap. At least now, he could do it inside the ropes.

I had got a lot of my own players in by the time Curtis left. I had signed a French lad called Laurent d'Jaffo from Stockport County in February 2000. He was a centre forward and probably the best header of the ball that ever played for me. He did some work for me as a valued scout when he retired and has become a good friend. I signed Patrick Suffo in June 2000 from Nantes only to find out that he had been banned for six months for spitting at a referee. So he couldn't play until the beginning of 2001. I got George Santos, who was from Marseille, from West Brom in July 2000. I signed the veteran defender, Keith Curle, and the forward David Kelly, too, both of them on free transfers.

We went to Hillsborough for my first Sheffield derby in the Worthington Cup in November 2000 and we played fantastically. The Hillsborough band was playing and I hated that band but we were doing so well that I was banging my feet in time to the music on the side of the dugout. But the Wednesday goalkeeper, Kevin Pressman, pulled off save after save after save and Efan Ekoku won it for them in injury time.

It was funny with me and the Wednesdayites. I always got on all right with them, really. I think they had had such nightmares over at their place in the time I was at Bramall Lane that they almost admired the job I had done. I got more respect off them than I did off a lot of Unitedites actually. The Blades fans were always fairly grudging with their affection for me. They very, very rarely chanted my name, even when we went up to the Premiership. I don't know why. I think it was something to do with me being a fan. In a strange way, maybe they didn't respect me quite as much because of that. Maybe an outsider would have commanded more affection. I don't know.

One of the best moments of that 2000-01 season came a couple of games from the end of it when we played Burnley at Bramall Lane. Stan Ternent was the Burnley manager and they were on the verge of making the play-offs. Ternent was even more wound up and aggressive than usual that day. He was desperate to avoid giving me the satisfaction of ruining his only chance of getting to the Premiership. I had always known he was a dickhead but, even by his standards, he behaved like a deranged lunatic that day.

There's a corridor at Bramall Lane that runs from the ticket office down past the back of the away changing room and past my office to some toilets and more offices. At half time, every Tom, Dick and Harry can walk down it. On the day of the Burnley game, our physio, Nigel Cox, was walking through from the ticket office when Ternent came flying out of the back door of the away changing room like a madman, screaming and shouting at Cox.

'You eavesdropping twat,' he was yelling.

Next thing, he's pitched up at the referee's room, accusing us of listening at the door and moaning about some of the first half decisions. I had told Kevin Blackwell to keep an eye on Ternent because I knew he would be trying to put pressure on the ref, so when Ternent came round the corner, frothing at the mouth, Blackie had a word.

'Leave it, Stan, will you?' Blackie said. 'You're always at it, you.'

In his demented state, that was all the encouragement Ternent needed. He launched himself at Blackie and head-butted him. Blackwell swung a right hook back at him and smacked him on the nose. He sploshed him good and proper.

In Ternent's autobiography, he tells how he went back into the Burnley dressing room and said he'd given Blackwell a good hiding. He said there was no way Blackwell would be seeing the second half. He likes to portray himself as a hard man, Ternent. But we saw the incident differently – as far as we were concerned Blackie had a little cut on his lip. That was all. He seemed right as rain and Ternent was in bits. We beat them 2-0, by the way. Burnley never did make the play-offs.

By the end of that season, we had made real improvements. Some of the lads from the youth set-up were starting to come through. Phil Jagielka, Michael Tonge and Nick Montgomery were the Sheffield equivalent of Manchester United's class of 1992 with Ryan Giggs, Nicky Butt, Paul Scholes and the Neville brothers. Jagielka, Tonge and Montgomery were great lads who were the core of my team for the next six years. We had climbed to tenth at the close of the campaign and everybody sensed the club was heading in the right direction at last.

I started taking the lads to Cornwall for their pre-season tours around that time. We stayed at a golf club complex called Trethorne on the Devon-Cornwall border and played matches against Hayle and Bodmin Town. I stayed at my house down there, which was nearby, and one morning I arrived back at Trethorne to find that the boys had had a big night. Paul Devlin had been on one of his benders but for once he hadn't been the star of the show. That distinction went to a young Irish central defender called Colin Cryan, who had got so pissed that the lads had carried his bed out to the seventeenth green with him in it and left him there. A member of staff found him at 7 a.m. He was still asleep. As part of the tour, I always had a barbecue at my house. Derek Dooley would come down and do a bit of cooking and the lads would play pitch and putt on my grass. They took great pleasure in hacking big divots out of it. It'd take me a month to get the grass right again.

We didn't start the next season well. We only won one of our first nine games. It was the only time in my six and half years at the club that we even flirted with relegation. But we edged our way out of trouble until, by the middle of March, we were parked comfortably in mid-table and aiming to end the season on a high. West Brom, who were near the top of the table and heading for automatic promotion, were due at Bramall Lane on 16 March and I thought if I could put one over on them and their manager, Gary Megson, it would provide the platform for us to have a decent run-in and push into the top ten again.

I've hated Megson for years and years. He played for Sheffield Wednesday, for a start. But I began to dislike him seriously when I was manager of Bury and he was in charge of Stockport County. We played them at Gigg Lane in the FA Cup third round at the start of January 1999. Our side was decimated by injuries and we were well beaten 3-0. Megson was very condescending and told the press how easy it had been.

When we went to Edgeley Park a few months later to play them in the league, we were fighting for our lives in what would now be the Championship and we still had a lot of young lads in the team. So I decided to play it the Megson way. And in case you didn't know, the Megson way is boring. Believe you me, it's boring. The Megson way is never create anything, avoid defeat as best you can and try and snatch a win on the break. That day at Stockport, I played five across the back, just like he does, and we got a decent 0-0 draw.

After the game, he told the press that if a team of his ever played like that, he'd pack the game in. When I went up, the reporters asked me what I thought.

'He'd better call it a day then and do us all a favour,' I said. 'Does he not realise that we've only got half our players fit and that we were playing kids today? Does he want us to lie down like we did in January? Would he like us to get beat 3-0 so he could have a nice night out? It's not my job to help him out.'

Megson didn't have to say any of that. Just because of his team's own deficiencies, he tried to deflect attention on to my side and the young lads who were playing in it. So that started it off between me and him. I never rated him anyway. I always thought his teams were boring. I'd found it hard to believe, when I was interviewed for the Sheffield United job, that he was being considered as well. He was Sheffield Wednesday through and through. That would have been a real kick in the teeth for Blades fans if they had hired him. There's only going to be one winner there, I thought to myself at the time.

So there was a bit of tension when Megson and West Brom pitched up at Bramall Lane in March 2002. If the dislike between me and Megson wasn't enough, there was another feud simmering as well. The previous season, Andy Johnson had elbowed George Santos in the face off the ball when Johnson was playing against us for Nottingham Forest. Santos had his eye socket shattered and his skull dented. He spent several days in hospital and had to have an operation. Johnson had escaped punishment because no one had seen what he had done. And now he was playing for West Bromwich Albion.

I had a chat with George before the game. It was the first time he had come up against Johnson since the incident, which had happened almost exactly a year earlier, and I knew he would have revenge on his mind. I told him I had made him part of the squad because he was a good player and I wanted to get a result. I told him I knew how bad the incident had been but that I didn't want him going out there looking to exact retribution. I put him on the bench so that I could call on him if I needed to. I told him I wanted him to give me his word that the bad blood between the two of them wouldn't be an issue on the pitch.

'I give you my word, gaffer,' he said. He was a lovely lad, George.

'I'm putting you on the bench then but I don't want any problems,' I said.

'No problems, gaffer,' he said.

It was a lively game. Our goalkeeper, Simon Tracey, was sent off after nine minutes for handling the ball outside the box. I didn't have a substitute keeper on the bench so I sent on a Dutch lad called Wilko de Vogt, who was our second-string left back, and stuck him in nets. I had to sacrifice Peter Ndlovu in the process and I took him off for Wilko. Scott Dobie put them ahead nine minutes later and then, midway through the second half, Derek McInnes scored a belter to put them 2-0 up. I still thought we had a chance, though, so in the sixty-fourth minute, I used my two remaining substitutes and sent on George Santos and Patrick Suffo.

Less than sixty seconds after they had come on, someone played a loose pass to Johnson in midfield. Suddenly, I saw George Santos homing in on him like an Exocet missile. They both got to the ball about the same time and George launched himself at Johnson. He almost got the ball but he certainly got the man. Johnson went about twenty feet up in the air and when he landed, he lay on the deck like he'd been shot. It all kicked off then. There were players pushing and shoving and Eddie Wolstenholme, the referee, was flapping. Derek McInnes, ran up to Suffo and started taunting him and Suffo head-butted him as brazen as you like right in front of the ref. Santos had already had the red card by then. Now Suffo was following him up the tunnel. There was blood pouring out of McInnes from a gash over his eye but he'd known exactly what he was doing by inciting Suffo.

I might have just got the sack at Meadow Lane but I was determined to break open the bubbly with Mick Jones to celebrate everything we had achieved there.

I only had seventeen games in charge of Torquay but the players there, including Kevin Blackwell, wearing number fifteen, gave me back my love for football.

My Torquay players celebrated on the pitch at Carlisle's Brunton Park when we saved ourselves from relegation from the league on 1 May 1993. The fans deserved their moment, too, after the journey they had made.

Leading out my Huddersfield Town team with my daughter, Natalie, for the Division Two play-off final victory over Bristol Rovers in 1995.

Chris Billy scores the winner for Huddersfield at Wembley to put us up to the old Division One.

There are few better feelings than winning a play-off final and I shared the moment after the Bristol Rovers game with Huddersfield forward Ronnie Jepson.

Physio Dave Wilson, me, my best mate Paul Evans, and Mick Jones on the pitch at Wembley before Huddersfield's play-off final against Bristol Rovers.

Above: I jumped into the stands and sat with the supporters at Home Park after I was sent off in the second leg of Plymouth Argyle's play-off semi-final against Colchester United.

Left: Andy Booth, left, was the best header of the ball that ever played for me, and he and Chris Billy, right, got the goals that won Huddersfield the play-off trophy.

Left: Happy times with Dan McCauley.

Below: Ronnie Mauge, second left, scored the goal that brought me another play-off final victory over Darlington in 1996.

My dream came true when I was appointed manager of my home town club, Sheffield United, in December 1999.

Derek Dooley, who was the Sheffield United chairman at the time, is a man I admire tremendously so it was a special honour when he presented me with the Manager of the Month award for December 1999.

Me and William on a small tractor in the grounds of our house in Cornwall. My favourite form of transport.

We were down to eight men and we had no substitutes left. But the fun was only just beginning. I got Keith Curle over to the touchline to try to get him to calm things down but he started flying into tackles worse than anybody else. He got booked as well and then he went after McInnes, who had his head all bandaged up by now, like he was on a mission. Curley was going daft. Then Michael Brown started to limp. In the seventy-seventh minute, Dobie put West Brom 3-0 up and I started to think about trying to salvage something from this nightmare for our game against Millwall three days later. Brown was limping heavily by now.

'If you're injured, Brownie,' I shouted to him, 'lie down and get off. We've got a game on Tuesday.'

A couple of minutes later, he struggled off. One of their directors said afterwards that he had limped to the touchline and then sprinted down the tunnel. He was accusing Michael Brown of feigning injury. What a muppet. Brownie had to have a double hernia operation the following Wednesday. He didn't play for the club again all season. And if that was a sprint he was doing when he came off, I'd hate to see a West Brom player dawdle.

Now we were down to seven with ten minutes left. Rob Ullathorne ran for a ball and pulled up clutching his hamstring. It was obvious he'd pulled it. Anyone who knows the game knows you can't imitate that kind of action. The trainer went on to see him and said he was going to have to come off. There were eight minutes left. I didn't know that the rules said that if a team was reduced to six men, a game had to be abandoned. In all the excitement, I didn't even know how many players we had left. It was bloody mayhem out there.

Anyway, when our trainer said Ullathorne couldn't continue, Eddie Wolstenholme called the game off. In the aftermath, when I realised what had happened, I wondered why the ref hadn't just asked us if we'd leave Ullathorne sitting on the pitch and play out the game like that. We would have been happy with that. We had absolutely no desire for a replay so we certainly wouldn't have objected to that scenario. But we were never given the option. The match was abandoned and all hell broke loose.

Megson led the kerfuffle. He started ranting and raving about how disgusting the behaviour of our bench had been. He accused me and the players of orchestrating the chaos at the end with the late injuries. He said he had never seen anything as disgraceful as the events he had just witnessed in all his twenty-six years in the game. Blah, blah, blah. But then he said the thing I'll never forgive him for. He said on television he'd heard a member of staff shouting on to the pitch to Michael Brown. He said he had heard them instruct him to go down 'to get the game off'. The clear insinuation was he was referring to me.

'To get the game off'. Those five words caused me more upset and hurt than he could have imagined. Yes, I had told Michael Brown to go down but only because he was clearly injured. I never told him to do it for the purpose of getting the game off. I didn't care about trying to get a replay. We didn't want a replay. We were happy to give West Brom the points. We even said that straight after the game on the radio. We just wanted to try and put it behind us as fast as we could. It wasn't as if we were proud of what had happened.

But Megson and West Brom were panicking so much about the fact that we might try and demand a replay that they started spraying all these accusations around. Megson said his five words because he was having his silly little hissy fit but he unleashed a storm for me that nearly cost me my job. The press went ballistic about what he had said. I had more bad publicity that weekend than Osama bin Laden. Jimmy Hill took the prize for slagging me off when he said the next morning that the club ought to be relegated and I should be suspended for two years.

Jimmy Hill didn't phone me to find out my point of view or my version of events and yet here he was gabbling all this garbage. I saw him five months later when we played the first game of the next season against Coventry City at Highfield Road. I went over and introduced myself.

'Jimmy,' I said, 'Neil Warnock.'

'Oh, hello, Neil,' he said, bright as day.

'Jimmy,' I said, 'I just wanted to tell you how disappointed I was that you saw fit to say that I should have been suspended and my club should have been relegated without having the decency to contact me to find out my point of view. You have hung, drawn and quartered me before knowing anything about the facts.'

'Which game was that, Neil?' he said.

He hadn't got a clue. There was no point in pursuing it. I just walked off.

The couple of days after the West Brom game were terrible. Sharon and the kids couldn't go out of the house that weekend because of the press coverage. The kids were getting stick at school.

It was diabolical. That was a real low point for me. There were people telling Kevin McCabe that he should get rid of me. The self-appointed supporters' rent-a-quote Andy Nicholson was saying that if the accusations were true, I could not manage the club for another game and that I would have to go. It was horrendous. The Warnock-bashers loved it. They all came out from under the woodwork. They all had their twopenn'orth. I wasn't sure I had unanimous support on the board. I thought one or two directors might use it as an excuse to get me out. I thought it was a possibility.

It crossed my mind to pack it all in. I felt bitterness towards football at that time. I felt I didn't deserve the treatment I was getting and my family didn't deserve it either. Just because of Megson using five words that he didn't need to use, I was slaughtered. He didn't have to say those five words. He could have got his point across without crucifying me like that. He didn't know what my family had to go through because of him. My kids and all.

It wasn't as if we were glorying in the mess. On the Monday after the West Brom game, I told Santos and Suffo they would never play for the club ever again. And they never did. It's all right having disagreements and the odd punch-up in training. Every club has incidents like that. But when you represent the club on the pitch, you can't behave like that. I don't necessarily blame Santos for wanting revenge on Andy Johnson but I expected him to have the self-discipline not to go after him. So I told both of them they had humiliated me. They were nice lads off the field but what they did that day was beyond the bounds of acceptability.

I didn't pack it in. Derek Dooley was incredibly supportive of me, especially considering he had been friendly with Don Megson, Gary's dad, and I decided to carry on. I played a few of the kids in midweek against Millwall and we won 3-2 with two goals from Ndlovu in the last two minutes. That showed real character after all the flak we had been taking. A few days later, we played Burnley at our place. Megson and Stan Ternent at Bramall Lane within the space of a week. It's a wonder pest control didn't pop round to deal with the infestation. Anyway, we battered Burnley 3-0. Beating Ternent again cheered me up no end.

Some time later, we and West Brom had to attend an FA hearing into the events of 16 March, a match already christened by the press as the Battle of Bramall Lane. Mick Maguire, from the Professional Footballers' Association, represented me and he was a tremendous help throughout the whole episode. He dealt with it all with great calmness and knowledge.

Megson was still spouting off. He said that if the FA ordered a replay, West Brom would stand there for the kick-off and then walk off the pitch. Then he told anyone who wanted to listen that a member of my staff had phoned him to apologise and to say that what had happened was totally out of order.

Eventually, the FA fined Sheffield United £10,000 for the players' behaviour at the match. The Football League, following the FA's recommendation, let the match result stand. They gave me a £300 fine because some jobsworth noticed that I had come out of my technical area at some stage. It was the lowest fine I'd ever had in my managerial career and I've had a few. I wasn't even mentioned in Eddie Wolstenholme's report. I was absolved of any wrongdoing and the FA were almost apologetic about having to fine me at all.

'Megson says he's going to include all the details of what happened in his book,' one of the press lads said to me after the hearing.

'He's writing a book is he?' I said. 'Well, it'll be the best fucking cure for insomniacs that's ever been published.'

Megson's made a couple of attempts to make it up with me since. A few months after the game, I went to a pre-season LMA meeting at the Hawthorns and Mick Jones and I sat at the back of the room. When we broke for drinks, Megson came towards me as if he wanted to say something. I blanked him.

A couple of seasons later, we played at West Brom and I went to put the teamsheets in. He came round the corner and stuck out his hand as if he wanted me to shake it.

'Not a cat in hell's chance,' I said to him. 'I would never shake your hand in a fucking million years.'

I wouldn't either. I wouldn't piss on him if he was on fire.

14
CRUEL HEARTS AND CUP RUNS

I HAD NEVER really liked Cup games. I didn't buy the romance of them. Clubs that I was managing never had a decent chance of winning the FA Cup or the League Cup so what was the point? I had always thought that all a Cup run was good for was messing up your league form. My ideal was drawing one of the giants as early as possible, earning a good payday from it and then getting on with the business of trying to climb up the league.

But in 2002-03, I decided it was going to be different. I was getting on a bit and I had told myself I was going to retire at the end of the following season when I was fifty-five. I never did, of course, but I believed it at the time. Anyway, I thought if I only had a couple of years left, I might as well have a good crack at the Cups. I had a good side. I thought we could go on a bit of a run.

Our first Cup game of the season in that campaign was home to York City on 10 September in the Worthington Cup. It was the first of ten consecutive home ties we got that season. It was blowing a gale and tipping it down with rain. There were only 4,675 people there and we played poorly. It was a bloody miserable night all round but we sneaked a 1-0 win out of it. In the dressing room afterwards, I said wryly to the lads that they'd remember nights like that when we got to Wembley. I got a few bitter laughs.

We beat Wycombe Wanderers in the second round and Leeds in the third. We were 1-0 down and going out against Leeds when Phil Jagielka scored a cracker of an equaliser in the last minute and then Peter Ndlovu won it for us in injury time. It was always special beating Leeds because they are such a massive club. Our crowd went mad at the end. We beat Sunderland in the fourth round and Crystal Palace in the quarter-finals. We were in the semi-finals, two games away from an appearance at Cardiff. We drew Liverpool.

We played the first leg at Bramall Lane. Liverpool played us off the park for the first half hour and Neil Mellor, a lad I had tried to sign several times, put them ahead ten minutes before the interval. Liverpool were passing the ball around for fun. Not taking the piss, but not far away. They were keeping the ball and barely breaking sweat. The crowd was quiet. We were being outclassed. It was only a matter of time until they got another one and then the floodgates would open. I was watching the match from the stands. Voluntarily, for once. So I buzzed down to Kevin Blackwell, who was on the bench.

'Listen, Blackie,' I said, 'I'm coming down in a minute. When I get there, don't worry what I say or do because I've got to stir things up. Otherwise we're going to get battered.'

'Too right we are,' he said.

They had a bloke called Salif Diao in midfield who had just

committed a horrific tackle and got away with it. Then Michael Tonge had made an innocuous challenge and got booked.

As I came out of the tunnel, the Liverpool boss, Gerard Houllier, was on the edge of his technical area so I made sure I brushed his long black overcoat as I stormed past. He turned around to look at me.

'That's a fucking disgrace that, Gerard,' I yelled at him. 'How can Diao not get booked for a tackle like that? How much are you paying that ref?'

'No, no, no, no,' Houllier said. 'The referee is correct. He does not do anything wrong.'

He was a lovely man, Gerard, but I had to stir it up a bit more.

'Just fuck off, Gerard,' I said. 'That's a joke. He should be in the book.'

'No, no, no, no,' he said again.

'Oh, just fuck off, you,' I said.

Then, Phil Thompson, Houllier's number two, came storming out of the dugout. He acted like he was Gerard's minder. He started mouthing off.

'You can fuck off, Pinocchio,' I said. 'Go and get back in your fucking cupboard.'

Well, that got him going as well. It was a red rag to a bull with Phil. He started waving his arms and yelling and gesticulating and the fourth official got involved. Suddenly, it was absolute mayhem. When the half time whistle went and we were going down the tunnel, they were having a right go at me. They weren't bothered about the game any more or the fact they were winning 1-0. I took my time going to the dressing room so I could wind them all up a bit more.

I turned round and spoke to Blackwell.

'We've fucking got them now, pal,' I said.

'What do you mean?' he said.

'Just you wait,' I said.

We went into the dressing room.

'Listen lads,' I said. 'We were poor in that first half but all they're going to be talking about at half time is what a prick I am and what they want to do to me. We've got them rattled and we've got to believe we can get at them. I want us to get right in their faces now and let's see what happens. You lot can change this game if we get stuck in.'

Well, my lads got leathered into them second half and Michael Tonge scored two cracking goals in the space of six minutes late on and we won 2-1. At the end of the game, I went to shake Gerard's hand and Phil Thompson was still going mental. He wouldn't shake my hand.

'Wait till we get you back to our fucking place,' he said, 'we'll sort you out then.'

I was a bit worried about their place. Not because of Phil Thompson. But I knew it would be packed inside Anfield and the atmosphere would be fantastic. I was also aware that I didn't want to frighten the lads to death by doing too much work on how to try and deal with Michael Owen and Steven Gerrard. So on the day of the game, instead of getting on the bus to go for a light training session in the morning, I told the lads to turn left outside the hotel and we wandered down to the Pier Head, them in their boots and their track suits.

I'd got the fitness guy, Dean Riddle, to buy us tickets for the ferry across the Mersey and we jumped on the first one that came. We went up on the top deck and went through a couple of our defensive routines up there. We pretended that the space between two of the lifebuoys was the goal and we practised what our wall was going to be. We did all our set piece preparation on the top deck of a ferry across the Mersey. Poor Wayne Allison, our centre forward, was sitting on one of the steps on a stairway and had gone very pale. He was bloody seasick on a ferry across the river. The rest of the lads seemed to enjoy it though.

Not that it helped us get off to a good start. Liverpool went ahead after nine minutes with a goal from El-Hadji Diouf. Everybody thought they were going to batter us but they couldn't break us down again. Then late in the game, their goalkeeper, Chris Kirkland, came out of his box and dived on the ball. It should have been a straight red card. We watched and we waited while the referee, Alan Wiley, decided what to do. He fished a yellow out of his pocket instead. He bottled it, basically.

Wiley said he hadn't sent Kirkland off because his momentum had carried him out of the box and the offence was accidental. But we all knew that if our goalkeeper, Paddy Kenny, had committed an offence like that, he would have been straight off. That was just one among the many major decisions that have not gone my way in football because I have never managed a big club. But it had got to the point where I thought Alan Wiley had something against me.

Tommy Mooney took the free kick after Kirkland's handball. It was deflected about an inch wide. That would have put us into the final. It was unbelievably close. The game finished 1-0 to them after ninety minutes so – because we had won the first leg – we went into extra time. We pushed them all the way but then Michael Owen scored in the 107th minute and that was it.

After the game, I went on to the pitch with the players to applaud the fans and their dopey Swiss centre half, Stephane Henchoz, came towards me and spat at me. It only just missed me. I told the press about it. I said I expected better than foreigners spitting at me at Anfield. Patrick Collins called me 'a bigot' in his column in the *Mail on Sunday* for saying that. I didn't even know what a bigot was. But I was disgusted with Henchoz. I called him a few names, too. None of them was 'bigot'. Fortunately, he was that slow I knew he'd never catch me if he tried to run after me.

I saw another side of Liverpool, too, though. What pleased me that night was that Owen, Gerrard and Jamie Carragher were a different class with my lads. They walked round every Sheffield United player after the final whistle, shaking their hands one by one. They knew how much my lads were hurting.

It was the end of January by then and we had started to play well in the league, too. It looked like we would have a good shot at the play-offs, maybe even automatic promotion. I decided that, despite what I had told the lads at the beginning of the season, we should forget about the FA Cup now and concentrate on the league. We had beaten Cheltenham Town in the third round but we drew Ipswich Town in the fourth round and I made a load of changes. I left a few of the first team out and gave a kid called Tyrone Thompson his debut.

'For heaven's sake, no replays,' I said to the lads before they went out.

Ipswich dominated the game and yet somehow we were 2-0 up at the interval. This isn't going to plan, this, I thought.

I went in to see them at half time.

'If we're not careful, we're going to win this,' I said sarcastically.

We went 3-0 up after the break and I thought the game was over. Then Ipswich scored three goals in four minutes and the teams were level with twenty minutes to go. I didn't want to watch any more so I went down to the dressing rooms. I was so pissed off. We were looking at a needless trip to Ipswich when we were trying to win the league. Then I heard this massive cheer from our fans. Paul Peschisolido had scored the winner in the last minute. I went out into the corridor a few minutes later and saw the Ipswich boss, Joe Royle, looking totally crestfallen.

'We didn't even want to win, Joe,' I said, which probably didn't help much.

'You don't need to fucking tell me that,' Joe said.

We drew Walsall in the fifth round and I thought we might as well have a go for the FA Cup now. We beat them 2-0 with goals from Ndlovu and Mooney. Now, we were in the quarters. Either side of the Cup games, we lost four games on the bounce in the league. The Cup run was driving me daft but it had got this momentum all of its own. It felt like we had a charmed life. There was nothing we could do about it.

We played Leeds in the quarter-final at Bramall Lane. Terry Venables was in charge of them. It was a drab game and neither side looked like they were going to score. Twelve minutes from the end, our striker, Steven Kabba, put us ahead. I looked over at Venables.

'Get ready,' I said to Blackie. 'It's going to be like bloody Dunkirk for the rest of the game now.'

But they never had a shot. They never broke sweat. They didn't want to know. Apart from Alan Smith. He was running around like a madman trying to get everybody else going. We held out for the win but I went on the pitch at the end and I made sure I found Alan Smith.

'If there's one player I could sign out of your team, it would be you, son,' I said. 'I thought you were an absolute gem today. If they were all like you, Leeds wouldn't be in the shit they're in now. If you ever want a game, feel free to ring me.'

I was excited now. We were in the semi-finals and we had a real chance of going all the way. The other teams in the hat were Watford, Southampton and Arsenal. I fancied us against Watford or Southampton. We drew Arsenal. I was gutted. I knew we'd give them a game but it was still bad luck.

The game was to be played at Old Trafford. I rang Sir Alex Ferguson and asked if we could train on the pitch to get used to it. He was happy to oblige. He was ready to do anything he could to help us. United had a league game against Arsenal at Highbury a few days after we played them that was effectively a title decider.

'I tell you what, Alex,' I said, 'if you could have had a choice of us, Southampton or Watford to soften them up for you, I know which one you'd have picked.'

'I know, son,' he said.

'Don't worry,' I told him, 'we'll sort them out.'

It turned out we couldn't train at Old Trafford. The FA wouldn't allow it. They said it would give us an unfair advantage. Given that Arsenal played there every season, that seemed a bit daft. Anyway, Alex rang again. He said we could go and train at United's complex at Carrington and have a walk around on the pitch after. It was a generous offer. I took him up on it.

While we were at Carrington, I walked up to his office and had a chat. He asked me how I wanted the pitch cut for the semi-final.

'Do you want it long, short, wet, dry?'

'What do you think?' I said.

'If it's short and wet, the ball will zip and fizz along and they'll pass and pass and it'll be difficult for you,' he said.

'We better have it long and dry then,' I said.

We got stuck into them right from the start. Brownie caught the Arsenal captain Patrick Vieira a couple of times. One of them was a humdinger of a tackle. It was hard and fair but Vieira felt it. He went off early in the second half. He tried to play against United the following Wednesday but he didn't even the last the first half. United got a 2-2 draw and went on to win the title that season. I expected a medal from Fergie.

We didn't make it easy for Arsenal that day. Our work rate was phenomenal. We were holding our own until ten minutes before half time when Sol Campbell clattered into Wayne Allison from behind. It was an obvious foul but the referee, Graham Poll, didn't blow. Wayne stayed down. It was obvious he was hurt but still Poll didn't blow. The crowd were baying for him to stop the game but he wouldn't. He let Wayne lie there and Arsenal pressed forward. Their move should have broken down when they played a loose pass that was going straight to Michael Tonge. But Poll got himself in a bloody mess, got in the way of it and collided with Tonge.

Now Wayne and Tongey were both out of the picture and Arsenal broke quickly. Francis Jeffers whipped in a cross, Sylvain Wiltord knocked it against a post and had a shot blocked and then Freddie Ljungberg followed it up and crashed his shot into the roof of the net. Well, I went berserk. I couldn't believe what Poll had done. I couldn't believe he hadn't blown up on one of three occasions, including when he collided with Tonge. At his level, there's no excuse for that kind of shoddy positioning. It shouldn't happen. He just couldn't be bothered to be in the right position. Quite frankly, I don't believe Poll wanted to stop the game. I don't think he wanted to stop Arsenal scoring.

The worst thing for me was that at half time, he walked off the pitch smiling like a Cheshire cat. Great big grin plastered all over his face like it was the best day of his life. We had steam coming out of our ears and he was smiling and joking with his linesmen. He was loud and proud, Graham Poll, just like he always is. But then he hadn't seen how much work we had put into our Cup run. He hadn't been there when we'd got so close against Liverpool. And now he was grinning. Grinning. It was unbelievable.

He was smiling away as if he was enjoying it. But there is no way that goal would have happened if Graham Poll had been doing his job. We had chances after that, I know. David Seaman made a fantastic reaction save from Peschisolido's header in the dying minutes but we should have scored three times in the space of ten seconds in that sequence. Carl Asaba should have scored with a volley but he mishit it. Peschi should have scored the header and Jagielka should have scored when the ball broke loose. But I didn't blame any of them for our defeat. I blamed Poll.

15

REFEREES UNDER SCRUTINY

I AM A qualified referee. So was my dad. Me, Neil Warnock, the scourge of officialdom, the terror of men in black everywhere, part of a refereeing dynasty. When I was playing at Rotherham United, I refereed in the Sheffield Sunday League. I got to Class 2 but I couldn't go any higher because you had to do Saturday games to qualify for that and I was always playing. I used my refereeing as a way of having a warm-down on a Sunday. It was better than going out jogging on my own and I enjoyed the games. The league was always short of referees and I thought I'd help out.

The players knew who I was, knew I was a professional player, so I didn't get quite as much lip as the rest of the refs in the league. If I did get any lip, I'd tell them what to do. I'd swear at them like my dad used to do. He would give them some back and shut them up.

'If you'd made as few mistakes as me, you'd have had a good game, son,' I used to say to them.

The hardest teams I ever refereed were Arbourthorne EA,

which was a working men's club in Sheffield, and Hoyland Town Jags from Barnsley, who were the Rolls-Royce of the league. Arbourthorne's number six was the hardest man I have ever watched. I used to love refereeing that match because I knew it was going to be a difficult game. I got a lot of satisfaction out of my refereeing.

My dad was better than me. He was a Class 1 referee. I went to watch him quite a lot when I was a kid. He would swear at players and keep them in line. He would manage a game and the players respected him. But he had a chip on his shoulder about the fact that he never made it to the top of the refereeing ranks.

'I don't sell enough raffle tickets, son,' he said.

He was a bit envious of a mate of his called George McCabe who knew all the right people. George and my dad were the same standard but George got a lot higher up the ladder. My dad didn't say the right things to the people who could have helped him.

A psychologist could probably have a field day with me about that. I can understand what the theory might be: my dad didn't reach the top because he wouldn't bow his head and tug his forelock and therefore I resent the present-day referees who have made it. I don't respect them because I know some of them haven't got to where they are for the right reasons. It is possible, I suppose, that some of those thoughts are lurking somewhere deep in the recesses of my mind but, if they are, I've never been aware of them.

I do feel that when referees went full time it did change some of them, and not all for the better. My dad always said if you don't notice the referee they have usually had a good game, and he was right. There are referees now who like the limelight and talking to big name players, but I think they forget we haven't come to see them.

I remember going to see Graham Poll in his room at Old Trafford in the aftermath of Sheffield United's FA Cup semi-final defeat to Arsenal. He was just how I would have imagined him to be. Not a chance of him even beginning to think he might have made a mess of things. I told him I couldn't understand why he hadn't stopped the game. He said he didn't think the challenges in question were fouls. The collision with Michael Tonge was an accident, he said, and he didn't see any reason to stop the game even though we had lost our advantage. I said a referee of his calibre should have positioned himself better to avoid the collision. I could tell as I was talking to him that it was a waste of time.

He didn't seem to give a toss about Neil Warnock and Sheffield United. He had come to referee the semi-final of the FA Cup. It was his big afternoon out. It was a great occasion and he wasn't going to let Sheffield United or Neil Warnock spoil it. The hurt that I felt over that semi-final, I felt for years. I felt a sense of betrayal that day. Why did he laugh, why did he smile when he came off at half time?

Keith Hackett, the general manager of the Professional Game Match Officials Board, asked him once why he had smiled and he said it was because he was enjoying the occasion. I couldn't accept that. He was dismissive to me. I can't begin to tell you how long it took to put the disappointment away I felt for all my lads who had put so much in to get us so far and then were undone by this one incident. I couldn't get it out of my mind.

It took me three years to get some real closure on the unfairness of that day. I didn't feel gleeful when Poll booked the same player, Josip Simunic, three times during Croatia's draw with Australia in the 2006 World Cup. I didn't gloat when my mobile phone started beeping with message after message from people who were pissing themselves laughing about what Poll had just done.

But part of me was glad it had happened to him. I knew he'd finally be feeling the same kind of hurt I felt that day of the semi-final against Arsenal. Now he knew how it felt to be hurt and humiliated. I knew that he had set his heart on refereeing the World Cup Final that summer and suddenly his dream was gone and everyone was laughing at him. The incident with the three yellow cards was payback time for me.

He thought of himself as a showman. Usually, the referees don't feel the hurt. They just make their mistakes and go on to the next match. They are not bothered really. They don't feel hurt and pain. But he did when he showed those three yellow cards. Because it stopped him doing something that he dearly wanted to do. I thought it might teach him some humility.

When he quit refereeing at the end of the 2006-07 season, he wrote a long, self-pitying piece in a newspaper about all the terrible treatment he had received from the FA. And he said he had been 'bleeding internally' from the wounds of his 'three-card trick' at the World Cup. I laughed at that. So now he does know how I felt that day at Old Trafford.

I got to the point during Sheffield United's season in the Premiership where I hoped that we were handed Poll as referee in our matches against the big teams. That way, the decisions he was going to give against us wouldn't end up costing us the game because the odds were we were going to lose anyway. I hoped that maybe we could use up our quota of shocking decisions against Manchester United, Chelsea, Arsenal and Liverpool.

I didn't want Poll when we were playing Watford, Wigan and the like. It had been personal between me and him for several years. It was bound to be. When somebody like me confronts you and you don't like what I say and the way I say it, you are bound to remember things and keep things hidden inside. If I was a referee, I would do the same.

In my view we suffered at the hands of one of his decisions again in Sheffield United's promotion season from the Championship in 2005-06. Actually we were already promoted but I still wasn't beyond his reach. Three games before the end of the season, we played Leeds United at Bramall Lane and, even though we were already up, there was a lot of tension around the match because the clubs are fierce rivals and Kevin Blackwell, my old sidekick, was their manager. Poll was the referee.

It started kicking off on the touchline. The bloke who was Blackie's assistant, John Carver, is somebody else I have not got a lot of time for and he was mouthing off to the fourth official for most of the first half. They appealed for a penalty in the first half, which wasn't a bad shout, but the linesman didn't flag for it.

So John Carver devoted all his energy to abusing the fourth official.

He was calling him every name under the sun. I told the fourth official he shouldn't let Carver speak to him like that but he didn't do anything about it.

A couple of months earlier, the same fourth official invented something I said to Mark Halsey during our home game against Reading. What had happened was that the Reading winger, Bobby Convey, had taken a dive in the box and the referee had given a penalty. In the uproar that followed, Convey came sprinting past our dugout.

He held one finger up in the air and winked at me.

'It was never a penalty,' Convey said, laughing.

That sent me nuts, obviously.

'You cheating bastard,' I yelled at him as he ran off.

The fourth official told Halsey I'd been shouting at him instead but the match assessor had seen Convey wink and Halsey didn't take it any further.

Anyway, while Carver was getting stuck into this fourth official, the Leeds right back, Gary Kelly, did three terrible tackles in quick succession. One on Jagielka on the byline that was over the top. One on Kabba in central midfield that was over the top. And one on Craig Short that could easily have broken his leg. Poll looked at all of them and did absolutely nothing. So I shouted down the touchline at Blackie.

'If he keeps going like that,' I yelled, 'he'll break some fucker's leg. But he'll break his own leg one day and it'll serve him right.'

Carver went ballistic then. He came out with the old garbage about me telling my players to break an opponent's leg. That wasn't what I had said at all. Wally Downes came out with the same stuff when we played at Reading the following season. I've never told a player of mine to break an opponent's leg but I do get annoyed when honest professionals on my own team are subjected to shocking challenges that go unpunished by unknowing referees.

I think the first time I said something like that was when I was in charge at Notts County and Steve Bull took out our centre half, Dean Yates, somewhere just below the knee when we played against Wolverhampton Wanderers. I told Bull that he deserved to have his own legs broken if he tackled like that but he turned it round into saying that I told my lads to break his legs. Steve Bull should have thought about how he could have ended a bloke's career before he started mouthing off about what I was supposed to have said.

So against Leeds, Graham Poll came over and talked to the fourth official about my behaviour. Carver was there spouting.

'Get him fucking off,' he was shouting from further down the touchline.

Poll said the fourth official had explained certain things and that he was asking me to leave for the stands.

'Has he told you what Carver's been saying to him as well?' I asked Poll.

But, of course, he didn't want to know about that. I was just about to go down the tunnel in disgust when a policeman wandered over to lead me away just in case. I don't know what they thought I was going to do but I was very wound up.

The fourth official refused to say anything to Carver when I was convinced he too should have been told to leave the pitch.

I got a six-match touchline ban for that. Well, for that and for what happened at Carrow Road when we played Norwich a few weeks earlier. We lost 2-1 and, even though I was gutted, I went right across to the Norwich dugout and put my hand out to shake hands with Nigel Worthington, the Norwich boss. But Worthington blanked me. He caught my eye and then turned away. I put my hand out again and he blanked me again.

So I flicked him a V-sign.

'Wanker,' I shouted at him and went down the tunnel.

So for my behaviour against Norwich and Leeds, I was charged with improper conduct. I pleaded guilty. The six-match touchline ban wasn't too bad, particularly as four of them were suspended. I requested a personal hearing because I wanted my case heard. Barry Bright was the chairman of the disciplinary commission and he was fair, just as he always is. Mick Maguire has joked that I've been in front of Barry Bright so many times that he's almost like family. I got a £750 fine for the Norwich episode and £1,000 for the incident against Leeds.

Before he quit at the end of the 2006-07 season, I still thought Poll was the best referee for the big games. I'd have had him in charge of Chelsea v Man U or Arsenal v Liverpool every time. I just wouldn't have let him do anything else. It's hard on the players from the smaller clubs when it seems like the referees know the bigger players – the Shearers, the Rooneys, the Thierry Henrys.

After our game against Liverpool on the opening day of the

2006-07 season, Rob Styles gave an interview on television about the late penalty he had awarded to Steven Gerrard.

'Steven was impeded,' he said.

But he couldn't even remember Chris Morgan's name. He had to call him 'the centre half from Sheffield United'.

Some referees are nice people. I know that. Some of them are genuine. But, through no fault of their own, most of them have never played the game so they have no understanding of what is happening in certain situations. They can't spot the tricks of the trade. I can name a lot of referees who would get 90 per cent of the game absolutely spot on but when they have to make a major decision, they get it wrong because they have never played the game.

There is a group of manufactured referees and Steve Bennett is their leader. Steve is a good ref on rules but he has no feeling at all about the game and will never, ever do anything that bends the rules. He will never handle a situation by acting as a human being. If he had that human element – and I have told him this – he would be an absolutely top referee.

He booked Michael Tonge at Anfield in Sheffield United's Premiership season for coming back on to the pitch before he had given him permission. Technically, he was correct, but Tonge had looked across and seen Steve Bennett waving his arm towards him and assumed that was the signal. He had told Tonge he would wave him straight back on. Actually, Steve was signalling for the Liverpool keeper to take the goal kick. The goalie kicked the ball, Tonge headed it, Steve Bennett booked him. It was his fifth booking of the season. It cost him a suspension and it cost us one of our best players.

When Steve Bennett goes to sleep, he probably has dreams about the rulebook. I asked him if he thought his assessors would have marked him down if he had ordered the goal kick to be retaken and told Tonge to go back to the sideline. It was a genuine mistake from Tonge. But Steve couldn't grasp that concept. It was in the rulebook, therefore Michael Tonge had to be booked.

Mike Riley's the same. I've never been a fan of his. He's another rule fanatic. He's a timid type. I waited for him after a game once at Hartlepool when he was just beginning his refereeing career and he sneaked out of another door. I caught him in the car park just when he thought he'd got away. In one way, I've got to take my hat off to him: somehow, for reasons I cannot comprehend, he has got to a stage where he is considered one of our best referees.

I remember at West Ham in 2006-07, we scored an equaliser in the ninety-second minute and he disallowed it. He disallowed it because our right back Derek Geary, who is practically a midget and was certainly the smallest man on the pitch, went up for a challenge with Robert Green, the West Ham keeper. Green dropped it and Rob Kozluk put it in.

It was never a foul and I spoke to Mike Riley about it afterwards.

'Even now, Mike, when you've had time to think about it and see it again,' I said, 'do you still think that was a foul?'

'Yes, I do,' he said. 'Yes, yes.'

'That's fine,' I said. 'I'm not fucking surprised.'

I'll never forget one of the first referees' meetings I attended. It was at Filbert Street. Cloughie was there and Graham Taylor. Somebody was talking about the laws of the game and Philip Don, who was in a referees' overseeing role at that time, interrupted.

'Excuse me,' he said, 'but could I just make it clear to everyone in the room that there are no grey areas now. You have asked for consistency, so there are going to be no grey areas. Common sense will not come into it.'

I saw Cloughie shake his head and look at Graham Taylor as if to say that if common sense can't come into refereeing then we are never ever going to improve.

There are some referees who want to understand. I raved about Mark Clattenburg when he first started officiating in the Championship and tried to get him on the Premiership list straight away. But I have seen him change over the years. He was more humble when he started out. He knew he wasn't always right. But now, even if he's wrong, he's right.

Midway through the season, Clattenburg turned down a penalty shout against a Manchester United player. It was a good shout and he didn't give it. Gary Neville ran the full length of the pitch to harangue Clattenburg and argue with him. Twenty minutes later, Cristiano Ronaldo went down when he hadn't been touched and Clattenburg couldn't wait to give it. I had a chat with Phil Jagielka about it.

'Why don't you go and run fifty yards and get under the referee's nose?' I said to Jaggy. 'Why don't you yell at them when they don't get things right? Why don't you go and put pressure on them?'

'Gaffer,' he said, 'I don't do it because if Phil Jagielka ran fifty yards and gesticulated like Gary Neville did, I'd get a yellow card straight away.'

It took me aback because when he said it I knew he was right. The refs don't like Gary Neville because he stands up for himself and he doesn't indulge their fantasies about being his friend. But he is the captain of Manchester United so they're still scared of him. The top players get away with so much more than Blackburn Rovers or Bolton Wanderers or Sheffield United players can get away with.

The refs aren't all bad. I know that. I had a bee in my bonnet about Alan Wiley for a long time because of a string of his decisions that had gone against me but now I think of him as one of the best there is. When we had him against Charlton towards the end of the 2006-07 season, he was always close to the incidents and he was always in charge but he wasn't in the headlights. He just went about his job. He didn't want everyone talking about him. That's how my dad used to referee.

Rob Styles has good days. After one of them, when he refereed the 2005 Arsenal-Manchester United FA Cup Final, I wrote to him and told him I couldn't believe it was the same person out there in the middle as the man who had begun his refereeing career so uncertainly. He didn't book everyone and he actually man-managed the game. In fact, he was outstanding.

But he has bad days, too. He very rarely admits he is wrong, even if it's obvious. When Steven Gerrard went down at Bramall Lane late on in the first game of our Premiership season, Rob gave a penalty and at first he said that Chris Morgan, our captain, had made contact with Gerrard. But after the game, his associates and the TV people had told him there was no contact so he changed his story. He did an interview saying he had given the penalty because of Morgan's intention to bring Gerrard down and the fact that he hadn't actually touched him didn't matter. The television interview made him look stupid. If you gave free kicks for intent, you'd never finish a game. I'm sure the refereeing top brass cringed when they saw that interview. But, anyway, he gave the penalty and it cost us two vital points.

Then, near the end of the season when we were playing Manchester United, our striker, Luton Shelton, was brought down by Gabriel Heinze at Old Trafford and Rob didn't give a penalty.

'That should have been a penalty and a red card. I hope it doesn't cost us later,' I told Rob afterwards. 'Little did I know that we'd be relegated by one goal. I wonder if Rob thought about it later.'

'I wasn't one hundred per cent sure, so I couldn't give it,' he said.

'Well, surely you could have asked your linesman,' I said. 'He had a good view.'

'It was my decision,' Rob said, 'not the linesman's.'

That confused me totally. I always understood that if a referee wasn't sure, he looked to his assistant for help. Anyway, if he couldn't see it, surely he must have seen the intent, because it was even more obvious than Chris Morgan's intent on the first day of the season. Couldn't he see there was intent there at Old Trafford, too? Rob Styles goes round the houses that many times that he trips himself up.

Mark Halsey? He tries to handle everything. He is not great positionally. Because he is better at handling things, he doesn't get as close as he might to incidents. But I never worry about having him. You always know that he is going to have a rapport with you. He will admit it if he is wrong. He is not an arrogant referee. If he makes a mistake, he will put his hand up.

Peter Walton? I've always liked him, even though he gets slaughtered in some quarters. If he could just be a bit stronger personality-wise, he could become a very good referee. Because he looks small, he probably doesn't blow his whistle loud enough. He does try to manage games, though. He's not a Steve Bennett-style robot.

Martin Atkinson? He's a genuine person who hasn't got any airs and graces.

Lee Mason? I like him. He's fair. He treats you the same whether you are a big club or a small club. He's not star-struck like so many of them.

Phil Dowd? I like him, too. I sympathised with the Wigan Athletic manager, Paul Jewell, when he went ballistic at him, because I've seen Phil miss major things but, in general, I like the way he talks to players. He has my respect. His style reminds me a bit of the way Neil Midgley used to referee. He used to make the decision he thought was right, irrespective of whether his assessor would mark him up or down.

Howard Webb? Another good ref, but because he's local we don't get him. A few times in our Premiership season, he let the linesman make major decisions where he could have done it himself. But I would still like to have him refereeing us.

Overall, I think the standard is much of a muchness. We had a good group of referees a few years ago and we have got another group threatening to come through now. I don't think we will see too many of them come to the fore until some of the others have retired, but men like Watson and Mason are a bit more human than the ones who have gone before.

They all need more help, too. Goal-line technology has got to come in now. I think penalty box technology has got to come in. I'm in favour of giving bans to people for diving on retrospective evidence. We should do divers. They are too clever for referees. They are too clever for a lot of us. So we should do them with the help of television evidence. They should be banned for five or six games. They could soon stop it.

There should be two referees at every match or there should be video technology. If a fourth official had looked at our penalty claim at Old Trafford, it would have only taken him ten seconds to see that it was legitimate. What is wrong with holding the game up for ten seconds? It is the major decisions that win you games and get you relegated. I can tell you all about that. Jim Devine's decision that allowed a goal for West Ham at Blackburn Rovers to stand in March 2007 when the ball hadn't crossed the line was one of many factors that contributed to sending us down. The fact that we haven't got goal line technology in the year 2007 in a hi-tech age and a billion pound league is an absolute joke. It's beyond me.

Even if they had more technology at their disposal, what they really need to improve standards is an ex-player or an ex-manager to advise them about the way situations develop on the field of play. The biggest problem with referees is that they don't have anyone educating them from our side. No one from the shop floor. No ex-players. No ex-managers. It's farcical when you think about it. It's negligent.

It should be common sense that the people who have played the game and lived with it at close quarters for most of their lives will know it the best. They will know its nuances and its rhythms. They will see things that others won't be able to see. They will see problems arising quicker than anyone else. They will have a sixth sense about the game of football. Keith Hackett has moved mountains since he took over but the situation is still essentially the same: referees are educating referees. The mistakes are inbred. All they are doing is passing on their errors to new generations.

What they need is somebody who has played the game but who is not a threat to them. I was a big fan of the idea of full-time refs for a while but I am not sure it is the answer. When good new refs start training with the big hitters, they just become one of them. They go over to the dark side. For that reason, I am not sure it is beneficial to have them all together when they have their training weekends. But I do think they have to be educated. They have got to have a Graham Taylor-type that has played the game or managed the game educating them.

I'm a qualified ref. Like I said, I'm part of a refereeing dynasty. Sometimes, I'll go to matches and it will be the ref who catches my eye. I went to watch a reserve match between Chesterfield and Man

City at Saltergate in the spring of 2007 and there was a young Geordie officiating.

I went in at half time and told him I was really enjoying watching him referee. He wasn't fussy and he handled everything. He helped the game. He didn't hinder it.

'Don't tell any of your mob I've been down here paying you compliments,' I said, 'or they'll fucking blackball you.'

16
FALLING BACK

I N THE DAYS after the FA Cup semi-final defeat to Arsenal in 2002-03, I had nightmares about Graham Poll. Specifically, I had nightmares about him grinning. His big grinning face kept coming to me in my sleep. He was grinning like that doll in the horror movie. It woke me up in a cold sweat a few times. It was bloody horrible.

But somehow, we had to try and lift ourselves again for the league. Portsmouth and Leicester City were well clear at the top in the two automatic promotion places but we were right in amongst the chasing pack and I wanted to make sure we didn't slip out of the play-off places. We got a lucky break straight away. We asked Nottingham Forest if they would put back our Tuesday night match with them after the FA Cup semi-final to the Wednesday to give us an extra day's recovery time. They refused. I used that to gee my lads up before the game. I told them Forest thought we'd be tired and that we wouldn't run. Well, we battered them that night. It was the worst 1-0 beating a team ever took.

We finished third that season. And there, waiting for us in the play-offs, were Forest. The first leg was at their place. What a fantastic club, Forest. They get 25,000 whatever division they are in. It was always lively for me at the City Ground because of my Notts County connections and, to add a bit more spice to it, there wasn't a lot of love lost between our staff and theirs. I didn't mind their manager, Paul Hart, but I didn't like his assistant, Ian Bowyer. I didn't have much time for him at all. We got out of there with a 1-1 draw after Michael Brown equalised a goal from David Johnson.

The second leg was one of the greatest games ever played in my years at Bramall Lane. There were 30,000 in the ground and the atmosphere was unbelievable. Then David Johnson broke after half an hour and put them 1-0 up. We laid siege to their goal after half time but then they put a cross in, we didn't clear it and, bang, Andy Reid had put them 2-0 up. Everyone thought it was all over then. The crowd was deflated. It was doom and gloom. We were feeling sorry for ourselves and I yelled to Brownie and Jagielka to get things going again.

When Forest had taken the lead, their bench were dancing about on the touchline, hugging and celebrating. I could see Bowyer cavorting about out of the corner of my eye. When they went 2-0 up, they came even further out of their dugout, throwing themselves around on the touchline and all that, shaking their fists and pointing their fingers. I could see Bowyer having a go. I gritted my teeth.

Then, two minutes after they had gone 2-0 up, Michael Brown got us back into the game and I knew we had a real chance. Bowyer and the rest of their mob retreated a bit into their dugout. I had brought Steven Kabba on at half time and he had galvanised everyone. He put us level after sixty-eight minutes with a fabulous goal. Bowyer and the rest of them slunk further back into the shadows.

We took the game into extra time. Midway through the second period, Peschisolido put us 3-2 up and the scenes when he scored were amazing. The Forest boys disappeared so deep into their dugout it looked like they were trying to tunnel out of the back of it. Three minutes before the end of extra time, Des Walker stuck a leg out and deflected a shot into his own net that made it 4-2 for us. We gave them a bit of a sniff when Robert Page scored an own goal to make it 4-3 and they missed a sitter at the death that would have taken it to penalties.

What a game. It was mind-blowing. The emotions were incredible. Up, down, up, down. Desperation turning to elation and then back to desperation again. It was the most amazing game I had been in charge of up until that time. Later on, I came out of our dressing room and saw Paul Hart sitting on the steps in the tunnel with his head in his hands. I felt sorry for him. I liked him. I didn't like his staff but I liked him.

That'll finish him, that, I thought to myself. It'll break his heart. It did, too. Forest never got over it. Neither did Paul. They got relegated at the end of 2004-05 and he slid out of the top echelons of the game.

We played Wolves in the play-off final at Cardiff. I was confident we could beat them. We'd finished two places above them in the league and I thought we were all going to get our shot at the Premiership. It didn't happen. It turned into one of the worst days of my career.

Part of it was my fault. I made a mistake in my team selection. Brian Clough had once told me always to pick what I felt in my head was my strongest team and never to let sentiment get in the way. But for the play-off final, I felt obliged to play Steven Kabba from the start because of the impact he had had in the second leg of the tie against Forest. I felt we owed our place in the final to him and that it would be unfair to leave him out. Unfair shouldn't have come into it.

In my heart of hearts I knew that when we played one up front against Wolves, we always beat them. If we were strong in midfield, we caught them on the break. We had beaten them that season at Molineux 3-1 and drawn with them 3-3 at Bramall Lane. I wanted to play one up but I didn't want to leave Kabba out. I should have played Asaba up front on his own but I changed it to accommodate Kabba. That was fatal.

Wolves set out to kick us off the park in the opening ten minutes. They went after Michael Brown and caught him with two whoppers. Steve Bennett, the referee, did nothing about it, even though one of the challenges was worth a straight red. For the one and only time in his refereeing life, Steve Bennett decided to be lenient. His wiring must have had a temporary malfunction.

And to be fair to Wolves, they were too good for us after that. They were two up after twenty-two minutes with goals from Mark Kennedy and Nathan Blake. We never got going and Blake destroyed us for half an hour. We couldn't cope with him. He turned us inside out. He was brilliant. They scored a third on the stroke of half time through Kenny Miller and that was it.

I waited for Steve Bennett as he was coming off at half time. I told him he was a disgrace. Why had he let the fouls on Brown go unpunished, I asked him. I protested fairly vigorously and one of his lackeys came to see me in the changing rooms a few minutes later and said the referee had asked him to tell me to stay away from the dugouts and the technical area in the second half. I had been sent off. So I went upstairs and watched it from a box.

We got a penalty early in the second half and I believe to this day that if Michael Brown had scored that penalty, we would have given them a right game. But he missed it. And then there really was no way back. I was pleased for the Wolves manager, Dave Jones, because he's a smashing lad, but what a terrible anticlimax that was. What a terrible night. We had already arranged to stay at a hotel in Cardiff and all the staff were there, and there had obviously been a celebration planned in the event we had won. I just wanted to go to bed.

I felt incredibly low. It had been a great season but ultimately we had got nothing out of it. That even applied to me at the League Managers' Association annual Manager of the Year dinner. They had sent the voting forms around earlier in the season and I had shouted down to Blackie to ask who we should vote for.

'Dario at Crewe,' he said, 'or Moyesey.'

David Moyes had had a great first full season at Everton. He was a top man as well.

'Yeah, Moyesey,' I said. 'We'll put Moyesey down.'

We gave him our top choice, which was worth six votes.

Towards the end of the season, I got a phone call from the LMA telling me to make sure I came to the dinner because I had been short-listed for the main award.

At the end of the evening, the compère announced the winners.

'In third place, Sir Alex Ferguson,' he said.

Then he said the first two were only separated by two votes.

'Second place goes to a manager who led his team to two semi-finals and the play-off finals,' he said. 'Neil Warnock.'

I went up and got my claps.

As I was making my way back to my seat, the compère started speaking again.

'And the winner of the Manager of the Year award this season is David Moyes,' he said.

Bloody typical. The nearest I ever came to a big accolade and I'd voted myself out of it.

I was thinking about packing it in by then. And then things got worse. A few days after the play-off final, I got a call from a journalist who told me Kevin Blackwell was leaving to join Peter Reid at Leeds United and he was taking the fitness guy, Dean Riddle, with him. Blackie was my mate. I trusted him. We had been together for sixteen years. And I was hearing this from a journalist. I tried to pretend I knew all about it but I felt sick.

I had brought Blackie up from nothing. He was a great lad who did everything for me. He was good to have around the place, a very bubbly character. I liked him. He would do anything for me at any minute of the day. I let him do a little bit of coaching at Plymouth and from then on, I took him everywhere with me. He was a superb lad and I looked after him.

If he had come to me and said he wanted to go to Leeds with Peter Reid, then I would have wished him good luck. I would have been disappointed but I would have respected his decision. I wouldn't have stood in his way. But to have to hear it from a journalist was like a twist of the knife.

He rang me up when the news began to leak out but he wouldn't come clean.

'Gaffer,' he said, 'I don't know anything about these rumours about Leeds.'

I knew everything that had happened by then anyway. After I got the call from the journalist, I had made some enquiries.

'Things like this don't just happen, Blackie,' I said. 'I know you've been planning it for a while.'

When I began to think back, all the pieces fell into place. I looked at the pictures of us all celebrating after the Forest semi-final victory and there was something about Blackie even then that told you his heart wasn't in it. He was on the pitch celebrating with me but he wasn't really there. He wasn't the same.

He definitely wasn't with me in Cardiff for the final. Rob Styles, the fourth official, warned him before the game that they were ready to do me if I stepped out of line. But Blackie didn't pass the message on. He never told me to be careful. He never told me they were gunning for me. I don't know why. I just think his mind was elsewhere. He was already thinking about Leeds.

I know it sounds excessive but I felt in those first days after I found out about his Leeds move as if a member of my family had died. My friends still dislike him for what he did and the way he left me in the lurch but the two of us are okay again now. After he got sacked by Leeds, he started showing up at Bramall Lane again and wandering into my office. He's still my mate but it will never be the same as it was.

I felt totally let down. There was a group of fans who wanted me out and suddenly I had to find a new assistant, a new fitness guy and new players. I had to lift the club after we had come so near and ended so far away. I didn't know whether I wanted the hassle.

I mean, where could I go from there? How do you follow two Cup semi-finals and the play-off final? There's only one way to go from there unless you get promotion. There were these fans who wanted shut of me so I knew it was going to be hard. Maybe that is how Blackie felt. Maybe he felt it was the right time to jump.

Soon after the journalist phoned me, Alf Arton, a bloke who was mates with me and Blackie from our Scarborough days, confirmed that Blackie and Dean Riddle were going to Leeds. We were both shocked about how it had all come about. And then, on the phone-ins, a lot of people started speculating that Kevin Blackwell was the reason why we had got to two semi-finals and the play-off final. People started to say it was all down to him and maybe the board should have kept him and let me go. Do they not understand who the hell the manager is? I thought. And in a strange kind of way, the fact that Blackie was leaving and the manner in which he chose to leave made me think twice about quitting. It gave me a new determination to make sure that people didn't think it was Kevin Blackwell who was responsible for everything we achieved.

It had been an exhausting season and now I only had a few weeks to regroup before the start of the new one. I moped around a bit down in Cornwall. I brooded about Blackie. It gnawed away at me. In the end, Sharon said she wanted to have a chat.

'I know you don't want to hear this,' she said, 'but don't you think it's about time you stopped feeling sorry for yourself? You're a lucky person. You've just had a fantastic season, you're one of the best managers around. Are you going to let Blackie destroy everything when you know you can get the club back where it belongs. You keep on about showing people, so start showing them.'

That got my chin off the floor. That night, I let the dog out and went into the garden. It was a clear sky. I thought I saw a shooting star. She's right, I thought. The next day I got up and started making calls. I got myself off my backside. I drove on.

17

THE FINAL PUSH
TO THE PREMIERSHIP

S O I STARTED AGAIN. I had three weeks to get ready for pre-season training. I appointed David Kelly, who had previously been on the playing staff, as my assistant, and he suggested Tony Daley, the former Aston Villa and England winger, as a new fitness guy. Tony was with Forest Green Rovers in non-league football so it was a bit of a gamble for me. I snatched a week's holiday in Cornwall and asked him to come down.

I got him to put a session on at Duchy College which is near my house in the West Country. They always let me have the facilities when I went down there with the team. So I got a group of students out of their classes and Tony put a session on for them. He was young and he was raw and he hadn't worked at anywhere near Championship level but he was such a nice lad and I thought he might as well start somewhere. It might as well be at Sheffield United. I gave him a chance and he grabbed it. He worked very, very hard.

The first game of the new season was Gillingham at home. I knew it was going to be horrible. The last match the fans had seen was a Wembley play-off final so there was bound to be a hangover from that. The sense of anticlimax was everywhere. We drew 0-0 and I sensed in the crowd that some were going to cause me problems. I knew already that that season was going to be about stopping the club going into freefall. We had expended so much effort the previous season that it would have been incredibly easy to let it all go.

When we drew our second game 0-0 as well, this time away at West Ham, the muttering increased. The supporters were saying on the phone-ins that maybe the club shouldn't have let Blackwell go. Just like when he left, they were saying maybe they should have let me go instead. But I wasn't going to cave in now. I stuck two fingers up to all the doubters and showed them who was really in charge. New staff, new start.

Things picked up after that. It wasn't as good a season as the year before but it wasn't bad. We got to the quarter-finals of the FA Cup where we lost to Sunderland at the Stadium of Light. And in the league, we were there or thereabouts all year. In fact, we only missed out on the play-offs on the last day when we failed to win at Preston.

The next season was very similar. I tried to make improvements but they didn't always work. In December 2004 I paid Brighton £250,000 for a central defender called Danny Cullip. I bought him because I thought he was a leader and a talker and we needed a talker. Well, he was a talker all right. It was just that he didn't really say the right things.

He talked for effect, basically. Nothing was ever his fault. It was obvious very quickly that he wasn't fitting in with the rest of the lads. It came to a head one morning when he had words with Michael Tonge at training. Tonge asked him to give him a simple ball but Danny Cullip thought he was Franz Beckenbauer. He didn't play it simple so Tonge said something to him and Cullip laced into Tongey. I knew it wasn't working. I pulled him into my office one morning and told him I didn't want him around any more.

'You don't fit in with us, Danny,' I said. 'I think it would be best for all of us if we sold you on.'

Well, he went ballistic then.

'You're the worst fucking manager I've ever had,' he said. 'You haven't got a fucking clue.'

'Thanks, Danny,' I said.

But he wasn't finished.

'You're the luckiest man I fucking know,' he said. 'You're so spawny to have a group of players like this playing for you.'

'Well, I signed most of them, Danny,' I said.

'I don't mind going,' he said, 'because this club's only going one fucking way with you in charge.'

'Thanks for the kind words, Danny,' I said. 'I'll do my best to get you away as quickly as possible.'

I sent him out to Watford on loan at the end of March 2005. He only played eleven games for us. Then in the summer, I got a right stroke of luck. I sold him to Gary Megson at Forest. Talk about a win double. Two for the price of one. It was like winning the lottery. I didn't speak to Megson, of course. Terry Robinson did all the negotiations.

'Tell them Danny's an example to everyone,' I told Terry. 'It's just that he hasn't fitted in.'

I'm sure Danny and Megson were very happy together. They were made for each other.

That winter, something else happened that made a huge difference. Sharon and the kids had been living in Cornwall for a couple of years because we thought that the quality of life for the children was so much better down there. I drove down there every Saturday night after the game and then drove back the following Monday. It was a punishing schedule but we thought it was worth it.

But when we were sitting around the table having our Christmas dinner, Amy, who was five then, started asking questions about our situation.

'Why can't we be a family like this all the time, daddy?' she said.

'Look, love,' I said, 'you don't want to live in a concrete jungle when you can live down in the country.'

'I'd rather be a family, daddy,' she said.

So the next day, we went to see a school for the kids, and Sharon, Amy and William moved back up to Sheffield. I felt a lot happier. The season was going okay as well. We had another good run in the FA Cup. We beat Aston Villa and West Ham and then we got bloody Arsenal again in the fifth round. We drew at Highbury and took the replay at Bramall Lane to extra time and penalties. I had started to dream of Cardiff again by then but Arsenal beat us 4-2 in the penalty shoot-out and went on to win the Cup.

We were still well placed for the play-offs. We beat Leeds 4-0 at Elland Road at the beginning of April, which felt particularly sweet, and then beat QPR at home. But then we began to fade. We drew at Forest, lost at home to Derby and drew at Watford. We had slipped down to eighth place. We went into our last home game of the season against Millwall needing to win to have any chance of squeezing into the play-offs.

Jody Morris scored after five minutes for them and they beat us 1-0. When the final whistle went, a group of about a hundred Sheffield United fans in the main stand behind my dugout started chanting 'Warnock Out' and shouting abuse. We had all gone straight down to the changing room but I told the lads they had to go back out and acknowledge the majority of the fans for their loyal support during the season.

'What about those other bastards, gaffer?' one of the lads said.

'That's not your problem,' I told them. 'It's me they're yelling at. Go out and stand up to them. Wave at them and smile at them.'

So the lads went out and did a reluctant lap of honour. Mick Jones and I sat there like Glum and Glummer.

'I'm not going out there just so those bastards can slaughter me,' I said.

He didn't say anything. We both had a cup of tea. I started to think.

'Why should I let a hundred fucking people destroy me?' I said to Mick suddenly. 'I'm going to go out there and you're coming with me.'

By the time we got out of the tunnel, the lads were on the other side of the pitch. I could hear the catcalls straight away. They had spotted me, the same group who'd been chanting at me at the final whistle. There was steam coming out of their ears by now. They were spitting blood, faces contorted. I smiled and clapped them and waved at them and gave them the thumbs up.

I looked at their little group.

You haven't got a fucking brain between you, I thought.

The rest of the ground were fabulous with me. I think they were pleased I had defied the mob.

My elder daughter Natalie was in the stand near to this group of thugs and she was crying her eyes out. She was distraught. She came down to my office later and she was still upset. I told her that for some of the supporters, for whatever reason, it was the only way they had of expressing themselves and that it hurt them more when I waved at them and smiled even if inside I was thinking, you bastards.

It was a horrible time. I was beginning to think it wasn't really worth it. It wasn't even as if we had had a bad season. I hadn't had much money to spend and I had still got the team to the verge of the play-offs and the fifth round of the FA Cup. But everybody was saying surely it's time for a change now, he can't take the club any further forward. And, you know what, I began to feel the same.

That's when I went to see Kevin McCabe.

'Listen, Kevin,' I said, 'if you can't give me some money to spend on new players now, I think you're better off getting a new manager. I can keep us in the top ten on nothing, like I have done for the past five years, but that's not enough for this lot any more. I know it's only a minority of fans, but I'm going to get slaughtered if I don't take us up and I can't do it on thin air. If you don't give me money to spend, we won't go up because we're not good enough.'

I knew that if I didn't get new players in and I lost the first couple of games of the following season, I would get a lot of stick. I had seen what had happened with Natalie and I didn't want any more of that. I didn't want it turning really nasty.

He asked me how much I wanted. I told him at least £2 million Not exactly a king's ransom but I already had a couple of players in mind who I thought could make a real difference.

'I don't want you to go,' he said. 'I'll give you some money to spend.'

So I went up to my post-match press conference and told the reporters I had no intention of packing it in. I was going to turn the club round and get them promoted, I told them. In the first two weeks of the close season, I bought Paul Ifill from Millwall for £800,000 and Danny Webber from Watford for £500,000. Clubs tend to buy their players towards the end of the summer so they don't have to pay their wages but I knew that if we didn't sign those two straight away, we wouldn't get them. I got David Unsworth on a free transfer from Portsmouth, too, and Keith Gillespie, who had been released by Leicester City.

As the new season approached, the talk was still that I would probably get the first six games and then I'd be out. Or, at best, that I'd get until Christmas. And then I'd be out. But I had confidence in the lads that I'd had with me for a few years and I was pleased with the players I had bought, particularly Keith Gillespie. He had had a trial at Leeds United, but Blackie didn't want him. Craig Short asked me if I'd take him. Keith was down on his luck but Short said that, despite his reputation, he was a good lad. So I took him up to Scarborough with us and played him in a reserve match up there on a Wednesday night. He played in a team of kids and first half he had a nightmare. He couldn't dribble, he couldn't cross, he couldn't pass.

At half time, I told him if he wanted a contract he was going to have to show me he could cross a ball. I told him I wasn't bothered how many times he lost it and I told everyone else in the team that every time they got the ball, I wanted them to give it to Keith. Well, the second half, he must have crossed sixteen balls. Six of them were crosses I thought it was impossible for him to make, when it seemed that the full back had closed him down or that the ball was running out of play. He was magnificent.

He'll do for me, I thought.

He had listened to me get stuck into him at half time and then he had responded. I pulled him after the game. I told him I was going to give him a contract. He thought I meant a month but I told him it was going to be a year. He looked at me in amazement. This was a lad who had been bombed out totally, nobody wanted him and there was no chance of him finding anywhere else and I was giving him a year on the strength of a second half at Scarborough.

A few weeks later, we went to Shrewsbury for a Carling Cup game and Gillespie played with all the kids on a shitty night. It was 0-0 and we won on penalties. When we got back to the ground at Sheffield, he was helping us unload the kit bags like all the senior players do even now. I told him that night that I was extending his contract to two years. He repaid me with his form that season and in our season in the Premiership.

In fact, he started repaying me the first league game of the 2005-06 season. Inevitably, it was against Leicester, the club that had released him after all the shenanigans in La Manga. I desperately needed a good start and we got one. I brought Gillespie on for Danny Webber after seventy-seven minutes with the scores level at 1-1 and he electrified the game. It had been a bit dreary until then but Kabba put us ahead with a penalty and then Gillespie crossed for Ifill to score a third. Leigh Bromby grabbed a fourth in the last minute to round things off.

And then something amazing happened. Something even I found hard to believe. We won ten of our first eleven league games. The only blip was QPR away. Apart from that, we ripped through them. By the beginning of October, ourselves and Reading were way, way clear of the rest. Reading beat us but we didn't waver. We only lost two of our first twenty games and stayed top until 22 November. We gave ourselves a real cushion. We needed it later.

Our start to the season turned a few heads. At the end of November, Portsmouth asked if they could speak to me. They had just parted company with their French manager, Alain Perrin, after a fairly disastrous spell in charge. I talked to Peter Storrie, their chief executive, and Milan Mandaric, the chairman. I met Milan somewhere near Oxford, halfway between Sheffield and Portsmouth, I suppose, and I was very impressed with what they had to say. I enjoyed talking to Milan. I liked him.

They offered me a three-year contract on top money in writing. It threw me into a dilemma. We were going well at the club but we had got beaten 4-2 at Leicester on 26 November and it should have been more than 4-2. I looked around the squad and I thought, I'm doing miracles here. That was the strength of our squad on a bad day. It was a reality check for me.

I was ill that week so I sent someone down on my behalf to speak to them about terms. I wanted it all sorting that week because we were playing Sheffield Wednesday at Bramall Lane on 3 December and I couldn't go into a match that important with the Portsmouth issue hanging over me. One way or another, I wanted it resolved before the Sheffield derby.

I told Kevin McCabe about Portsmouth's offer.

'You've got to stick it through here,' he said. 'This is your club. We are up there now. You have got to see it through.'

I showed him the fax with my offer from Portsmouth. It was more than twice what I was on at Bramall Lane.

'I'll sort you out,' Kevin said. 'If you get us up, I'll make sure you'll not be far off that next season.'

Some of the lads asked me to stay but, to be fair to Craig Short, he remembered what had happened at Notts County when I had got the offer from Chelsea and the lads had begged me to stay. He had had that on his conscience for a while. He told me he thought I ought to go to Portsmouth.

But things didn't go smoothly. George Best, who was a close friend of Milan Mandaric, had died on 25 November and his funeral had been arranged for the same day as the Sheffield derby.

Milan, quite understandably, was preoccupied with that. I spoke to him on the Wednesday and he said he was going to Best's funeral on the Saturday and he would like to leave the announcement of my arrival until the following Monday.

'That's no good to me, Milan,' I said. 'Not with Sheffield Wednesday at home on Saturday. I couldn't do that to the players.'

'So what shall we do?' Milan said.

'If you want to leave it until Monday, I think we should call it a day,' I said. 'I don't want to leave my team in the lurch and I don't want to leave Kevin McCabe in limbo.'

I would have been able to take charge of the game against Wednesday but I didn't want to do that if I knew I was going somewhere else. That's just not me. My head wouldn't have been right. On top of that, the kids had found out what was going on and Amy was getting morally blackmailed in the playground with people telling her there was no way her dad could leave. People were ringing us, people were walking up the school driveway with the kids and talking to me. It was emotionally draining for all of us. Sharon said she would support me but she made one very good point.

'You've always said you'd like to come back to Bramall Lane with William to watch games when you're not manager any more,' she said. 'But if you left the club when they were top of the table and they didn't go up, you wouldn't be able to go back because they'd always blame you.'

I phoned Milan.

'I don't hold it against you or anything, Milan,' I said, 'but I'd rather call it a day. We've got a big match on Saturday and I want to get my head round that. It's your club and you can do exactly what you want.'

When I had finished speaking to Mandaric, I called Kevin McCabe. I told him I was going to stay put. He told me I wouldn't regret it.

And I didn't regret it. I resented it when Kevin McCabe didn't keep his word and I wished I'd had the money that Portsmouth had been offering me but I didn't regret it. How could I regret immersing myself in the battle to get my club, my home town club, promoted to the Premiership against all the odds and with one of our fiercest rivals, Leeds United, chasing us all the way.

The press thought Leeds were bound to catch us. There was a bit extra riding on that issue for me because Blackie was still the Leeds manager then. There were a whole host of younger managers in the chasing pack, too. There was Iain Dowie at Crystal Palace and Aidy Boothroyd at Watford. But I stayed optimistic, even when our advantage began to shrink. While you are chasing, there is no pressure on you. There were no expectations for them at that point. But as soon as they caught us up, they couldn't cope with it. None of them. That's when we took off again.

We did have a very dodgy spell. Reading had disappeared into the distance at the top of the table and for part of February, going into March, there was a run of games where we only took six points out of a possible twenty-four. All the press were saying the bubble had burst and that Warnock had blown it. And, yes, obviously there were more calls for me to go.

Part of the problem was that, in an attempt to seal promotion, I had made a couple of signings in January and February. We were a bit short up front because we only had Neil Shipperley, who was a veteran, and Steve Kabba. So I had splashed a bit of money on Ade Akinbiyi from Burnley and Geoff Horsfield from West Brom to bolster our forwards and provide the final push over the finishing line and into the Premiership. But it didn't quite work out like that.

I tried to play Akinbiyi and Horsfield together and it didn't work. I tried to play one and not the other and that didn't work either. That's when we went on our bad run. Leeds, Watford and Palace started to catch us up and began mouthing off about how we were tying up.

I watched Geoff in training and it just wasn't what I wanted. I had no problem at all with him as a person but he just didn't fit into our style. Ade scored a winner against Sheffield Wednesday which was a great goal but he was struggling with the expectations at a big club. He's another lovely lad but it just wasn't happening.

Geoff and Ade didn't really hit it off or fit into the team. So I left them out. If I had been a younger manager, I couldn't have done that. I had spent more than a million quid on each of them and, if I'd been less experienced, I would have felt obliged to play them because your directors would have given you so much stick if you didn't. But I didn't do that. I told myself I had made a mistake but the bigger picture was that I could rectify the mistake and get promotion. That's why it didn't worry me.

I had one other trick up my sleeve. In the third week in March, with seven games to go, I brought in the former Olympic high jumper, Steve Smith, to give the lads a talk. He spoke for about twenty minutes and he was brilliant. His presentation was called Raising the Bar and it was based on his belief that you need to push yourself outside of your comfort zone.

He talked about how, during his competitive career, he often took risks when he was deciding what jumps to go for. If he only had one jump left, he would pass on achievable heights that would have placed him fourth or fifth and go for heights above his personal best in an effort to get the gold. He talked about making sure you left the competitive arena without any regrets. It made the hairs on the back of my neck stand up.

Leeds got to within two points of us at one stage. If they had beaten Palace at Elland Road on 21 March, they would have gone level with us. But they lost. By that stage, I had decided that, if I only had seven or eight games left, I was going to go back to Mr Reliable, Neil Shipperley. If we missed out, we would miss out fighting with the team that had got us where we were in the first place.

I got Shipperley into my office one day after training.

'Ships, I'm coming back with you,' I said, 'and I'm going to stick with you.'

And that was when we took off again. We started romping it. We won four out of our last seven and stayed unbeaten. All the others fell by the wayside. We beat Southampton, drew at Stoke and then beat Hull. We went to Cardiff City on Good Friday knowing that if we beat them and Leeds failed to beat Reading, who were already promoted, at Elland Road the next day, we were up.

It was a tense game at Ninian Park in bright sunshine. It looked like it was going to be a draw and I would probably have settled for that. We had Leeds at Bramall Lane the following midweek and we had to back ourselves to beat them. But then, with fourteen minutes to go, Danny Webber scored a great goal to give us the lead and we hung on for the victory.

I had my car at the ground and, after the game, I drove straight down to Cornwall. I wanted to go back up to Sheffield with the lads really but it wasn't mathematically certain that we were up and I had got so many jobs that I wanted to do at the house. I had some work with the machinery to do. I had to get a grass-cutter serviced and some work done on the tractor and I had arranged it all for the day after the game.

The day of the Leeds-Reading game, I did some work in the morning. I knew I couldn't watch the telly in the afternoon because it would be too much. I would be too nervous. So about two o'clock, I told Sharon I was going to do some weeding with one of the machines in the fields. There were thistles there that needed to be taken out because they disturbed the cattle.

So I went out there without the phone and I rode around on the tractor, doing my best to concentrate on the thistles. I came back in about 4.30. Sharon said I might as well come back in because Leeds were beating Reading 1-0 anyway. I rang Stuart McCall, my assistant, who was at the game. He said Reading would never score in a million years. He said it looked like they had already been on their holidays.

So, we were in the kitchen having a cup of tea, watching Sky Soccer Saturday on the little telly we've got in there. It got to 4.45 and they hadn't mentioned the Leeds score for a while. On the news ticker at the bottom of the screen, it seemed to have every result except Leeds. It got to 4.50 p.m. and there was still nothing, so I thought the game must be over.

I was resigned to the fact that Leeds were going to keep the race alive by then. I was starting to plan for the game against them at Bramall Lane the following Tuesday. But then the camera went back to the presenter, Jeff Stelling, who had a gleam in his eye.

'There's been another goal at Elland Road,' he said.

'Please God, please God,' I said to myself.

'Will it mean Sheffield have to wait until Tuesday or are they already promoted?' Jeff Stelling said.

Before he had time to give the answer, they flashed the score up on the screen. It was 1-1. Stephen Hunt had equalised for Reading in the eighty-fifth minute. Sharon and I jumped up and started hugging and kissing. I couldn't believe it. The next five minutes seemed like a lifetime but eventually they announced that the final whistle had gone and that the result was final.

Sharon and I had a few minutes together and then the bloody front door bell went. Before we knew where we were, every Tom, Dick and Harry was at the gate. There were camera crews and loads of reporters. The TV people brought champagne and everything. It was exhausting. I was in shock. I couldn't grasp what we'd done.

It was six years of hard work. Six years of striving for something. Six years of ups and downs. Six years of trying to keep it going. Six years of refusing to be beaten. Six years of rising above the cynicism of others. Six years of relentless motivation and struggling. It was too much to acknowledge. The photographers kept saying, 'Could you smile, you're a Premiership manager.' But I felt numb.

In the end, we decided to go for a meal. The only place around is our local pub. I rang them up.

'It's Neil Warnock here,' I said. 'Could you fit me and my wife in tonight?'

The guy didn't have a clue who I was. He said they were full.

We drove into the local village and there was a new kebab take-away place that had just opened. A farmer with some great big bloody Wellington boots came in to buy something. I bought one kebab for me and one for my missus. I was a Premiership manager but the stardust hadn't been sprinkled on me yet.

I looked at my missus.

'Wherever he is,' I said, 'I bet Jose isn't having a kebab tonight.'

18

ENTERTAINING RAFA

W E PLAYED IN the first game of the 2006-07 Premiership season. The very first. We kicked off at 12.45, before any of the others, rushing out into our brave new world on a bloody red hot afternoon in Sheffield. An hour before the start, one of my coaching staff came in. He said the Liverpool manager, Rafael Benitez, was complaining because the air-conditioning wasn't working in their changing room. He had asked if we could turn it on for them.

'Go back and tell Rafa this is Bramall Lane, Sheffield United,' I said. 'There isn't any air-conditioning in his changing room. They can have an electric fan if they want.'

We had only just got air-conditioning in the home dressing room, let alone the away one. The season before, when we were going for promotion and the weather was getting hotter as we moved into April, we had had a portable air-conditioning unit for a while. There was this big tube that went out through the tiles in the ceiling and it was the noisiest thing you could ever wish to meet. I couldn't even do a team talk with that thing blaring away. It was either sweat cobs in silence or be cool in a racket.

In the close season, I had told the chairman we had to do everything properly when we were promoted. We had to make a priority of getting as much done for ourselves as we could. When I went down there early in the summer, they had done loads of work on the away dressing room, the new press box, the away toilets and the new television lounge, but nothing for my lads. I changed that around.

Sod the opposition, I thought. I started getting things done for my lads instead.

I knew we would struggle to get points on the board early in the season. Four of our first six games were against teams who had qualified for Europe and I was worried we might get buried before we had even started. But that first Saturday against Liverpool, there was a lot of optimism and excitement around Bramall Lane. We were entertaining the team who had won the Champions League fourteen months earlier. I was hoping against hope that we could get off to a flier.

Everyone else had us as the favourites to go down. We were the bookies' favourites to finish rock bottom. They gave Watford more chance of staying up than us. I knew it was going to be tough but I always thought we would stay up. Right to the last minute of that last game against Wigan, I thought we'd stay up.

One of the big things going for us was that there were a lot of young managers in the Premier League who hadn't got a lot of experience. That gave me optimism. Even though I knew some of their clubs would survive, Iain Dowie, Gareth Southgate, Glenn

Roeder and Stuart Pearce were all being thrown in at the deep end and I knew it wouldn't be easy for them.

We had kept the same squad, too, and our expectations were not as high as elsewhere. Charlton had spent £12 million pre-season and they were talking about getting into Europe. So were Manchester City and Middlesbrough. That meant added pressure from their supporters. For us in our first season, we were just aiming for survival.

In the close season, I had bought the centre forward, Rob Hulse, from Leeds United for £2.2 million and the central defender, Claude Davis, from Preston North End for £2.5 million. I wanted to spend more but we didn't have more.

I had already decided that we couldn't change everything just because we had got promoted. We had to go with the bulldog spirit. Keep the spine of the team English, as so many other leading clubs do. That's even more important at a club like Sheffield United where we had to rely on unity to help us try and bridge the gap in quality between us and many of our rivals. I wanted to preserve the sense of humour and the banter we had in the dressing room. I thought that would go a long way.

And we took a great spirit with us into the Premiership. Even over things like fines. I fined players for all sorts, me. If I was talking on the training pitch and the lads were sitting around and I could see out of the corner of my eye that somebody was not listening, I'd ask him what I'd just said. If he didn't know, it was £20. If I caught him again, it was double. If I asked a player and he started stuttering and trying to bluff his way out of it, one of the other lads would pipe up. 'He doesn't know, gaffer,' he'd say. 'Get him fined.'

I fined them heavily for being late on match days and for the bus on away trips. I've done what Roy Keane did to Anthony Stokes, Marton Fulop and Tobias Hysen when they were late for the Sunderland bus and he left without them. Fair play to Roy for that. That kind of strength and attitude is one of the reasons why he has made such a brilliant start as a manager. When I did it, just like him, it wasn't my main players involved. If Phil Jagielka had been late last season, I'm not sure I would have left without him.

My main aim at Bramall Lane, and throughout my managerial career, has been to avoid cliques. Cliques poison the dressing room spirit at football clubs. You have to weed them out. You can have people who are closer to some players than others but you can't have groups isolating themselves. Whenever I have brought players from abroad, I made sure they intermingled. I didn't want groups forming along national lines, be it English, Jamaican, Irish or whatever. I wanted comedians. I wanted characters. I wanted laughter. I have always gone for players who would put as much into their job as I put into mine.

That summer of 2006, I felt the same as I did on all the occasions I had been given a free transfer in my playing career: I wanted to prove all the people wrong who said we were going to go down. I wanted to prove the pundits wrong about us getting relegated. I felt it was an achievement to get us up to the top flight. To stay up would have been another step higher than that. I knew we'd need a lot of luck but I felt we could do it.

I wanted that first season in the Premiership to be the start of something. I wanted to put down a platform that we could build

Michael Brown was one of my earliest and best signings in my seven and a half years at Bramall Lane. Here he is scoring a crucial goal against our rivals, Sheffield Wednesday, which sealed the win.

I stood on the touchline and watched in disbelief as we lost to Arsenal in the 2003 FA Cup semi-final.

Patrick Suffo, left, becomes the third Sheffield United player to be sent off by referee Eddie Wolstenholme during the notorious Battle of Bramall Lane in March 2002.

Left: Paul Peschisolido celebrates after scoring the winning goal in the 2003 play-off semi-final victory over Nottingham Forest, one of the most dramatic matches I have ever been involved in.

Below: I was ecstatic after we beat Forest in the 2003 semi-finals, particularly as there w no love lost between me and many of the Forest staff.

Right: It was a great honour to be introduced to Her Majesty the Queen at a town hall reception given by the Lord Mayor Elect of Sheffield in May 2003.

Below: Celebrating Sir Alex Ferguson's twenty years in charge at Old Trafford with the Manchester United manager and former Liverpool boss, Roy Evans.

Above: William was a Sheffield United mascot when we played Arsenal at Highbury in February 2005, so Sharon brought her camera along to capture the occasion.

Left: Victories over Sheffield Wednesday were always special and I celebrated this one with Shaun Murphy.

Below: Danny Webber scores the winner against Cardiff City at Ninian Park on Good Friday 2006. When Leeds drew with Reading the next day, Sheffield United were promoted to the Premiership.

Above: Tens of thousands of people turned out to greet us when we arrived at Sheffield Town Hall after we clinched promotion to the Premiership.

Right: Standing with Nick Montgomery and Paddy Kenny on the top deck of the bus that took us through Sheffield to celebrate promotion in 2006.

Below: Celebrating with the lads after the last game of the season. I was already thinking about the scale of the challenge that lay ahead.

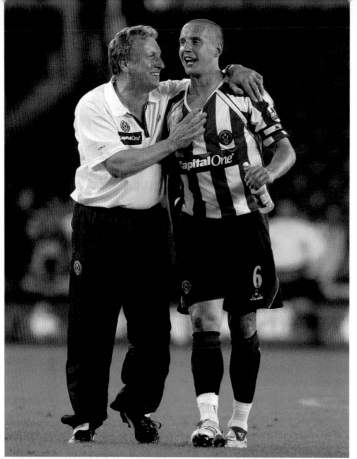

Left: The lads always used to say Phil Jagielka was my favourite and he certainly was when he scored the goal against Middlesbrough that gave us our first Premiership win.

Below: Making a point to the referee in the closing stages of our defeat to Jose Mourinho's Chelsea in October 2006.

Right: Officials often upset me and this one looks terribly pleased with his afternoon's work.

Below: I am not a fan of referee Mike Riley, something I made clear to him after he had disallowed our equaliser against West Ham in November 2006.

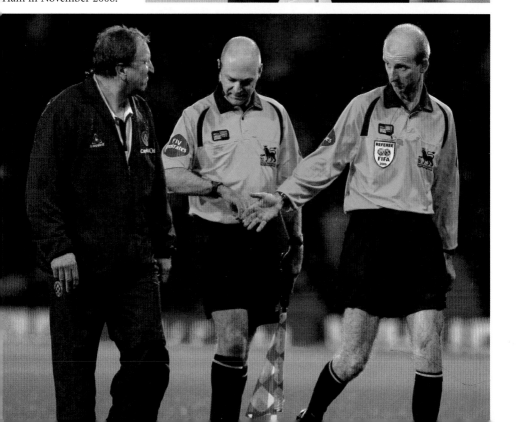

Me and my brother, John, and sister, Carole.

I won a bet with some of the Sheffield United players when I wore full tartan regalia for the Highland Games in 2006.

My wonderful kids, Natalie, Amy, William and James.

on. I wanted us to move on and begin to achieve something like Bolton have done. I spoke to people like Paul Jewell at Wigan and the Bolton boss, Sam Allardyce, about the situation in the Premiership. I spoke to Steve Bruce who had been up there and got relegated. I took as much advice as I could. I did a lot of listening and a lot of planning.

That included a pre-season trip to Inverness. The Highland Games were on while we were up there and, the day after the game, which we won, I decided I'd go along to have a look. Rob Kozluk and a couple of the others bet me £100 that I wouldn't wear a kilt. So I did. I put the full regalia on and I went along and watched the tossing of the caber and all the rest of it.

I turned round at one point and there were two very attractive young ladies behind me, each with a camera in her hand. They gestured that they wanted their picture taken with me. I thought Sheffield United must really be on the map if these two girls were aware of me, too. After the picture had been taken, I asked them who they supported.

They just smiled at me and didn't say anything.

I thought maybe they were shy in the presence of a Premiership manager.

'Who do you support, love?' I said again. They giggled a bit this time but that was it.

Turned out they didn't speak a word of English. They had no bloody idea I was a football manager. They just wanted a picture of a bloke in a kilt.

There was a full house at Bramall Lane for Liverpool's visit. We had sold 21,000 season tickets in the summer which was more than anyone expected. Because of the numbers, there were problems getting them out to everybody so there was a real hubbub outside the ground before kick-off. Liverpool put a decent side out which, crucially, included Steven Gerrard and Jamie Carragher. If those two are playing, they're worth ten of anybody else. But we still got a bit of a lift when we saw they had left out Peter Crouch and Xabi Alonso. I was forced to watch from the stands, courtesy of Graham Poll and that muppet, John Carver.

We were well organised and in certain situations we let them have it and in others we closed them down. If we were stretched, I didn't want us to go chasing the ball because they would pass through us. I wanted us to get back together and get organised. We would always let one of the centre halves have it who we didn't think were as good on the ball. Someone like Hyypia. Let him have it and let him give it away.

We should have been in front at half time. The lads were a bit disheartened when they came in at the interval and it was still goalless. But we talked about the need to stay positive and, as I was coming out for the second half, I heard a massive roar. Rob Hulse had headed in a great free kick from David Unsworth and we were ahead. For twenty-four minutes, we were top of the Premiership.

We were okay until midway through the second half. Then Liverpool started to dominate it and Gerrard roamed in off the wing. With twenty minutes to go, Gerrard surged through the middle of our defence and ran into the box. As he hurtled forward, he jumped over a tackle from Chris Morgan, aimed a weak shot at goal and fell over. Rob Styles gave him advantage and then, when he didn't score, he gave him a penalty. Later, he came out with that ridiculous line about giving the penalty for 'intent'. He had made a mistake but he wouldn't admit it. He would never have given that penalty for Sheffield United at Anfield, though.

Robbie Fowler put the penalty away and the match petered out into a 1-1 draw. Afterwards, I went into our dressing room and the lads were complaining about the penalty decision.

'Even he said it was never a penalty,' one of them said, looking up at the television.

By the time I'd looked round, Robbie Fowler was on the screen being interviewed so I assumed the lads must have been talking about him.

I mentioned what Fowler had said in my press conference and Liverpool were furious. It turned out that a split second before I'd looked up at the screen, Jamie Redknapp had been giving his analysis for Sky and it was he who said it was never a penalty, not Fowler. I apologised to Fowler for that. But there was no way it was a penalty.

I didn't see Benitez afterwards. I couldn't shake his hand after the game because I was up in the stand and when I came down he wasn't around. He'd shot off. I thought that after Liverpool got the equaliser, he could have gambled to get the win but he didn't. He seemed happy with a point and that was fine with me. It was more than we had expected but less than we deserved.

At least we had a point on the board. We only got one more in the next five games. That was a draw at home to Blackburn that felt like a defeat. They missed one penalty but we missed two, both saved by Brad Friedel. Two penalties in the last thirteen minutes and we couldn't score either of them. Rob Hulse missed one. David Unsworth missed the other. Unsworth got another penalty at Bramall Lane on the last day of the season. Unfortunately, he didn't miss that one. He was playing for Wigan by then.

It's funny now when I look back on that Premiership season and think of all the small things that would have made the difference. Every match I think back to, something jumps out at me and reminds me that if it had happened differently we would still be in the Premiership. If Unsworth had scored for us that day back at the beginning of September, we wouldn't have got relegated. If, if, if. It can drive you mad thinking like that.

I tried not to get too wound up by the search for our first win, even though the home defeat to Reading the week after the Blackburn game left us rooted at the bottom of the table. I had made up my mind I was going to enjoy the season and try and be a bit more relaxed. In the past I was a bundle of nerves before matches. The doctor prescribed me antacid tablets to stop the churning in my stomach and I'd have to take half a sleeping tablet the night before a game.

If we had an evening game, we would do a short morning training session and I would get home about midday. I would get a flask of coffee and a Bakewell Tart and drive out to Chatsworth about half an hour away. There was a little tea hut in the car park there and sometimes I'd buy a cup of coffee and a couple of buns. Then I'd try and park the car in a nice area where I could look across the valleys where the red deer were wandering. I'd lie the seat back and have a couple of hours' sleep and come back about 5 p.m.

On 23 September I took charge of what they said was my thousandth game as a league manager. We played Arsenal at the Emirates. I was waiting for a presentation but I never got one. It didn't really matter because I think it was actually about my thousand and twentieth. They hadn't counted the seventeen games when I was in charge at Torquay. I did have a bit of a laugh with Arsene Wenger before the game, though. Arsene and I had had a bit of an up and downer when we played each other in the FA Cup semi-final in 2003 so I pointed out to him that the dugouts at the Emirates were so far apart I might struggle to shout at him.

Wenger looked at me in that kind of quizzical sideways manner of his.

'I am sure that somehow you will find a way,' he said.

We both laughed our heads off. I know deep down Arsene respects somebody like me who has never had anything and has made the best out of what he's got. He said something later that season about how he respected some coaches in the French Third Division more than others who had won the European Cup because he knew what a good job they were doing against the odds. He knows his team is always in for a hard game when they play us. We held out for sixty-five minutes that day but, once they went ahead, the game was over. They beat us 3-0.

So we had two points from six games and we were rock bottom. Everybody had written us off completely by then. We had Middlesbrough at home next and I thought we'd be able to get at them.

Hulsey put us ahead but Yakubu equalised after a bad back pass just after half time and for a while we looked like we were hanging on for the draw. But we are hard workers and we stuck together and stopped feeling sorry for ourselves. The crowd was magnificent, too. Instead of panicking and picking on people, they did nothing but encourage us. They turned up the volume and I began to think they could win us the game.

Just when it seemed the chance of victory had slipped away, Jagielka scored this belter from way outside the box. As it was coming down to him, I was willing him to take a touch first but he just hit it and, as soon as he hit it, I knew it was going in. There was a split second where everything seemed to freeze. Then the ball bounced in front of their keeper and went through his dive and the net bulged.

Then it was absolute euphoria. I must have looked a stupid prat running round like a little kid. That's why I appreciate seeing Sir Alex celebrating because you can't put that feeling into words. That was special that day. It was our first win in the Premiership after so many people had written us off and dismissed us.

I said a few words to the lads afterwards about how proud I was of them and then I went and got in this little slipper bath that I have in the changing rooms. Derek, the old kit man, who has been there donkey's years, brought me a cup of tea. I lay back in my bath absolutely exhausted from the emotion of it all. I thought about all those fans going home that night and feeling the same way I felt.

I went back to my childhood for a few minutes while I lay there on my own. I thought about getting off the bus with my dad, walking up past the Territorial Army building, up to the stadium and through the Kop turnstiles and up the hill and watching my team. That feeling when Jagielka scored was just like when I was a kid. You never forget that. And I thought the people who had been at our game that day would never forget it, especially the kids who had never seen us win in the top flight.

I had told the board that I was going to New York the week after we played Middlesbrough. There was an international break and I wanted to fulfil one of my ambitions and see Barbra Streisand singing at Madison Square Garden. When I saw that her concert there fell at a convenient time, I booked four tickets for me and my best mate and our wives.

'I'm telling you now,' I'd told the directors before the start of the season, 'because we might be ten points adrift at the bottom by then and you might want to get rid while I'm away.'

The concert was unbelievable. We were four rows back. Tony Bennett was a few seats away. Oprah Winfrey was there. I was right on the edge of the stage so when Barbra looked down at the audience, I just thought she was looking at me. But you know what, pressure gets to everybody. Even her.

She had a heckler who started shouting at her while she was doing some sort of sketch about George Bush. In the end, she picked up the microphone and looked straight at him.

'Why don't you shut the fuck up and get out,' she said, which took everyone by surprise rather.

Just shows you, I thought. Everyone has it in them at some stage.

At the end of October, still struggling in the bottom three, we played Chelsea at Bramall Lane. When Sheffield United had got promoted, people seemed to think there might be a problem between me and Jose Mourinho. Either that I would try and wind him up or that his attitude would get under my skin. That was never going to happen.

I like Mourinho. He's given everyone in the Premiership a kick up the backside. Everyone was getting a bit bored with the Arsene-Alex confrontations and he has brought his own brand of cockiness and quality to English football. The only thing I hate about him is that he's such a good-looking bastard.

People say he's arrogant but when someone like him is dealing with players who are on the money his players are on, you've got to have a lot of confidence. If you know you're good at what you do, you can afford to be a bit blasé. If I was in his situation, I'd act the way he does, too.

Everybody talks about the money he has had at Chelsea but my answer to that is that he never had any money at Porto. He had nothing really and they won the European Cup. In comparison with the people he was playing against, he hadn't got better players, but they were organised, they fought for each other and they won because of the team spirit. Not because of the quality. That isn't lucky. We missed another bloody penalty and they beat us 2-0.

But we got a great win at Newcastle and drew at home to Bolton. Then, in the middle of November, it was the one we had all been waiting for: Manchester United at home. I was looking forward to it, too. I had always got on with Fergie, right from my earliest days in league management. There are no airs and graces with him. No high and mighty. He has always been a father figure to English managers.

He has sent me letters congratulating me when I've been in charge of a team that has been promoted. And he's sent me letters commiserating when I was in charge of a side that was relegated. Very few managers do that but he does it religiously. He is renowned for knowing everybody and talking to everybody.

There was a time when I was in charge of Notts County when I wanted to get some advice about a couple of Scottish players I'd been told about. I hadn't got a clue and neither had Mick Jones so Mick told me to ring Fergie about them. So I called him. He knew everything about both of them.

'Aye,' he said, 'good left foot but gets turned easily, not the best in the air, brave but doesn't read the game too well.'

You name it, he knew it about them. I was on to him for about half an hour. I put the phone down and looked at Mick.

'I bet he even knows who the fucking groundsman is at Dunfermline Athletic,' I said.

I was only joking.

'Ring him and ask him,' Mick said.

I thought I'd do it just for a laugh.

'Alex,' I said, 'I don't suppose you know who the groundsman at Dunfermline is, do you?'

And before I could laugh, he told me who it was. I just thanked him and put the phone down.

We played United in the middle of November. He came into my office at five past two. The teamsheets had been handed in. He picked the television remote control up and went straight on to the racing channel. He wanted to know why I hadn't got the pay-per-view racing channel. He had to put up with Channel Four. He had a glass of water or something. Then he had a cup of tea and a biscuit about quarter past two. He got straight into the biscuits.

It got to twenty past two. I nipped into the dressing room to do a couple of bits and bobs while the players were out doing their warm-up. When I went back into my office, Alex was still there. It was twenty-five to three by that stage. Well, my lads come back in at quarter to three for me to talk to them and I was getting a bit edgy.

'I'm sorry, Alex,' I said, 'but I'm going to have to ask you to fuck off now if you don't mind.'

He looked up from the racing.

'Look,' I said, 'if I'd got Ronaldo, Rooney and Giggs in my starting eleven, I'd be in here until three o'clock, too, but I have got to go and motivate my lot next door so can you fuck off now and let me have a few minutes?'

What a team United were in that 2006–07 season. And what a manager he's been. He's the guy who sets the standards. There won't be another one like him. I think his style of management where he controls everything at the club has almost died out now. People like Mourinho will stick around for a few years and then move on.

So Alex jumped up from his chair and off he went with a smile. After the game, he was back in there before five o'clock. He doesn't speak to the BBC or any of the written press so he was the first one back in my office. Rooney had scored twice. We lost 2-1.

19
REACHING FOR SAFETY

T HERE'S NO GRUDGE between me and the Reading boss, Steve Coppell. I like him and I respect the job he's done. What he's achieved at the club is something to be very proud of. Probably never to be surpassed. Sadly, I can't say the same for his assistant, Wally Downes. Wally, I don't like. If ever a name fitted a man, it's Wally for Wally Downes. Wally by name and wally by nature.

We played them at the Madejski Stadium in the middle of January when we were threatening to drag ourselves clear of the relegation struggle. Reading had taken the Premiership by storm. They were flying. They didn't have any relegation worries. They were thinking about Europe and playing with confidence and style. We didn't have a good recent record against them and I knew it was going to be a hard day. I didn't realise that, at the end of it, I was going to have to run for my life from a screaming mob.

Coppell's a super man but Reading aren't angels. They're just very clever. Every decision the referee makes, either Wally or Kevin Dillon, Steve's other assistant, is on the edge of the technical area shouting the odds at the linesmen or the ref. Everyone thinks they're do-gooders but they're worse than me. Reading get away with it because when there's a flashpoint, the cameras always go to Steve, who's sitting there calmly in the dugout, itching his chin.

By the time we went there, I had built up a bit of history with Reading. I was reported for using foul and abusive language to the referee, Grant Hegley, the season before, after he had denied us the clearest penalty you will ever see in your life. Their midfielder, James Harper, took out Keith Gillespie somewhere around the knee with seven minutes to go and he didn't give it. He didn't give it because he should have sent off our goalkeeper, Paddy Kenny, early in the game and he'd bottled it. He was trying to even things up by denying us a penalty. I let him know what I thought about him, he reported me and I was charged by the FA.

So it would be fair to say that my previous visit to the Madejski was rather fraught. Not quite as fraught as this one was going to be, though. We played well enough in the first half but Shane Long put them ahead a minute before half time and Ulises de la Cruz put them two up five minutes into the second half. I still thought we might be able to get something out of the game so I sent on Keith Gillespie.

Things were already tense. Steve Sidwell had got away with a disgraceful over the top tackle on Chris Armstrong that should have been a straight red and Reading's left-sided player, Stephen Hunt, had been goading Gillespie while Gillespie was warming up. As soon as Gillespie came on, Hunt gave him a few more verbals while they were waiting for play to restart and Gillespie smashed him in the face. Mark Halsey sent him off and all hell let loose.

I applauded Hunt from the sideline. He knew exactly what he'd been doing. Gillespie was stupid to fall for it but Hunt had got at him.

While Gillespie was walking down the tunnel, I also let Halsey know that even though what Gillespie had done was bad, it was nowhere near as bad as the tackle Sidwell had made on Armstrong. Not in the same league. I made a stamping motion with my foot to show what Sidwell had done and try and point out to Halsey that it was a leg-breaking tackle.

I was still looking at Halsey and swigging from a bottle of water when I turned around and saw this raging bull with bulging eyes pushing me out of the way and yelling and screaming at me. It was Wally Downes. I let him mouth off. He'd gone completely. I just turned away from him and shook my head while people wrestled him away. They should have stuck him in a straitjacket and put him in a padded cell to calm him down.

Afterwards, Wally came out with all the usual garbage about me telling my players to go and break someone's leg. Well, for a start, if my players took on board everything I shouted at them during a game, they'd be seeing a therapist for the rest of their lives. And anyway, I was effectively saying the opposite of what Wally was suggesting. I was telling the referee that my players were going to get their legs broken if he kept letting Reading get away with dangerous tackles like Sidwell's.

The thing is, Reading's game against Sheffield United is always Wally's chance to get his name in the papers. It's his big day out when Reading play the Blades. He hero worships Dave Bassett who was one of my predecessors as manager at Bramall Lane, so he's always rambling on about how Bassett was a far better manager than I will ever be. Wally played for Sheffield United actually. Briefly. He played a handful of games and got sent off twice.

After he'd come charging over and lunged at me, Halsey came to talk to us. He told me he was going to have to send me to the stand. He sent Wally off as well. Wally was charged with improper conduct and, for once, I wasn't.

I didn't want anything to do with any of the post-match pleasantries but some of my staff were invited into Steve Coppell's office. Wally was in there, holding court. He was sitting in the manager's chair, stark naked other than his T-shirt. For the fifteen minutes they were in there, all he could do was play with his bollocks. That shows you the class of the man. I can't say I was surprised.

Andy Leaning, our goalkeeping coach, had driven my car down to Reading so I could head off to Cornwall after the game. He told me he had parked it fifty yards away from the team coach. About an hour after the match had finished, a couple of stewards said they'd escort me to the car. Except, when we got outside, there were still hundreds of Reading fans milling around. When I looked around, the stewards had melted away.

I hurried over to my car but, before I got to it, I heard someone shouting.

'There he is,' one of the Reading fans yelled.

I sprinted over to my car and dived in. Before I could even get the key in the ignition, there were about ten yobbos all around the car, banging on the windows and hammering on the roof. Two of them were sprawled on the bonnet. I started the car and put my foot on the accelerator. The thugs who were on the bonnet slid off and the rest of them backed away. Another minute and they'd have smashed the car up with me in it. That's typical of the security operation at Reading. Other clubs are aware of the potential for a situation like that but they don't seem to be. It's amateur night down there. I thought it was appalling that they could leave an opposition manager in that kind of danger.

That defeat left us still in sixteenth place. We'd had a reasonable December so we had a small buffer between us and the bottom three. At the end of November, we stayed down in London for a few days for the matches against West Ham and Watford. Normally, I don't like the team staying down because it leaves them with too much time on their hands, but it made sense this time. I didn't want them all bored out of their pants so, after we'd lost at West Ham, we went straight off to Walthamstow Dogs in our jeans and roughnecks.

When we got there, we arranged a meeting point for later and then went our different ways. But as you always find with a good squad, they stuck together. I found them all on this terracing watching the bookies at work. In the second or third race there were two dogs neck and neck at the line and young Stephen Quinn thought his had won. So he went down to the bookie and the bookie paid him out. He won about £55.

Five minutes later, the same bookie came up to us and asked him for the money back. He said the dog had actually come second and he'd made a mistake. I told him that wasn't on. What would have happened if Quinnie had gone over to the other side of the track? The bookie wouldn't have got his money back then. It seemed a bit random. But he went on about it so much that Quinnie gave him his money back.

I wandered off for a bit after that. After a while, a punter recognised me and came up for a chat. He was a Spurs fan but he seemed to know the dogs inside out. He was an owner and he said he had a dog running in the 9.45 that was a surefire winner. I thanked him and told him if it won, he could be my guest at the game against Watford the following Tuesday. I'm not sure quite how excited he was by that offer but, anyway, I was grateful for his tip.

I went back up on to the terracing with the lads and put the word round. A couple of minutes before the race, I went down to the bookie who had cheated Quinnie and put £100 on the dog I'd had the tip about. A few of the other lads did the same. Then we watched. It started off near the back but gradually it moved up the field until it was third and then second and there was only him and one other in it. It won it by a nose and we were all jumping up and down and hugging each other.

After a bit, I gazed down to where the bookie was standing and he looked absolutely distraught. The lads went and got their money but I was determined not to go and collect mine until I caught the guy's eye. Eventually, I caught him sneaking a look up at where I was standing and I went down there and he paid me out. I won about £500. It must have been the most expensive fifty-five quid that bookie has ever taken when he nicked it back off Quinnie. I loved that because he had stitched young Quinnie up and he deserved everything he got.

The next night, we went to watch *Casino Royale*, the new James Bond film, and then we started to prepare for Watford which was the televised game on the Tuesday night. The previous season, Watford had been too physical for us, but this time we coped well with them and grabbed a 1-0 win through Danny Webber. It seemed like a huge victory for us.

We followed that by beating Charlton at Bramall Lane at the time they were in freefall under Les Reed. We battered them so badly that I felt sorry for Les. But not too sorry because now we were flying. We drew at home to Villa and won at Wigan. Then, in the last game of the year, we beat Arsenal in Sheffield. Christian Nade turned Kolo Toure beautifully about forty yards out just before half time and then ran on and lifted his shot over Jens Lehmann for the only goal.

What a night that was. It had been raining earlier and the ball was zipping around on the turf. It reminded me of one of those nights when I'd come to the ground as a kid, travelling down into the city and seeing the floodlights from miles around. It was almost like a play at a theatre. It was like the dry ice was clearing and then the players ran out. It was great drama. Paddy Kenny was carried off after an hour and Jagielka went in nets but they still couldn't get an equaliser. Jagielka even made a fantastic save in the last minute.

That's why we had a bit of a cushion when we went to Reading. And ten days after Reading, we beat Fulham 2-0 at Bramall Lane, which was probably the easiest match we had all season. We blew a point in the next match, away at Blackburn when David Dunn went down under a flimsy challenge from Michael Tonge in the ninety-third minute and Morten Gamst Pedersen bent in a free kick for their winner. But then we beat Spurs at home on 10 February and moved up to the heady heights of fifteenth. We were ten points clear of the relegation zone. Everyone thought we were safe.

I thought we deserved to be where we were. In fact, I thought we should have been higher. But I knew we weren't safe. We had Liverpool, Everton, Bolton and Chelsea in the next four games. We lost 4-0 at Liverpool and I got slagged off afterwards on the phone-ins for not picking a more attacking side. Not picking a more attacking side against a team who were heading for the Champions League final? Fine.

So then it was Everton. I know I've got a tendency to blame referees and linesmen for bad results but it's very rarely I blame newspapers, particularly a newspaper as respected as *The Times*. But in the week leading up to the Everton game, I had allowed Paddy Kenny to do an interview with Pete Lansley, a decent lad who writes for *The Times*. I didn't think it would be a problem, but it was.

Paddy had had a few personal problems. He'd had his eyebrow bitten off in a curry house in Halifax after an argument about his wife, who he'd split up with. I'd told him not to go out in Halifax but what can you do? It never occurred to me that *The Times* would want to get into stuff about a scrap in a curry house but about a quarter of an hour after Paddy and Pete Lansley had sat down together, Paddy stormed in to my room at the training ground.

He was raging. He said all the man from *The Times* wanted to talk about was his personal life and his divorce. Paddy was going crackers so I went outside and told Pete to lock himself in his car while I calmed it all down. It would be fair to say that was the end of the interview.

Paddy seemed okay going into the game and Rob Hulse put us ahead with his eighth goal of the season soon after half time. But then, with quarter of an hour left, Paddy came racing to the corner of his area near the byline to try to claim a bouncing ball that Andy Johnson was challenging for. You only need to breathe on Andy for him to go down but Paddy did a lot more than that. He was all over him. Even when Johnson wriggled away, there wasn't that much danger because we had two men on the line and Johnson was going to have to shoot from a tight angle. But before he could get his shot off, Paddy clipped his ankle. Mikel Arteta scored from the penalty and we'd thrown away another couple of points.

Next up, we lost at Chelsea. But it wasn't the losing that really hurt us at Stamford Bridge. Far worse than the 3-0 defeat was the injury sustained by Rob Hulse after twenty-five minutes. He tried to get on the end of a cross from Keith Gillespie, collided with Petr Cech and broke his leg. It was one of those awful accidents in football where no one is to blame. It was just two committed, brave players going for the same ball and one came off a lot worse than the other.

We were disappointed with the medical facilities at Stamford Bridge, which was ironic, given the complaints Chelsea had made about Reading when Cech was injured at the Madejski Stadium. Hulse was lying injured in our dressing room for a long time while we waited for an ambulance. We felt strongly enough about it to write a letter of complaint about what we thought was an unacceptable delay. There were other issues, too. The stretcher got stuck in one of the corridors, which wasn't wide enough. Stuff like that. When they'd come to Bramall Lane, Drogba got injured and we x-rayed him during the game and told them there was nothing wrong. But they hadn't even got an x-ray machine at the ground. I was taken aback.

That was Hulse out for the rest of the season. He was our leading scorer with eight goals in the league at that point and he was the man who led the line for us. He was a terrific worker and a great lad, an unselfish player who everybody else respected. I've been told since that he was close to getting a call-up for an England squad when he was injured. Other people had noticed his contribution, too.

Straight away, commentators and analysts predicted that we would struggle without him. They were right. It's obvious that a team like ours is going to miss a player of Hulse's quality. We lost our attacking focal point when we lost him. And although Jon Stead stepped up and scored some crucial goals for us, we still missed Hulse's contribution alongside him for the rest of the season.

I sensed other things turning against us around that time, too. In fact, if you want me to name the most significant day in the battle against relegation for a whole number of clubs, including us, it was that day: Saturday 17 March. It was the day someone strapped a pair of concrete boots on to our feet and threw out a lifeline to some of our rivals.

Up in the north-east, Gareth Southgate rested some of his first-choice players for Middlesbrough's match against Manchester City at the Riverside. No Jonathan Woodgate, no Julio Arca, no Mark Viduka. All saved for an FA Cup replay with Manchester United a few days later. City were in freefall but Southgate's act of generosity gifted Stuart Pearce and his side a 2-0 win after five straight defeats. That turned their season around and took them out of our reach.

I knew Southgate was a friend of Pearce but I thought that was taking it a bit far. If I could have picked three players not to play against Sheffield United, it would have been Viduka, Arca and Woodgate. It would have been nice to see Middlesbrough lose the next six games and see how Gareth reacted then. I thought it showed disrespect to the other clubs fighting relegation. Sadly, it wasn't the last time I felt that as the season rushed towards its climax.

Meanwhile, at Ewood Park, Bobby Zamora scored a goal for West Ham that won them a game they had been expected to lose and gave them hope where previously they had had none. It wasn't any old goal, though. It was a goal that should have been disallowed three times. Let's forget the first two because they wouldn't have mattered if the linesman, Jim Devine, had spotted that Zamora's shot hadn't crossed the line when it hit Carlos Tevez and bounced out. But he didn't spot it, Howard Webb gave the goal and West Ham started off on their great escape.

I thought we'd put West Ham back in their box a month later when we beat them 3-0 at Bramall Lane. We played incredibly well that day. Then we got a vital point at the Valley a week later which broke their spirit and put them down and then we scrabbled our way to a nervous home victory over Watford.

We needed one point from our last two games away at Aston Villa and home to Wigan Athletic and we would be home free. West Ham were away to Manchester United on the final day and, even though United were in the FA Cup Final the following week, I thought Sir Alex's side should still be way too good for them.

After all, we had played them a few days before we drew at Charlton. They started with Ronaldo, Scholes, Carrick, Rooney, Scholes and Giggs. Rooney, in particular, was too good for us again and, after Carrick had opened the scoring early on, Rooney got a second four minutes into the second half. But with about twenty minutes to go, Luton Shelton, our reserve forward, who I'd signed in the January transfer window and who had played an absolute blinder on his debut, was brought down from behind in the box by Gabriel Heinze.

It was the most obvious of penalties and the most obvious of red cards. Everybody said so but Rob Styles didn't give it. Let's face it, he doesn't give much against the big teams. He hasn't quite got the courage. If he had had the courage, they would have been down to ten men and we would have only been 2-1 down and right back in the game. Who knows what might have happened?

But he bottled it. He didn't even ask his linesman. And all we were left with was the consolation of having played well in a 2-0 defeat and the memory of the gallows humour that had spread round our dressing room at half time when we were all marvelling at Luton Shelton's debut performance in the opening forty-five minutes.

'Luton,' I said, 'I can't believe how good you are. But you must be knackered. How long can you last in the second half. Ten? Twenty? Thirty?'

'I don't know, gaffer,' he said.

'Look,' I said, getting my white handkerchief out of my pocket, 'take that with you and when you've had enough, start waving it at me and I'll bring you off.'

A smile spread across Rob Kozluk's face.

'Then pass that fucking hanky round to the rest of us,' he said.

20
EIGHT DAYS TO WIGAN

O N THE WEDNESDAY before the Wigan game, I got a call from Alan Curbishley's agent, Phil Smith. He went through a few pleasantries and tossed around the names of some players I might be interested in for the following season. Then, as casually as he could, he got down to the real reason for the call.

'Alan's hoping there won't be any collusion on the last day,' he said.

He was referring to the so-called 'flat-cap conspiracy' theory that had been doing the rounds, the idea that if West Ham were losing at Manchester United on Sunday afternoon, Sheffield United and Wigan would contrive a late win for Wigan so both the northern teams could stay up.

It made me laugh. I was still thinking about Fergie presenting Curbishley with those first-class tickets to New Zealand the year before. I was thinking about Rio Ferdinand playing against Anton Ferdinand. I was thinking about how West Ham would have been down already if the Premier League had done the right thing and docked them points for fielding an ineligible player, Carlos Tevez.

And Phil Smith was telling me Alan Curbishley was worrying about collusion.

'Well that's fucking two of us then,' I said. 'Don't forget those air tickets for New Zealand.'

'Look, Neil,' Phil said, 'Alex has rung Alan and he's told him he's going to have to pick a strong side.'

And I believed him. I really did. I believed all the stuff Sir Alex said publicly, too, about how he had a duty to the legitimacy of the Premiership and to all the teams fighting against relegation to pick his strongest possible side. As I said after the Wigan game, Sir Alex sold me a dummy there. He sold everyone a dummy.

I hadn't really been worrying about West Ham too much up until that point because I had always assumed they were going to get out of it anyway. With Watford and Charlton down, I thought either Wigan or Fulham would be the third team to be relegated. They were both on terrible runs and I couldn't see Fulham, in particular, getting another point. Then, as we arrived at Villa Park to get ready for our evening kick-off match against Aston Villa on the penultimate weekend of the season, I walked into the dressing room, looked at the television and saw the team Rafa Benitez had picked for Liverpool's visit to Craven Cottage that afternoon.

Liverpool had beaten Chelsea in the Champions League semi-final the previous Tuesday and I'd been curious about how they would approach the game. But I never thought Benitez would stoop as low as he did. I thought they would still play Carragher and Gerrard and, with Carragher and Gerrard, they're always going to be in with a shout. But Benitez left out nine of his first-team players. Nine. The Champions League Final against AC Milan was still more than two weeks away. I couldn't understand it. I hadn't even heard of two of the players Benitez picked. Seriously. I hadn't.

That showed total contempt for us. I know he has got to look after the interests of his own club first, but why rest practically his entire team then, when the final was still so far away? He brought them all back a week later for their last game of the season against Charlton, which was a match with nothing riding on it. I hated Benitez when I saw that Liverpool team flash up on the screen in our changing room at Villa Park. I never thought I'd feel hatred like that for someone like him. I know that sounds horrible but I did hate him. Of course, they lost. Robbie Fowler missed a great chance but Fulham won 1-0. I felt sick inside when they scored. I felt cheated.

I hope AC Milan win that Champions League Final now, I thought, so Benitez has got some pain and some hurt to go with mine.

It was still in our hands, I know. In fact, if we were dismayed by what had happened at Fulham, we were buoyed by the news that Wigan had lost at home to Middlesbrough. Our goal difference was four better than theirs and we were three points ahead of them with two games to play. We needed a point at Villa Park to be absolutely sure of safety. A 1-0 defeat would have been almost as good because there was no way Wigan were going to beat us by three clear goals at Bramall Lane the following Sunday. When my lads ran out to face Villa, we knew we could almost touch safety.

Maybe I should have played a more conservative formation that evening. Maybe I should have done what I did against Manchester United and played five across the back. But we were so pleased about the Wigan result before we played that no one thought about our goal difference. Neither me nor Brian Kidd nor Stuart McCall, my assistants, thought about the ramifications of that until long after the game. In hindsight, we should have done. But there were only fifteen minutes separating the end of Wigan's game from the start of ours. If we'd played five at the back, perhaps we would have stayed solid and only lost 1-0. I don't know.

Even though there was nothing really riding on it for Villa, they were pumped up. It was their last home game of the season and, before the kick-off, they'd brought out the Villa team that had won the European Cup in 1982 as part of the twenty-fifth anniversary celebrations. The crowd was going wild and Villa ripped into us from the start. We were open and full of ourselves and thought we could get a result. We got our backsides kicked. They could have been 4-0 up at half time. They played that well. And the nerves got to some of our lads. I could see it in their eyes. That happens when you get close to a target you've been aiming at for so long.

We lost 3-0 in the end. Villa were the best team we played all season. We ran into them at precisely the wrong time. Patrik Berger's goal, their third, was probably the best goal we conceded all season, too. We were still three points ahead of Wigan but our goal difference was now only one better. That meant that if Wigan beat us at Bramall Lane, they would stay up and we would go down. The margin of our defeat at Villa changed the whole dynamic at the bottom of the table going into the final weekend.

It wasn't a particularly difficult week in terms of preparing the team for what lay ahead. I had plenty of experience behind me and I knew how much nerves would play a part against Wigan. I knew, too, that the Wigan boss, Paul Jewell, was a good manager who had been in this situation before. I knew he wouldn't make it easy for us and I knew that Wigan would probably raise their game. Despite all that, I was still confident we would get the result we needed. If I had been told on the first day of the season that we could go into the last day needing a point at home to Wigan to stay up, I would have taken that.

What I found more troubling that week was the speculation about my future. I batted all the questions away well enough and said, truthfully, that Kevin McCabe and I had put all negotiations about a new contract on hold until after the end of the season. That didn't stop the *Yorkshire Post* running stories, presumably put out by Kevin, to the effect that he would offer me a new contract whether we were relegated or not. But that didn't do anything to soothe the resentment I had been nursing for some time about my treatment by Kevin and the board.

When I had rejected Portsmouth's approach in the middle of the previous season, Kevin had made promises about how he would improve my pay once we were promoted. So when we went up at the end of 2005-06, I thought I'd be on something close to what I would have been on at Portsmouth. That seemed like a reasonable assumption. That was what Kevin had promised me and I'd believed him. Then I spoke to Terry Robinson, who I knew from Bury, who was the football club chairman at Bramall Lane.

'They're not going to want to give you a lot more money, you know,' he said.

'You are joking, aren't you?' I said.

But Terry knew what was coming.

A couple of days after the end of our promotion season, I got a letter from Kevin McCabe congratulating me on my achievement. It said he was taking up the option in my existing contract which meant he offered me 20 per cent more than I'd been on in the Championship. That was a nominal figure that had been in my contract but I'd assumed that if I got the club up to the Premiership, the club would pay me Premiership wages on a new deal. I was wrong about that. The letter said I'd be able to earn a lot more with bonuses if I kept the club up but, even with that bonus, I'd only just about reach what I had thought should be my basic wage. As an example of their attitude towards me, I was still on the same bonus for winning a game as I had been in 1999.

Kevin knew I was in a weak position and he took advantage of that. He knew I didn't want to leave. He knew I was desperate to manage the club I had supported as a boy in the Premiership. I worked so hard to get them up that I didn't want to walk away once I got them there. He was right about all that but I felt I was being shown a lack of respect for what I had done. He was abusing my love for the club. I was only basing my pay requests on what Paul Jewell, Steve Coppell, Alan Curbishley and Iain Dowie had been earning. I knew what wages they were on and I wasn't even seeking parity with them. What I was asking for would still have left me the lowest paid manager in the Premiership but Kevin wouldn't entertain it.

I wondered then whether Kevin wanted me to leave. I asked if I could have more on my basic. I said he could take it off my bonus for staying up. I got another letter from him. It said they had agreed to give me an increase and that they would take it off my bonus. I had hoped they might recognise that I was upset and reconsider their original offer. They didn't. They just tweaked it. They moved some numbers around. So now I was in a situation where I was on a smaller bonus for trying to keep the club up than I had been for getting them promoted to the Premiership. It was small-time thinking from a chairman who said he wanted Sheffield United to be a big club. I'm sorry if it sounds spoilt, but I felt insulted. I thought it was disrespectful. It gnawed away at me. I knew a promise from Kevin had been broken. I felt betrayed.

I felt that if anyone else had done what I had done at Bramall Lane, they would have been able to write their own contract. If anyone else had done what I had done, they would have been treated like a king at the club. But the fact that I was a Sheffield United fan, which should have been in my favour, worked against me. I didn't get the respect that people like Paul Jewell and Aidy Boothroyd got for similar jobs at other clubs. So I went to see the chairman and I told him how disappointed I was, especially after all the conversations we had had around the time of Portsmouth's offer.

'I should be on a lot more than what you've offered me,' I told him, 'but I'm not going to let it affect me now. I'm going to put it to bed and get on with the contract you have offered me. I will do my damnedest to keep us up and I don't want to talk about money again.'

And that was how it stayed for most of the Premiership season. I was only on a one-year contract again, which was hardly a statement of faith in my ability from the club. Then, in April, I got an offer of a new contract from Kevin. It was presented as a two-year contract on condition that Sheffield United were a Premiership club, and there was only six months' notice included in it. In football, that means it was a six-month contract. I don't know why he did that. If that was his idea of motivation, it flopped. It didn't motivate me. If anything, it demotivated me.

Things hadn't been quite the same between us as they were in the early years. Kevin had moved abroad as a tax exile some time in our promotion season and I had less contact with him. He'd also been heavily involved with our Chinese connections, which were taking up even more of his time. When he's away it's harder for him to see what's going on, and it's amazing how many people tittle-tattle. You get a lot of gloom and doom merchants bending his ear. I felt he had listened to a lot of nobodies. I also blamed myself for not making more of an effort to make sure I contacted him. We had drifted apart more than we should have done.

The way the new deal he offered me in April was constructed, we'd have to finish high up in the Premiership in 2007-08 for me to earn the money I should have been on two years ago. I know you can only spend so much. I'm certainly not complaining about my lot in life. I know I'm a fortunate man. But in any walk of life, you want to be paid what you are worth. You want to be paid the going rate. If that doesn't happen, whether you're a fireman, a lawyer, a miner, a doctor, or a journalist, you feel aggrieved. At Sheffield United, the whole club was a reflection of what I did. I stamped my personality on it and that is one of the reasons it was successful in recent years. Other clubs I have managed have realised that when I've gone. I think Sheffield United will, too.

I suppose that's football. Across the spectrum, the chairmen of football clubs always believe that when you have success, it's down to them, not the manager. Derek Pavis believed that at Notts County. He thought he didn't need me any more. Terry Fisher at Huddersfield, too, and Dan McCauley at Plymouth. And Kevin McCabe believed it as well. They don't understand what managers do at a club and I don't think they ever will. They are businessmen. They might be supporters, too, but first of all they are businessmen.

I was surprised at Kevin's attitude, though. It was almost like being let down by a friend. That's how I felt. If I had been messed around like that at another club, I would have walked out. Sometimes, it hasn't done me any favours, but I've always walked out on a matter of principle. But because it was Sheffield United, I didn't want to do that. I was hurt by the lack of respect but I wanted to manage my own club in the Premiership. I wanted to manage them and I wanted to keep them up. I desperately, desperately wanted to keep them up.

I tried to make the week leading up to the Wigan game as normal as possible but I got the lads together on the Monday and had a chat with them.

'You're all going to be nervous on Sunday,' I said, 'and you're not going to want to make a mistake that costs us Premiership football but you have all got to want the ball and be a team. We have to give it our best shot.'

It was the biggest game I'd been involved in, too. I'd only rank one other alongside it and that was Scarborough's match at Sutton United when we effectively clinched promotion from the Conference and Barry Fry and the Barnet players were sitting in the stand, willing us to lose. I know people will think there's no comparison between the magnitude of the two games but there is in my mind. I knew Sunday 13 May would be either the most enjoyable and satisfying day of my life or one of the most miserable ones. There's nothing in between.

I tried to do stuff with the kids to take my mind off it. We had a pool competition on the Wednesday night. We had a cricket match in the back garden. But the kids knew a lot was at stake, too.

I was driving Amy home from school one day. She was quiet but I knew she had heard Sharon and me talking about the fact that we might have to move if we were relegated.

'Whatever happens, daddy,' she said suddenly, 'nothing can change the fact that we're a happy family and that we love each other and wherever we go, we'll be okay.'

I could have cried.

I was going to tell the players the team on the Friday before the game, but on the Thursday night, I got a call from Nick Montgomery. He wasn't in my plans because he'd dislocated his shoulder against Watford a fortnight earlier and was told he would have to have surgery the next week.

'Gaffer,' he said, 'I feel I'll be fit.'

'What are you talking about, Monty?' I said. 'They've just told me you've got to have a pin put in your shoulder next week.'

'I have,' he said, 'but I've taken the sling off and I've been doing press-ups and exercises and all sorts and I'm okay.'

'But I was going to tell them the team tomorrow,' I said. 'You better get in early and have a training session in the morning and make sure.'

I almost filled up as he was telling me. Bloody hell, here was a lad who had dislocated his shoulder the week before and had to go to hospital under anaesthetic because he was in that much pain when it was being put back in and he was telling me he wanted to play in one of the toughest games anyone will ever play in. If he proved his fitness to me, I knew I had to play him. Games like Wigan, you want all your leaders. He came through everything fine. I stuck him in.

I had a few more nerves than normal the night before the game. My tummy was churning when I got up. I got to the ground about 1.30 p.m. I didn't want to get there too early. I got there feeling positive and confident. People were saying a lot of strange things would have to happen to send us down but I knew it was still all up for grabs.

21

MESSAGE ON
A BILLBOARD

THE TELEVISION WAS on in the dressing room. I wasn't watching it but suddenly I became aware of the lads staring up at it and looking shocked.

'I can't believe it,' Michael Tonge said.

'Fucking hell,' Andy Leaning, the goalkeeping coach, said. 'No Ferdinand, no Vidic, no Scholes, no Giggs, no Ronaldo. I thought Ferguson said he was going to play his strongest team.'

I didn't say anything. I went back into my office. I sat down and looked at Sky Sports. The Manchester United team to play West Ham was still up there on the screen. I stared at it in disbelief. I felt really let down. I've got so much time for Sir Alex but he had left a lot of players out against Chelsea a few days earlier and he'd said he'd play his best side against West Ham. This wasn't his best side. This was nowhere near his best side.

I found it hard to grasp.

He must know what a lift it gives to his opponents when they see players like that left out, I thought. He must know that there'll be jubilation in the West Ham dressing room when they see that side.

Some people might say I should just have been concentrating on our game. They might say I shouldn't have been worrying about Old Trafford and that I should just have been getting on with making sure Sheffield United got the result we needed against Wigan. They've got a point, but I was as prepared as I possibly could be for our game anyway. I was confident we could do our job but, as I looked at that screen, I knew that our insurance policy was going up in smoke.

This wasn't just any old relegation battle either. It will go down as the most controversial fight there's ever been to avoid relegation from the top league. There were the vast sums of money involved, for a start, but there was also the fact that West Ham had played almost the whole season with a striker who was ineligible. That striker, Carlos Tevez, was the guy who had dug them out of trouble. He was the reason they even had a chance going into the last day. He was the reason why we were still worrying about relegation. So I think I could be excused my dismay when I saw that Manchester United team.

Let's face it: if Sheffield United or Wigan or Charlton had done what West Ham had done with Tevez and Javier Mascherano, their other Argentine signing, any one of us would have had points deducted by the Premier League commission. Everyone knew that. But even though the Premier League found out about the irregularities at the end of January, they didn't hold their hearing until the end of April. This is supposed to be a blue-chip organisation we're talking about here and they behaved like rank amateurs. How the chief executive, Richard Scudamore, has had the cheek to stay in that job, I just don't know.

For West Ham everything was a bonus by that stage. They had thought they were down because they knew they should have been docked points. When they weren't, they realised they had a second chance they didn't deserve and they went out and grabbed it. They had nothing to lose and they played with a freedom the rest of the clubs down at the bottom could never feel. And now this. Now they had got a United team with all the best players missing. Now they had been given another chance, another unfair advantage. It was unbelievable.

I went back into the dressing room and I could tell the lads were a bit deflated. That was part of the reason we started the game slowly, I think. Wigan had to win so they were always going to come flying at us but we were very flat for twenty minutes. People have said maybe we shouldn't have had a telly in the dressing room but the players would have found out what was going on at Old Trafford anyway. Someone would have come in and told us.

Emile Heskey dominated us in the early stages. Paul Scharner put them ahead after fourteen minutes. We didn't even start until then. But we fought our way back into it and Jon Stead equalised with one of the bravest headers you're ever going to see seven minutes before half time. That should have steadied us. That should have been enough for us. We had had our warning with their first goal. We should have kept it tight and let them start to feel nervous and edgy. We were back in the driving seat. But we threw it away again.

We had almost reached half time. If we'd gone in at 1-1, we would have stayed up. I'm convinced of that. I could have settled them down and breathed more confidence into them. Instead, in the fifth minute of added time at the end of the first half, Derek Geary had a chance to head a ball into touch and he headed it back into play. Derek had been one of our best players that season. He was playing for Stockport County reserves when I signed him and he has turned his career around to such an extent that he had been named in the Ireland squad that week. But he made a mistake against Wigan, they got possession and Michael Tonge gave away a free kick. When it was crossed in, Phil Jagielka handled it in the box and David Unsworth stepped up and scored the goal.

David Unsworth, who had missed that penalty for us against Blackburn earlier in the season. David Unsworth, ex-Sheffield United. David Unsworth sending us down. I knew he'd score it. The one he missed against Blackburn was the worst pen he'd ever taken. I knew he wouldn't hit one like that again. I didn't feel bitter towards him. That's just the kind of cruel coincidence football throws up now and again. He's a great lad, David, actually. Good luck to him.

When the whistle blew for half time, I went down the tunnel and into my office. The television was still on. West Ham were leading 1-0 at Old Trafford. Tevez had scored. The bitterness came flying back. I never thought I'd want Chelsea to beat Manchester United in the FA Cup Final but at that moment I found myself thinking I'd be cheering Chelsea on. I felt so let down.

In the second half, my mind drifted. I thought back to the

opening day of the season and Rob Styles giving that ridiculous penalty against us. I thought about the team Benitez had picked at Fulham. I thought about Michael Brown, Fulham's best player, head-butting a Liverpool player early in that game and Steve Bennett not seeing it even though he was five yards away. I thought about Unsworth's missed penalty against Blackburn. I thought about the Premier League ruling over Tevez. I thought about him blocking that shot against Blackburn and Mr Devine, the linesman, saying it had crossed the line. I thought about the penalty we'd been denied at Old Trafford. My mind was crowded with images of our year in the Premiership. I felt like I was going mad with the injustice of it all.

I didn't feel it slipping away right until the very end. I always thought we might claw it back. Danny Webber went clean through and lifted his shot over the goalkeeper and, after what seemed like an eternity, the ball hit the post and rebounded away to safety. Maybe if he hadn't been a bit ring-rusty, he would have scored. We had other chances, too. We should have had a penalty when Jagielka was fouled in the box. We didn't get it. Surprise, surprise. All the time, I stood there on the touchline in the pouring rain. All the time, I couldn't shake the thought that this was funeral weather.

When the final whistle went, I felt dazed. I wanted to shake Paul Jewell's hand. I went over towards him. He'd been submerged by his jubilant staff and crowds of people, all congratulating him. He's a fine manager. He'd done a brilliant job. I waited for him to emerge from the scrum and shook his hand. I went round every one of my lads to try to comfort them a bit. I was oblivious to the crowd. I didn't even say anything to some of the players. I just patted a few of them. It was like being in a fog. It was like when you press the mute button on the television. You're seeing the pictures but you're not hearing the sound.

I went in the shower. The lads were slumped in their seats in the changing room. I talked to them for a few seconds. I wanted to say hurtful things to them. I wanted to scream at them for mistakes they had made. But I knew it was the wrong time. I knew there was no point. And I knew they were great lads, lads who had given me everything and who deserved better.

'Every one of you knows that we should have had twelve or fifteen more points than we've got this season,' I said to them. 'It's not been West Ham or Wigan or any of the other teams that have cost us. It's been us. But you're a credit to me. You run your bollocks off, you chase, you tackle, you train well, you make me proud to be your boss. I can't bollock you for anything but we messed this up ourselves.'

I walked out and went back to my office to see Sharon and the kids. I felt desperately low. I felt so much bitterness.

Why me? I kept thinking to myself.

I felt like a child when people have ganged up on him. I felt the rage you feel when you've been done an injustice.

Then I realised, I'd felt like that once before. I was thirteen and I was standing outside my house in Frecheville and my mum was lying in a coffin in our front room. The wind was blowing in my hair and I closed my eyes and lifted my head up.

How can God do this? How can he take my mum away from me

when all the other lads have got their mums? It just doesn't make sense.

I know some people might think that's inappropriate. Some people might think it shows I haven't got things in perspective. Well, I'm just being honest about it. That's how I felt. The pain didn't last for as long as when my mum died, obviously, but in that moment I felt the same kind of intense despair. Just like then, I couldn't do anything about it. If I could have cut my hand off or cut my leg off to stop the pain, I would have done. But you can't do anything for that kind of pain. You can't take a tablet for it. There's nothing you can do to ease it.

I got back to my office and my best mate, Paul Evans, was waiting there for me. Sharon, Amy and William were there, too. Sharon had been crying and the kids knew why she was so upset. It wasn't just the football. Not just because of the result. Twenty minutes or so after the game had ended, Sharon and William were sitting in my office when the film actor, Sean Bean, who is a Sheffield United board director, burst in with his girlfriend. He was obviously the worse for wear.

He wanted to know where I was. Sharon told him I was doing a press conference and I'd be back soon. So Sean Bean started swearing at her and my five-year-old son.

'It's your fucking husband that got us relegated,' he said, pointing at her. 'He's a fucking wanker.'

That's Sean Bean, the tough guy actor. Some kind of tough guy, eh, reducing a five-year-old kid and his mum to tears. Kevin McCabe apologised to me when he learned what had happened and said he wouldn't tolerate that kind of behaviour. He would consider taking action regarding Sean's position as a director. Well, I won't hold my breath.

I was livid to begin with. I wanted to go and find him but Paul told me not to waste my time with him. He might be a film star but he wasn't in my eyes that afternoon. At a board meeting once, he made a big show of how he wanted to make an important point about something he had spotted to improve the club's fortunes. We all waited expectantly.

'Do you think Captain Blade has served his purpose and should be removed?' he said as if he'd unearthed something vital. 'I think we should get rid of him.'

That was it. That was all he wanted to talk about. The team mascot. The fluffy thing that stood on the touchline. Captain Fucking Blade. That was the extent of his contribution.

The next day, I flew to see Kevin McCabe in Brussels. I had a lot of text messages on my mobile from other managers. A lot were highly critical of Sir Alex. You'd be surprised at the identities of a couple of the senders. I spoke to Kevin and I thought we'd resolved everything amicably. Then a couple of days later, after we'd held a joint press conference to announce my departure from the club, I heard he'd done an interview on Radio Five Live.

'Neil Warnock is a great motivator,' he had said, 'but we can reflect now maybe he wasn't quite right for our Premiership ambitions. But he gave it his all.'

I thought his words were a disgrace. I rang him up straight away.

We've been friends for twenty years and friends don't say things like that. It was almost as if he was saying he hoped I didn't get another job. It was disrespectful and patronising. It was typical of Chairman's Syndrome. They always, always, have to have the last word. Anyway, I asked him what he had been thinking when he'd said what he'd said. He sounded flustered. He said he'd been misquoted and he apologised to me. I told him I'd checked it and he hadn't been misquoted. He still insisted his remarks had been taken out of context. He said he'd write to every paper that had reported his remarks and ask them to put the record straight and he would phone the radio and TV stations, too.

'Don't bother,' I said.

The afternoon after the press conference to announce that I was no longer manager of Sheffield United, I picked up some of my belongings from my office and drove home.

There was a billboard for the *Sheffield Star* outside a newsagent's shop on the Abbeydale Road.

'Warnock's Dream Is Over,' it said.

One is, but there'll be others to fulfil.

EPILOGUE

WHEN YOU LEAVE somewhere after so long, you want to shut yourself away and, for one or two days, I was no different. Donna, my wonderful secretary at Bramall Lane, phoned to tell me hundreds of letters had arrived for me at the club. She told me I ought to read them. I went down to collect them and I found a lot of them very moving. It took me more than a week but I replied to every one. I'll always keep them. They reminded me that 95 per cent of Blades fans had been behind me all the way and appreciated everything I'd done.

I'd promised William I would take him to the first FA Cup Final at the new Wembley. All the family travelled down to London the day before the game and William and I drove up to Wembley on Saturday morning. He was so excited when he saw the arch towering over the stadium. We got closer and closer and, even though it was only 11.30, the place was buzzing.

It took us a while to find the right entrance. It was a long walk for a five-year-old. Come to think of it, it was a long walk for a fifty-eight-year-old, too. I got recognised by a few West Ham fans along the way. They started singing for me.

'There's only one Carlos Tevez,' they yelled as I went past. I had my picture taken with some of them. They're a loyal bunch, West Ham fans. I've always enjoyed their humour.

We bumped into Steve McClaren outside. He was struggling to find his way, too. I introduced him to William, who looked incredibly dapper in his new suit, and William shook the England manager's hand. William's not stopped talking about that ever since.

We had lunch in one of the hospitality areas and then went out into the stadium. The first look at the new Wembley was amazing. What a sight. I know it was late opening but it was worth the wait. I sat with William and we talked. He's a good little player already and I told him one day he'd play down there on that pitch. Then I thought about when I started in management. My ambition was to manage a team at Wembley and I did it five times. Now I was thinking I'd love to do it again at the new stadium.

We were sitting with the Chelsea fans. I was glad about that. After the events of the previous weekend, I wanted Chelsea to win. William had found a blue Chelsea balloon and he wouldn't let it go. Then I saw Sir Alex walking out on to the pitch.

I'm sorry, mate, I said to myself, I'm not bothered how well you play today because I know you're going to lose. Just like I know Liverpool are going to lose against AC Milan.

Then I did something I very rarely do. I phoned a bookmaker. I rang my ex-wife, Sue, whose partner, Malcolm, knows a bookie. I asked him to put me a few hundred quid on a double: Chelsea and AC Milan to win. Then I sat back and watched. United were the better team in the final but I knew what the result was going to be. Just when it seemed like pens, up popped Didier Drogba to win it for Chelsea. The fans around us went mad with joy. I just sat there motionless.

I cleared out my office the week after and said my goodbyes. I had some great staff at that club. Then it was on to William's sixth birthday party and two hours with twenty-five kids to entertain. That's what I call real work. No wonder I was looking to get back into football as quickly as possible.

Sheffield United announced that Bryan Robson was going to be their new manager a couple of days later. Bryan rang me a couple of days after that to pick my brains about the players and I told him he was a lucky man to have inherited such a great bunch of lads because I was sure they'd go straight back up as champions. I wished him well but it occurred to me as I put the phone down that I had only ever taken over at clubs where confidence was rock-bottom.

It's not like that for Bryan. Being a former England captain gives you certain privileges, I suppose. That's why I knew Kevin McCabe would be happy. He had always wanted someone like Kenny Dalglish, Glenn Hoddle or Bryan to fit the image of his expanding Sheffield United empire.

We packed up and went to Cornwall. I felt my spirits lifting again as we went over the Tamar Bridge. Then Sharon and I did something we've been planning for a long time. We went to a wonderful place called Trevigue on Cornwall's north coast to renew our vows after ten years of marriage. The weather had been poor but on this day there was just sunshine and blue skies. Amy did a couple of readings, which was special.

And then we had a party back home. A party with some wonderful friends, many of whom I'd known all my life. I wanted to celebrate. I wanted to celebrate moving on and a new beginning. My old mate from my Chesterfield days, Tony Moore, was there. He's fought cancer and come out the other side. Some people from our local village were there, too, people who've made us feel welcome in the place we think of as home now. My best friends, Paul and Julie, came, too, and so many other friends I couldn't mention everyone. But they were all special.

The music was good. A little bit loud, but good. We got the usual complaint about the noise from the usual person. But nothing stopped us enjoying it. We danced all night and, as everyone drifted away, Sharon and I were left alone on the dance floor. Gary Sinclair, the DJ and a good pal of ours, played us some of our favourite slow records and, as we danced, we knew we had finally put everything that had happened in the last weeks and months behind us. We knew we could move on to the next chapter.

NEIL WARNOCK

Career Record

Born 1 December 1948, Sheffield

PLAYING CAREER (LEAGUE)

	P	GOALS
Chesterfield (July 1968-June 1969)	20+4	2
Rotherham (June 1969-July 1971)	46+8	5
Hartlepool (July 1971-Feb 1972)	58+2	5
Scunthorpe (Feb 1972-March 1975)	63+9	7
Aldershot (March 1975-Oct 1976)	35+2	6
Barnsley (Oct 1976-May 1978)	53+4	10
York (May 1978-Dec 1978)	1+3	0
Crewe (Dec 1978-May 1979)	20+1	1
TOTALS	296+33	36

MANAGERIAL CAREER

Gainsborough Trinity	July 1980-January 1981
Burton Albion	January 1981-February 1986
Scarborough	July 1986-January 1989
Notts County	January 1989-January 1993
Torquay	February 1993-May 1993
Huddersfield	July 1993-June 1995
Plymouth	June 1995-February 1997
Oldham	February 1997-May 1998
Bury	June 1998-December 1999
Sheffield United	December 1999-May 2007

LEAGUE RECORD

Season	Club	L	P	W	D	L	F	A	Pts
1987-88	Scarborough	FL4	46	27	14	15	56	48	65
1988-89	Scarborough	FL4	21	10	7	4	34	24	37
	League Total		67	17	21	19	90	72	102
	League Cup		5	1	3	1	12	12	—
	FA Cup		3	1	0	2	2	4	—
	Play-off		0	0	0	0	0	0	—
	Other		4	1	1	2	5	5	—
1988-89	Notts Co	FL3	25	13	5	7	41	28	44
1989-90	Notts Co	FL3	46	25	12	9	73	53	87
1990-91	Notts Co	FL2	46	23	11	12	76	55	80
1991-92	Notts Co	FL1	42	10	10	22	40	62	40
1992-93	Notts Co	FL1	24	4	8	12	24	44	20
	League Total		183	75	46	62	254	242	271
	League Cup		11	6	1	4	18	19	—
	FA Cup		9	5	0	4	13	8	—
	Play-off		8	5	3	0	10	3	—
	Other		10	3	4	3	9	10	—
1992-93	Torquay	FL3	9	3	4	2	11	10	13
	League Total		9	3	4	2	11	10	13
	League Cup		0	0	0	0	0	0	—
	FA Cup		0	0	0	0	0	0	—
	Play-off		0	0	0	0	0	0	—
	Other		0	0	0	0	0	0	—

Season	Club	L	P	W	D	L	F	A	Pts
1993-94	Huddersfield	FL2	46	17	14	15	58	61	65
1994-95	Huddersfield	FL2	46	22	15	9	79	49	81
	League Total		92	39	29	24	137	110	146
	League Cup		8	2	2	4	8	13	—
	FA Cup		5	2	1	2	6	4	—
	Play-off		3	1	2	0	4	3	—
	Other		12	7	3	2	22	13	—
1995-96	Plymouth	FL3	46	22	12	12	68	49	78
1996-97	Plymouth	FL2	29	7	11	11	31	42	32
	League Total		75	29	23	23	99	91	110
	League Cup		4	0	1	3	1	4	—
	FA Cup		6	4	0	2	14	6	—
	Play-off		3	2	0	1	4	2	—
	Other		4	2	0	2	3	4	—
1996-97	Oldham	FL1	16	4	3	9	20	25	15
1997-98	Oldham	FL2	46	15	16	15	62	54	61
	League Total		62	19	19	24	82	79	76
	League Cup		2	1	0	1	1	5	—
	FA Cup		4	2	1	1	4	3	—
	Play-off		0	0	0	0	0	0	—
	Other		1	0	0	1	0	1	—
1998-99	Bury	FL1	46	10	17	19	35	60	47
1999-00	Bury	FL2	19	5	9	5	29	26	24
	League Total		65	15	26	24	64	86	71
	League Cup		7	3	1	3	10	8	—
	FA Cup		5	1	2	2	4	7	—
	Play-off		0	0	0	0	0	0	—
	Other		0	0	0	0	0	0	—

Season	Club		L	P	W	D	L	F	A	Pts
1999-00	Sheffield U	FL1	25	9	9	7	35	33	36
2000-01	Sheffield U	FL1	46	19	11	16	52	49	68
2001-02	Sheffield U	FL1	46	15	15	16	53	54	60
2002-03	Sheffield U	FL1	46	23	11	12	72	52	80
2003-04	Sheffield U	FL1	46	20	11	15	65	56	71
2004-05	Sheffield U	FLCH	46	18	13	15	57	56	67
2005-06	Sheffield U	FLCH	46	26	12	8	76	46	90
2006-07	Sheffield U	PL	38	10	8	20	32	55	38
	League Total		339	140	90	109	442	401	510
	League Cup		24	15	3	6	42	25	—
	FA Cup		19	9	4	6	28	16	—
	Play-off		3	1	1	1	5	7	—
	Other		0	0	0	0	0	0	—
TOTALS	LEAGUE		892	347	258	287	1179	1091	1299
	LEAGUE CUP		61	28	11	22	92	86	—
	FA CUP		51	24	8	19	71	48	—
	PLAY-OFF		17	9	6	2	23	15	—
	OTHER		31	13	8	10	39	33	—
	TOTAL		1052	421	291	340	1404	1273	1299

HONOURS

Promotions

1986–87: Conference winners (promotion to Division 4)
       – Scarborough

1989–90: Division 3 Play-off winners (promotion to Division 2)
       – Notts County

1990–91: Division 2 Play-off winners (promotion to Division 1)
       – Notts County

1994–95: Division 2 Play-off winners (promotion to Division 1)
       – Huddersfield Town

1995–96: Division 3 Play-off winners (promotion to Division 2)
       – Plymouth Argyle

2005–06: Championship Runners-up (promotion to Premier League)
       – Sheffield United

Manager of the month

2002–03: (Championship): January

2003–04: (Championship): November

2004–05: (Championship): December

Cups

1982-83: Northern Premier League Challenge Cup – Burton
       (19 April 1983 v Macclesfield at Maine Road)

2002-03: FA Cup semi-final – Sheffield United

2002-03: League Cup semi-final – Sheffield United

Other

Winner, Hartlepool FC 'Player of the Year' 1971-72

Nominated, BBC Yorkshire Sports Personality Awards 2006

Winner, ITV Yorkshire Awards Sports Personality of the Year 2006

INDEX